SILENCED

International Journalists Expose Media Censorship

Edited by
DAVID DADGE

Prometheus Books

59 John Glenn Drive
Amherst, New York 14228-2197

Published 2005 by Prometheus Books

Inquiries should be addressed to
Prometheus Books
59 John Glenn Drive
Amherst, New York 14228–2197
VOICE: 716–691–0133, ext. 207
FAX: 716–564–2711
WWW.PROMETHEUSBOOKS.COM

09 08 07 06 05   5 4 3 2 1

Library of Congress Cataloging-in-Publication Data

Silenced : international journalists expose media censorship / edited by David Dadge.
    p. cm.
Includes bibliographical references.
ISBN 1–59102–305–X (hardcover : alk. paper)
    1. Freedom of the press. 2. Government and the press. I. Dadge, David
PN4736.S55 2005
323.44'5—dc22

          2005012213

Printed in the United States of America on acid-free paper

*This book is dedicated to journalists everywhere
who refuse to tread the easy path.*

CONTENTS

8   **CONTENTS**

FOUR LITTLE WORDS

DAVID DADGE

What does it feel like to be prevented from writing or speaking the truth? To be censored? Americans tend to be more fortunate than most. Four little words in the First Amendment to the United States Constitution, "or of the press," and a number of crucial Supreme Court decisions have prevented the government from overtly censoring the media. Of course, this is not to say that media censorship does not exist in America. It does—it exists in every society—but it is far subtler than the government simply trying to prevent the publication of an embarrassing story.

American playwright David Mamet perhaps said it best: "We live in oppressive times. We have, as a nation, become our own thought police; but instead of calling the process by which we limit our expression of dissent and wonder 'censorship,' we call it 'concern for commercial viability.'" Mamet's words are a striking acknowledgment that, in present-day America, calls for censorship are as likely to come from an editor, a publisher, a broadcaster, or a major advertiser as they are from a politician.

Silenced: International Journalists Expose Media Censorship touches on these pressures in America. Stacey Woelfel, news director of KOMU-TV in Missouri, tells the story of his battle to prevent displays of patriotism in the newsroom from over-whelming the actual story of the September 11 attacks. He describes how he faced threats from the state legislature to cut his budget and calls from the public demanding his resignation. Similarly, former city editor of the *Texas City Sun* Tom Gutting also lays out why he was dismissed by his publisher after writing an opinion column criticizing President George W. Bush shortly after the September 11 attacks.

This view of censorship is not, however, the true story of *Silenced*. The real story behind the book is how the rest of the world censors the media. While American journalists most often face corporate pressure, there are other parts of the world where journalists are still fighting with governments to establish the truth. Indeed, if *Silenced* can be best summed up, it is the story of those four little words—"or of the press"—and how their absence affects media around the world.

The first chapter of *Silenced* tells the story of Hans-Martin Tillack's experiences in Brussels reporting on corruption in the European Union. While one might expect a media environment similar to that of America's, this is not the case. Awakened early one morning to find policemen at his door armed with a search warrant, Tillack has faced continuous harassment from the very institutions whose job it is to stem the flow of corruption.

When being questioned, Tillack had an Orwellian conversa-tion with a policeman. Why not reveal the name of his source, the policeman asks. Because nobody would ever provide me with confidential information again, replies Tillack. The policeman tells Tillack that burning one source would not stop him from receiving information from other officials. Tillack retorts, "What kind of journalism would that be where you could only base your reporting on official press releases and the words of those who govern us?" His reply is a statement of intent for every investigative reporter with the hunger and desire for a good story.

Tillack is a German journalist working in Belgium. Both countries are bound by Europe's equivalent to the Supreme Court, the European Court of Human Rights, and yet Tillack found himself mired in a Belgian court system that has little regard for press freedom. Would those four little words have helped him?

More importantly, would those words have assisted Tim Lambon, a senior foreign video producer for the United Kingdom's Channel 4 News, had they appeared in the Liberian constitution? The temptation is to say probably not. Former dictator Charles Taylor presided over a regime that had no regard for the niceties of legal decisions or the separation of powers.

Part of a camera team sent on a poorly planned trip to Liberia to film Taylor's diamond mine operations, Lambon found himself roughed up and thrown into prison. Lambon's chapter aptly describes the cruel actions of the Taylor regime, the attempts by the international community to free the camera crew, as well as the powerful emotions of fear and uncertainty felt by the journalists, all of whom, at one time or another, thought they were facing death or long-term imprisonment.

Agence France-Presse journalist Michael Field provides a chapter on the much-ignored and underreported Pacific region, where tribal loyalties and local tradition undermine journalists' attempts at scrutinizing the many island societies. Field provides a look at the way the media behaved during civil war on the Solomon Islands and an attempted coup on Fiji, and he outlines the events that led him to be called the most "banned" journalist in the world.

Extreme government pressure on journalists is examined in two chapters written by journalists Andrew Meldrum and Jasper

Becker. Meldrum paints a savage picture of the destruction of the independent media in Zimbabwe at the hands of dictator Robert Mugabe and the events that led to Meldrum's forcible ejection from the country despite a last-minute court order allowing him to stay.

Becker, formerly the Beijing bureau chief of the *South China Morning Post*, talks frankly of his politically motivated dismissal from the newspaper and how Hong Kong newspaper owners often curtailed their criticism of the Beijing government in the hope of benefiting financially from the country's embrace of capitalism. As Becker rightly says of this desperate need to ingratiate, "The mentality of Hong Kong's elite was that they felt they should anticipate what Beijing wanted. They seemed desperate to be seen as more Catholic than the Pope."

With additional chapters on two journalists' investigations into police corruption in Melbourne, Australia, and how an editor-in-chief in Russia found that his office building had been taken over by thugs, *Silenced* traces the arc of censorship—in all its different manifestations—throughout much of the world.

The final chapter concerns the ultimate form of censorship—murder—and it offers proof, if any were needed, that there are journalists still prepared to risk their lives in order to ensure that information reaches the public. Telling a story he knows well, journalist and consultant to the Haiti Support Group Charles Arthur writes about the murder of Jean Dominique outside his Haitian radio station. Arthur describes the unwillingness of the police to find the perpetrators and the failed attempt to assassinate Dominique's wife. Dominique's experience is one repeated in many places around the world, and it serves as a reminder of how far removed some journalists are from the safety and protection of those four little English words.

What if those four words had never been written? Indeed, let's go one step further—what if journalism as a profession had never existed? If there were no newspapers, radio, television, or even the Internet? Such an exercise serves to show just how much we rely on journalists and their essential role: the dissemination of information.

For a start, it is likely that our views of events would be much more limited than in the real world. Our ability to make decisions concerning the events around us would rest on what we saw with our own eyes or on what others told us. Societies in such a world would be at the mercy of conspiracy theorists as facts became mangled and confused with each telling. If this is difficult to appreciate, try to imagine how a description of the assassination of President John F. Kennedy would have sounded after its fiftieth telling.

Moreover, it is likely that our busy lives, predominantly spent earning a living, would make us insular and inward looking: We would be relatively uninterested in the events of the outside world. We would not have the time to investigate the events around us. It is highly unlikely we would find the time to go to a local council meeting or travel to a presidential candidates' debate. Would we have the time to investigate the conditions in a children's home or a hospital? How many of us would be prepared to give up our spare time to see if a landfill site was being used properly? Probably very few of us.

As time went on in this make-believe world, governments and politicians would become increasingly more confident about their ability to evade scrutiny of their actions. It is more than likely that these governments would begin to base decisions on their own self-interest and self-preservation and not on what was best for the people. The altruism that may have existed at the beginning would swiftly disappear. No government is perfect, and the ability to escape the consequences of one's actions would, in turn, encourage their repetition. After all, would the internal inquiries of politicians be sufficient to promote change without the media publicizing these events? Furthermore, who on the "outside" of government would know?

Our ability to assess the actions of government during a time of crisis would also be severely hindered. How could we assess the correctness of going to war, of sacrificing our soldiers, of spending enormous amounts of money on defense without some assessment of these actions? How could we judge that the cause was just or that our interests were being best served? Would we travel to Senate hearings and ask for budget details, or would we rely on others to do that job?

Naturally, such an alternative world would be of interest only to crooked politicians, but it reveals the importance of the media's work: the difficult, and often thankless, task of scrutinizing the government on our behalf. For this reason, it is clear that their fight for information is our fight for information and that their censorship is ultimately our censorship. *Silenced* shows this struggle taking place in many countries far away from the United States. It is a struggle we should better acknowledge.

David Dadge

Chapter 1

FROM BRUSSELS TO BURMA

HANS-MARTIN TILLACK

Hans-Martin Tillack was born in 1961 in a small city close to Berlin in what was then the German Democratic Republic (RDA). He studied sociology and political science in Marburg and West Berlin before becoming a staff writer with the left-of-center Berlin daily *Tageszeitung* (*Taz*) in 1988. From 1992 he covered national German politics in Bonn (then the seat of the federal government), first for *Taz* and since 1993 for *Stern*, one of the three big German newsmagazines. From 1999 to 2004, he was the EU correspondent for *Stern* in Brussels, Belgium. From August 2004 to March 2005, he worked in the political department at *Stern* headquarters in Hamburg, Germany. Currently he covers national politics in the Berlin office of *Stern*. For his reporting on the European Union, he received the Leipziger Medienpreis.

I t was seven o'clock in the morning and I was still fast asleep when my doorbell rang. On the third ring, I opened the door to six men who introduced themselves as plainclothes officers of the Belgian Federal Police.

The men briefly showed me a search warrant and said that the EU Anti-Fraud Office had sent them. They wanted to know who had given me some highly confidential documents about fraud and irregularities in the European Commission, the executive arm of the European Union. The police informed me that I was suspected of having bribed an official to obtain these documents.

This must be a bad dream, I thought. As the Brussels correspondent of the German magazine *Stern,* I had written extensively about fraud and waste in the EU Commission. It was true that I had often benefited from leaked documents, but why would I be so stupid as to commit corruption myself while writing about it?

Unfortunately, the policemen were not part of a nightmare— they were real. The police officers took my private computer, mobile phones, diary and address book, bank account statements, and even a copy of the book *Spaceship Brussels,** which I had published with Andreas Oldag, a colleague from *Süddeutsche Zeitung.*

After the search, I was driven in an old Ford Mondeo to the *Stern* office in the Brussels International Press Center. The officers wanted me to show them where I had filed some specific documents. I refused and reminded them that the European Court of Human Rights had recently condemned Belgium for violating freedom of expression and the protection of journalists' sources.

My statement failed to impress the policemen. Because I had refused to cooperate, they decided to take nearly everything in my archive at the *Stern* office. The (British) *Daily Telegraph* would later call it the "biggest archive of investigative files of any jour-

---

Raumschiff Brüssel: Wie die Demokratie in Europa scheitert (Berlin: Argon, 2003).

nalist in Brussels."* The police used seventeen boxes to transport the material to their headquarters.

On several occasions, I asked to be allowed to call both a lawyer and my wife, Katja, who at the time worked in Estonia. But the policemen refused. I had not been cooperative, one of them explained to me. When I complained, I was told I should be happy that I was "not in Burma" or "central Africa." "In these places," one detective said, "journalists could be treated much worse."

I had been thrilled five years earlier, in August 1999, when I had first moved to Brussels. Until then I had worked for *Stern* in Bonn, the seat of the German federal government at that time. *Stern* had later sent me to Brussels to open our first office in the capital of Europe.

That was an interesting time to be in Brussels. The common currency, the euro, had just been introduced. With a budget of 100€ billion, and a staff of twenty-five thousand, the EU Commission was already by far the biggest and most powerful supranational authority on the planet. Its authority stretched from the Arctic Circle in northern Finland to the Canary Islands, not far from the African coast. Gone were the times when Brussels's decisions concerned little more than discussions on cucumbers or the technical details of tractor seats.

Now, the European Union also dealt with foreign and immigration policy and had supremacy over nearly all matters of economic policy, consumer protection, and environmental law. Brussels, it was said, was now responsible for every second new law that the 375 million citizens in the member states of the European Union had to respect—and soon the European Union would also encompass ten new member states in eastern and southern Europe, which would boost the EU population to 450 million.†

Going to Brussels was one of the most exciting challenges of

---

*Ambrose Evans-Pritchard, "Reporter Following Trail of Corruption in Eu Arrested," *Daily Telegraph*, March 20, 2004.
†On May 1, 2004, ten new countries joined the European Union.

my professional life as a journalist. As with so many continental
Europeans, especially Germans, I was enthusiastic about building
a closer union among the EU member states. Only by doing so
was I convinced that Europeans could become an equal partner
with the United States. Indeed, when I caught sight of the blue
EU flag with its twelve gold stars, I sometimes felt a sort of patriotic shiver—a feeling that Germans of my generation do not
often have when looking at the German flag.

Of course, I knew about the shortcomings of the EU project,
especially its gaping democratic deficit. It is difficult to explain to
non-Europeans how the union works, especially when many
European citizens struggle to grasp it. Most of the legislation happens behind the closed doors of the commission and the Council
of Ministers, where officials from member states negotiate with
each other. By comparison, the powers of the European Parliament remain weak. The EU Commission resembles a government
in many ways, but unlike a democratic government, the commission is not an elected body. The heads of the administration are
not called ministers but commissioners. The commission—now
numbering twenty-five men and women—is appointed by the
governments of the member states. It is, however, no secret that
the complicated Brussels bureaucracy is run by long-serving
senior civil servants. Because many of the decisions are not made
in public, the old boy networks and lobbies of all kinds have far-
reaching influence.

But, five months before my arrival in Brussels, an earthquake
had shaken the political landscape of the union. The twenty-five
men and women who then headed the EU Commission were
forced collectively to step down in March 1999. Journalists and
Members of the European Parliament (MEPs) had revealed an
embarrassing number of fraud cases in the EU administration.

Millions had gone missing. Sometimes the money would end
up in the pockets of officials or their wives, husbands, mistresses,
or friends. Bribes of all kinds, from free Formula One tickets to

shiny new cars, had been paid to civil servants. Well-organized networks of officials invariably seemed to benefit from the protection of the highest levels of the commission, and the leading directors general of the commission services always appeared eager to avoid any scandal that might harm the institution's reputation. Hardly anyone seemed to care where the money transferred from Brussels ended up.

Stern had reported on these scandals. Now, the ability of the newly appointed commissioners to clean up Brussels was a major story for *Stern*. My first story in Brussels included an interview with Michaele Schreyer, a Green politician from Germany. She was the new commissioner responsible for fighting fraud. On the question of fraud and the actions of the previous commission, Schreyer said it was shortsighted to try to cover up corruption and promised never to do so.

I believed her, especially as I knew her rather well. Schreyer dubbed me her "old friend" when she once called me soon after we both arrived in Brussels in the summer of 1999. When I had worked with the left-of-center daily *Taz* in Berlin in the late eighties, she was—briefly—regional minister of environment and town planning. Schreyer had no experience at the national or European level, but many thought, as someone with a fresh outsider's perspective, she might be the right person to clean up Brussels.

While still new in Brussels, I also met Paul van Buitenen. He had been instrumental in bringing down the previous commission. The assistant accountant and low-grade EU official from the Netherlands had watched for years while his superiors sought to avoid drawing conclusions from even the most obvious cases of fraud and financial irregularities. Frustrated, in December 1998, he finally informed the Green group in the European Parliament of what he knew about the fraud and cover-up in the commission.

How did Paul van Buitenen feel now? The solidly built guy smiled shyly. He was not too optimistic. All the officials who had been responsible for the wrongdoings were still there, van Buitenen warned me. No real regime change had occurred.

Van Buitenen's attitude was understandable. The old commission had suspended him with half his pay. The new commission had given him another job but continued with the disciplinary case against him. We held a reception at the newly opened *Stern* office in October 1999. Schreyer was among the guests, along with van Buitenen. He tried to approach the commissioner in order to shake hands—after all, they were both members of Green parties, she German, he Flemish. A photographer turned quickly toward the couple, but Schreyer backed away as if she had been addressed by Osama bin Laden. Schreyer's head of cabinet and personal aid, Eckart Guth, was an old commission hand. Guth accompanied Schreyer nearly everywhere and quickly warned me off van Buitenen. Nothing that van Buitenen had revealed was new, Guth confided to me.

Guth was a clever man. He must have known better. Official reports had concluded that the commission had failed to draw conclusions from even the most obvious cases of wrongdoing. Van Buitenen had been right. Why did Guth believe he could mislead me? And was he trying to do the same thing to Schreyer?

That would have been worrying. Schreyer and the commission president Romano Prodi had not only promised to fight fraud with a "zero-tolerance" approach but also announced reforms that would help to "break completely with the past," as Prodi pledged. Financial controls would be reinforced and critical officials encouraged, not harassed.

But soon I received information that the complete opposite was true. Only weeks after having taken office, Schreyer closed down an important audit department—the same one that had discovered nearly all of the big scandals that had brought down the old commission. It was the same department where van Buitenen had worked.

Of course, it had not been Schreyer's idea to dissolve the auditors' unit. It had apparently been the proposal of the director general of financial control, Isabella Ventura. Strangely enough, Ventura had been responsible for financial control under the old commission. She had largely failed, but Schreyer had allowed her to stay. Some said that the reason for the closure of the audit unit was that Ventura was settling her accounts with those officials who had created trouble in the past.

Fresh doubts about Schreyer's reform pledge occurred when I wrote a number of stories about another fraud case. The French company Fléchard had—before Schreyer and Prodi took office—benefited from a favor worth 14€ million. Fléchard received the money despite the fact that it was involved in fraudulent exports of EU butter. Nearly all of the high-ranking officials who had been responsible for this case were still in office. Mysteriously, the minutes of a high-level commission meeting on the case had disappeared. In an internal letter to Schreyer, published by *Stern*, three senior officials signed an astonishing joint statement. The minutes of the meeting, they wrote, had been "taken away" under "completely bizarre circumstances" from each of their three offices.

It had the appearance of organized crime. But why was it so important for them to make these minutes disappear?

Nobody really cared. With the exception of *Stern*, no other newspaper wrote about this strange case of theft. The Anti-Fraud Office searched for the document but never found it. Some MEPs looked at the case but soon lost interest. And Schreyer and her colleagues had already publicly declared that the case was to be closed. The story made me wonder! Documents disappearing in German federal ministries had created scandals. Why not in Brussels? Apparently, the standards were different.

One day, I found an internal audit report in my mailbox that revealed serious discrepancies found in the awards procedure of the EU research program. The program was worth 4€ billion and the report was—as I was able to verify—authentic. In vain, the auditors had considered disciplinary measures against the responsible officials. When I wrote an article about the audit report, hardly anyone was shocked. The commission did not reject the facts of our story but claimed that there was no need to worry. Once again, no other media took up the story.

When I first arrived in Brussels, another spokesman (of the social democratic party group in the parliament) tried to explain to me how journalists were supposed to work here. "There are no scoops in Brussels," he told me. "Whatever is new is always already known to all of the journalists."

At first, I did not understand what he meant. Then I started to publish my news stories—only to learn that my fellow journalists did not find them interesting enough to print. "The commission had denied it," one told me. "I could not believe that that was true," another reporter said to me, after the research story had come out. The reporter continued, "One German MEP said it was a non-story." On another occasion, a German radio reporter gave me some advice about a story of mine that concerned a big German bank and a multi-million-euro deal with the European Parliament that the bank had obtained in contravention of the tendering rules.

Had the radio colleague read the *Stern* story? "No," she said. The word of the MEP—whose party was linked to the bank—was enough. Finally, I understood the message of the spokesman. News was what my German colleagues collectively had decided to be news. They apparently contacted each other on a regular basis to reach an agreement about what would and would not be covered. In their view, information released or approved by the commission was newsworthy. What conflicted with the commission perspective was often not worth printing. So it was not news.

In January 2002, Schreyer hired a new chief accountant. But, after only five months, Schreyer suspended Marta Andreasen—after the experienced accountant refused to sign the commission accounts because she found them open to manipulation and fraud. The Andreasen case quickly became a huge issue in the European press, from the United Kingdom to Italy—with the exception of nearly all of the German dailies, TV stations, and news agencies.

A colleague of the highly respected German *Frankfurter Allgemeine Zeitung* even publicly attacked Andreasen at a press conference because she had blown the whistle. Besides, the representative of the newspaper claimed, the commission would already be under increased pressure from some Euro-skeptic governments. Therefore—so his argument went—one should not deliver ammunition to the enemies of greater European integration.

The situation was quite bizarre, I thought. Although it was the German commissioner Schreyer who was under growing pressure, I was virtually the only German correspondent who was writing about what had happened.

The commission administration did what it could to feed the eight-hundred-strong press corps. Every day at noon, the correspondents were invited to the press briefing. I often went but used the time as an opportunity to meet colleagues and exchange gossip. The briefing invariably started with the commission spokespeople proudly presenting some new achievement that would range from a new study on European space policy to a European-wide passport for pets. It was not uncommon for the commission spokespeople to state beforehand what questions they were prepared to answer. The correspondents normally accepted such pronouncements.

Although it was clear that the commission spokespeople called the shots in the pressroom, the atmosphere often resembled a gathering of friends. Spokespeople and journalists were all supposed to be on first-name terms. The briefings always ended with the chief spokesperson wishing "bon appetite" to everyone.

"Journalists and spokespeople shared the same goal," a senior colleague of *Frankfurter Allgemeine Zeitung*, Michael Stabenow, claimed in a ceremony for an outgoing chief spokesman. "Whether journalists or officials, we are all there in order to [provide information] about Europe," Stabenow said.

Overall, the situation looked similar to embedded journalism during the US-led invasion of Iraq. However, the journalists had managed only to adapt to the specific nature of Brussels politics. Nobody expected public debates on the performance of individual commissioners or the pros and cons of a new commission proposal. When the German government presents a new scheme, it immediately comes under attack from the opposition. In Brussels, there is no opposition. Most MEPs support the commission.

I was often told that I had broken the unwritten rules. When the commission claimed in 2001 that EU enlargement would be very cheap, most colleagues presented that as a fact to their readers. I wrote the opposite, based on internal figures and the in-depth studies of well-known economists. By accident, I later ran into commissioner Günter Verheugen (another German). I said hello—but he started to shout at me. I had missed the point completely, he told me. "Don't you see that you are completely isolated among your colleagues because none of the other journalists takes up your stories?"

Apparently, he thought that journalists should decide the truth by majority voting among their peers instead of by checking the facts. Three years later, the commission would nevertheless present a budget proposal for the upcoming seven years and ask for an additional 40€ billion per year. My colleagues would explain to their readers that this was quite okay, as no one could have expected that enlargement was available for free. As a result of these experiences, I learned to cooperate with my British, French, Polish, and Danish colleagues to ensure that a story was published in more than just one language. This approach increased the chances of people reading the story, and working with these colleagues was a clear indication that my reporting had not gone unnoticed.

Once I complained to a commission spokesman about how long it took him to reply to one of my interview requests. His answer was very telling. "We treat all journalists equally," he told me, "[including] . . . those who are Commission friendly . . . [and]," he said, looking at me, "those who are hostile to us."

"Do you have blacklists?" I asked him in astonishment. And what had I done to deserve the title of an official enemy of the commission?

Of course, you could hardly miss the problem: The commission was unused to critical coverage in the media. It was a logical consequence of the fact that there was no opposition in parliament and very little pressure from the media. One British MEP described the attitude of the commission people very well: They behaved like "spoiled kids." Even before the Santer Commission had been forced to step down in 1999, the public relations officers had tried to fight off critical coverage by applying all kinds of pressure. One journalist had been accused—unfairly—of being a right-wing extremist. Investigative journalists even found fake documents with allegations against a commissioner in their letterboxes; fortunately, they checked the facts and did not publish the story.

Naturally, all over the world, spokespeople do what they can to mislead journalists. But never before in my career had I received so many flatly wrong statements as I did in Brussels. This was possible because the commission's spokespeople got away with telling untruths.

Nevertheless, I still could not understand why journalists were anti-European if they wrote about people who broke European law or wasted the money of European taxpayers. As a result, I carried on reporting irregularities.

Over time, I began to receive more and more internal documents from people working in the various European institutions. Sometimes I found an anonymous letter in my mailbox. Sometimes officials were ready to talk to me in their offices, while others preferred to meet me in private, for example, in a small restaurant somewhere on the outskirts of Brussels or in their private apartments.

"This is a devilish world," one source explained to me over coffee. "You have to keep in mind that there are extremely strong networks in place, run by senior officials who have known each other for many years."

"The commission is sick," another source told me. "They were never under any real control, so networks could spread and gain control. The downfall of the Santer Commission came as a shock to many. So afterward they had one main aim: to finish with those who had caused this accident."

"There is a dinosaur living in the commission," the European Ombudsman Jacob Söderman confided to me. He was Finnish and used to Nordic transparency. Now he was responsible for handling citizens' complaints about the EU bureaucracy. "After the Santer crisis, the dinosaur was weakened," Söderman said. "But that is over."

Not that everything remained unchanged. Under pressure from the European Parliament, a new and more independent Anti-Fraud Office was set up in summer 1999. It was called OLAF, the French acronym for *Office Européen de la Lutte Anti-Fraude*. Since March 2000, the former German public prosecutor, Franz-Hermann Brüner, leads the organization. He has powers unlike any other EU investigator before him. He can raid any office in the European Commission without the prior approval of a judge. He would not even have to stop in front of the office of the commission president. He commands a budget of 50€ million and a staff of more than three hundred.

I met Brüner shortly after he had taken office. The small, bearded man was apparently not very good with words and constantly mumbled while smoking his pipe. He told me how important it was to cooperate with journalists. After all, it was the press who would have to protect him if the commission tried to interfere with his independence.

Brüner soon realized that the commission officials felt uncomfortable about OLAF's powers. After his initial months in office, the German even publicly criticized the commission for withdrawing its earlier commitments against fraud. The commission had accepted OLAF when it had been weakened, Brüner told deputies. Now, however, some officials were trying to recover the ground that had been lost.

I wrote about this conflict between Brüner and the commission, but, once again, I was the only one to do so. The OLAF boss also realized that he was not increasing his own popularity by investigating the wrongdoings of the commission.

The European Parliament had wanted OLAF to focus on internal fraud cases. This was a direct consequence of the failure of the Santer commission. But Brüner's investigators did not concentrate on Brussels fraud. Many of the investigators worked on the fight against cigarette smuggling or customs fraud—cases that concerned the illegal import of Chinese tiger nuts or frozen shrimp from Bangladesh.

As important as these crimes are, the authorities of the member states were already responsible for investigating them. OLAF could do little more than assist them in their investigations; sometimes their work annoyed national investigators who felt that the OLAF people were trying to meddle in matters that did not concern them.

But, by choosing this policy, Brüner clearly pleased Romano Prodi's people. Pia Maria Filippone, a high-ranking Italian EU official (and protégé of the commission president) openly admitted as much in an internal meeting in 2001. Filippone said that in 99 percent of cases OLAF's job would be to fight fraud in the member states, and, as a consequence, the inquiries would be "no real problem" for the commission officials.

Brüner followed this line. In 2003, he assigned no more than thirteen people to internal corruption cases. It was the smallest unit within OLAF. "Even [Brüner's] press service is bigger," the Austrian MEP Herbert Bösch used to joke.

Whenever one met OLAF investigators, they either bragged

about another strike against cigarette smugglers or they mysteriously failed to do their job.

In the summer of 2000, OLAF proudly announced a successful investigation of companies that had smuggled impure butter, which contained no real butter but a considerable amount of chemicals. Among the companies involved was the French enterprise Fléchard—the same company that had been suspected of fraud in the past but had been whitewashed by Commissioner Schreyer. Now, once again, the commission and OLAF were quick to promise that everything was under control. They said there was no danger for the consumers and no need for the powerful European dairy industry to worry! All the dubious butter products—on sale in Italy, France, and Belgium—had been seized, Brüner's spokesman Alessandro Butticé claimed.

The statement was untrue. But Butticé would only admit this after a *Stern* investigation (which would not have been possible without the help of Italian Brussels-based investigative journalist Marcello Faraggi). As it turned out, not all of the so-called Mafia butter had been seized. Apparently, questionable dairy products had even been delivered to the German company Bayernland. The enterprise denied any wrongdoing—and it was well connected to politicians in Brüner's German home state of Bavaria. The chairman of the Bayernland board was a member of the German Parliament for the political party that governed Bavaria. Had Brüner tried to play political games?

Paul van Buitenen also grew impatient about the work of Brüner's fraud busters. In August 2001, he delivered a 232-page report with fresh allegations of fraud and irregularities in the commission. But Brüner quickly downplayed the importance of the report. It contained little news, he wrote to an MEP in early 2002.

No one could question Brüner's assertion, as no one outside the commission knew of the report's existence. But, on a cold February evening in 2002, one official—"never mention my name," he said—handed me two confidential documents: first, van Buitenen's report, and, second, an even more confidential internal OLAF memorandum containing an analysis of the van Buitenen papers. One thing was clear from the reports—the OLAF experts did not share their director's opinion that van Buitenen had not delivered any sensitive information. On the contrary, the investigators recommended that OLAF open four new investigations and relaunch a number of dormant cases.

The story I wrote with the help of these documents made headlines all across Europe. It was quoted in the (London) *Guardian* as well as in *Le Monde* of Paris. The information we had obtained suggested that under Prodi and Schreyer the Commission had treated accusations of fraud and irregularities lightly. Gone was the much-heralded "zero-tolerance" approach. Based on what was contained in the report, even high-ranking commission officials such as Secretary General David O'Sullivan and Prodi's chief spokesman Jonathan Faull had apparently taken part in activities that could be described as an attempt to cover up financial scandals.

The commission reacted with unprecedented anger. Never again did he want to read such "nonsense," the normally well-controlled Briton Jonathan Faull hissed at a press conference. Nevertheless, he never took the trouble to outline the so-called nonsense in my articles. OLAF boss Brüner hurried to Faull's assistance. He wrote to my editors that my article had been "factually incorrect." In fact, the OLAF chief promised, the documents did not contain any criticism of Faull's behavior.

Brüner told a lie and he knew it. Two years later, in February 2004, in their complaints to the prosecutors in Belgium and Germany, which triggered the police raid, the OLAF investigators quoted precisely the same *Stern* article on Faull and added that we had quoted him correctly. Ominously, my article now served as proof to OLAF that *Stern* had possessed the confidential documents.

But, in March 2002, it was more important for Brüner to be economical with the truth in order to protect Prodi's spokesman.

Subsequently, the commission and OLAF did what they could to label me as a maverick journalist. Commission officials warned correspondents that they should not collaborate with me, as it would be harmful for them. A Prodi spokesman confided to me, that many in the commission saw me as a "lone rider with a mission."

Finally, on March 27, 2002, OLAF published a press release on the leak of the van Buitenen memoranda. OLAF said it would now investigate the possibility that "the journalist" who had received the papers paid officials in order to obtain them. I was completely shocked when I read that. Immediately, *Stern* published a press release in which we rebutted any suspicion of wrongdoing. Afterward, I briefly benefited from another leak: I got hold of an internal e-mail by OLAF spokesman Alessandro Butticé to all OLAF staff. In the e-mail, Butticé admitted that there were only "rumors" to support the bribery claim.

Looking back, I doubt there was even a rumor to bolster this claim. Two years were to pass before I learned that the then newly appointed spokesman of Commissioner Schreyer, Joachim Gross, was behind the false allegations. Gross had met OLAF spokesman Butticé for dinner on March 22, 2002. At the dinner, Gross (who worked under the direct authority of Prodi's chief spokesman, Faull) claimed he had heard something interesting, namely, that I had paid for internal documents. How much? Allegedly, 8,000€—or was it perhaps deutsche marks? Who could have told him? Gross declined to provide a name. For Butticé that was enough to put the allegation in a press release—a mere five days after his dinner with Gross.

The OLAF spin doctor presented his allegation in an extremely tricky fashion. He published it in such a way that we could not challenge OLAF in court. The lawyers at *Stern* headquarters told me that because my name was not explicitly mentioned in the OLAF press release, we could not sue. However, everyone understood that the accusation was directed against me—the same conclusion that the European ombudsman drew in November 2003. After hearing a complaint I had introduced, he slammed OLAF for a severe case of "maladministration." You should not publish an accusation without presenting any evidence, the ombudsman argued. It was a principle understood by every journalist but not the European Anti-Fraud Office.

Clearly OLAF was running a twin-speed judicial system. High-ranking commission officials—like Jonathan Faull—were immediately cleansed of any wrongdoing, even though the evidence said otherwise. But the journalist who wrote about the irregularities was publicly attacked by OLAF without a shred of evidence to prove the allegations.

Nevertheless, I carried on my investigations, especially into Eurostat, the statistical agency of the commission. In early 2001, I had received documents showing that a major EU trade union had complained to the responsible commissioner about widespread irregularities and fraud at Eurostat. But everyone in the commission denied there were problems.

In February 2002, I knew much more. Eurostat figured prominently in the van Buitenen memoranda. Since 1999, OLAF had apparently been informed on many occasions, and by different sources, about widespread sleaze in the statistical agency. There was talk of contracts for the husband of a Eurostat director, as well as slush funds and the harassment of those officials who had opposed the local management culture. According to the confidential documents, OLAF had opened several cases since 1999 but had never started a proper investigation or even properly "filed" the evidence.

From March 2002 on, I had spent many days and evenings in Luxembourg, checking the company register and meeting the Eurostat officials of different nationalities. Nobody could avoid the fact that there was something seriously wrong in the commission department. I wrote about dodgy statistics, dubious tendering procedures, and apparent nepotism in favor of a number of Greek companies (under the responsibility of a Greek Eurostat director). But, despite all the promises of "zero tolerance," President Prodi and his officials did not pay much interest to the allegations. In fact, the commission did its utmost to protect Yves Franchet, the head of Eurostat.

A Frenchman, Franchet had only recently been praised by the commission vice president Neil Kinnock for his approach to "total quality management." Based on this, it was no wonder that Kinnock had also turned down the complaint of a Danish Eurostat official. As *Stern* reported in May 2002, the Danish official had tried to prevent inflated payments to an obviously fraudulent company. Her superiors had not only insisted on the high payments but also stripped her of responsibility for the contract.

In March 2003, we revealed in our book *Raumschiff Brüssel* that OLAF was running no fewer than six fraud investigations into Eurostat and that Prodi's new spokesman, Reijo Kemppinen, continued to defend the "proactive" reform policy of Franchet.

This changed only after the *Financial Times* broke the story on the front page in May 2003. The *Financial Times* had some exciting news about a complaint OLAF had finally sent to the public prosecutor in Paris. Now, more than one year after my first reports on this case, my colleagues were suddenly becoming interested in these stories. As a result, the commission reacted, finally opening its own inquiry. The commission found itself being misled by Franchet and later removed the whole upper management of Eurostat.

It later transpired that the Eurostat management had manipulated tenders and favored a small number of companies with contracts worth millions. In turn, these undertakings employed friends and family members of the Eurostat officials, and they created slush funds out of inflated payments from the commission. These funds were, in turn, exploited by commission officials—though, allegedly, only for official purposes. However, these official purposes included cocktail parties, expensive restaurants and hotel bills, as well as payments to a horse-riding center and a volleyball club.

Several commissioners were under pressure from the European Parliament, including Michaele Schreyer. The services under her authority had issued damning audit reports about Eurostat as early as the autumn of 1999. They had warned about possible "fraud," but Schreyer claimed she had never been informed.

Sadly, that was an acceptable excuse in the eyes of most of the deputies and journalists. And what about the fraud investigators at OLAF? Since early 2000, they had known of official reports that denounced possible "fraud" at Eurostat, but the investigation only really started after my story, and those of other journalists, was published in the world's media.

"Why could OLAF only act after 'the press [had] reported' and the Parliament had asked for it," the Danish MEP Freddy Blak wondered.

Eurostat was not the only internal case where OLAF had failed. Supervisory officials noted in an internal memo that all too often OLAF would produce nothing but "simulated investigations." My sources continued to deliver me material that left me with no choice other than to conclude that Brüner did not really want to investigate internal fraud cases. Why not? My sources told me that it was for fear of being reappointed.

Brüner had never hidden his ambition to stay in office for another five years—until 2010. And the reappointment procedure was to be opened shortly, with the commission as the responsible body.

In November 2003, I published a detailed account of the work of Brüner and OLAF. *Stern* reported about fraud cases where OLAF simply did not take the trouble to investigate properly, in spite of overwhelming evidence of organized fraud. I also outlined a case where OLAF had evidence of criminal conduct by a leading Belgian politician that Brüner decided not to pass on to the Belgian judicial authorities. (Later, in my particular case, he would argue that he was "obliged" to transfer all evidence of illegality to the prosecutor).

"Brüner catches the small [ones] and lets the big ones run," I quoted a frustrated OLAF official. I also reported that European deputies were discussing whether to replace Brüner when his succession became due in 2004.

The article made considerable waves, at least by Brussels standards. Newspapers in Britain and Italy took up the story. At the OLAF headquarters, a postmodern glass tower in the European quarter of Brussels, the spin doctors once again reached for their telephones. OLAF spokesman Butticé even asked Prodi's people to confirm how much they trusted Brüner, and a Prodi spokesman subsequently obliged.

Apparently, the OLAF mandarins missed the irony of what they did! Brüner was supposed to investigate Prodi and his officials. In spring 2000, Brüner had told me that if he felt threatened he would call on the journalists to help him. In late 2003, the opposite had happened—Brüner felt frightened by the journalists and was seeking the help of the commission.

"They are obsessed with you," an OLAF agent warned me in early December 2003. He also claimed something that I could hardly believe, that Brüner's investigators had reopened a much-neglected investigation: "Special Case Number 3"—also known as the investigation against me.

Now, the OLAF investigators remembered Joachim Gross, the former Schreyer spokesman, who had pretended to know that I paid officials for information. On January 6, 2004, they interviewed him again. This time he provided the investigators with a new revelation. The source for his information on me was none other than one of my superiors at *Stern*, managing editor Wilfried Krause.

Later, the former spokesman (he had left the commission in July 2003) would admit that Krause had given him no information about my bribing officials. He would later claim that his source was another person in Brussels. When asked to reveal this source, he refused to provide the name of the mysterious character. A court would later ban Gross from repeating that Krause or any other *Stern* colleague was his source.

In January 2004, the OLAF investigators did nothing to verify the accuracy of Gross's statements. Had they even properly examined them? OLAF rushed into action. About one week after having talked to Gross, the OLAF investigators met with prosecutors in Brussels and Hamburg (where *Stern* has its headquarters) to discuss how to proceed against my editors and me. On February 11, they filed detailed complaints with the prosecutors in Brussels and Hamburg. They suggested "parallel searches" in the *Stern* offices of both cities.

There was an apparent need to act urgently. Alberto Perduca pressed the prosecutors because I was about to move to Washington, DC, as *Stern*'s correspondent.

The statement was a complete fiction. In fact, I was about to move to Hamburg, and OLAF Director Brüner was aware of this. But, without this fiction, it would have been difficult to explain why there was such "urgency," particularly because Hamburg was well within the reach of European prosecutors.

Of course, I learned about all of this—including that the responsible judge in Hamburg refused to grant a search warrant—only months later. OLAF had a better relationship with the public prosecutor's office in Brussels. A search warrant was signed on March 12, 2004. Just one day earlier, I had published a new story that made some noise and angered a number of people. The story said that EU deputies were suspected of having sent assistants, or other individuals, on their behalf to sign the official attendance list in the European parliament to fraudulently obtain the daily allowance of 262€. The German tabloid *Bild* put the revelation on its front page, and newspapers in France, Britain, Belgium, Austria, and Denmark followed suit.

It was eight days after the publication of this story that the police came to my door. Many thought there was a link between the two events. Perhaps someone at OLAF believed I had made so many enemies in the European Parliament that they would not have to face any substantial criticism from the deputies. But OLAF had underestimated the reaction of my colleagues.

The policemen accompanied me to my office in the International Press Centre. While walking down the corridor, I ran into a German colleague from the magazine *Focus*, Ottmar Berbalk. "Call my wife, call the news agencies, call *Stern* headquarters!" I yelled at him while the police tried to drag me away.

Ottmar and his *Focus* colleagues did what they could. A crowd of photographers, TV people, radio journalists, and other reporters gathered in front of my office door. Whenever the police opened the door, there were flashes lighting up the corridor. After the raid, newspaper and TV journalists in European countries—from Britain to Italy and from Finland to Bulgaria— called, interviewed me, and reported about the case. The line they chose was nearly always the same: Why did OLAF use all its powers to get back at a journalist when it had failed to show any interest in following the fraud trail inside the commission? Why had there been no OLAF searches of the private homes of the Eurostat directors? Why were there no OLAF searches of the commission offices?

German national deputies called me to express their support. The House of Lords in London discussed the case, and a leading deputy in the French Assemblée Nationale, René André, protested in letters to Schreyer and Pat Cox, president of the European parliament.

In addition, some EU deputies—the Austrian Herbert Bösch, the Dane Jens-Peter Bonde, and the Briton Chris Heaton-Harris— attacked OLAF for this unprecedented assault on press freedom. Unfortunately, they remained minority voices.

Cox told a TV interviewer of the BBC quite bluntly that he had no criticism for the OLAF investigators. Perhaps, he suggested, one should ask questions of the Belgian police. "This case stinks, no?" the BBC interviewer said to Cox. He replied that OLAF deserved no blame.

Helmut Kuhne, a German MEP and spokesman for the social democrats in the Budget Control Committee, even attacked those colleagues who had questioned OLAF's actions. It was an "absolute scandal" that people had tried to help me, he shouted.

Many people seemed to share Kuhne's view. The EU Commission—normally a defender of press freedom in remote areas of the globe—first tried a "no comment" policy. Next, it tried to wash its hands of the situation. The commission had "no role" in the story, Prodi's spokesman asserted.

Then word spread that the commission was in it up to its neck. Schreyer and Faull had apparently even encouraged Gross to testify against me in front of OLAF investigators. The commission finally decided to back OLAF openly. "You are their bête noire," an OLAF official told me. "They will not do anything to help you."

When I went to court to protest the actions of OLAF and the commission, the EU administration insisted that the Anti-Fraud Office was right to instigate a police inquiry into my sources. The arguments of the commission lawyers were revealing. In their eyes, we had neglected to realize how our reporting had affected "the reputation and the privacy of dozens or hundreds of EU officials who should have a right to fair internal investigations and [a] defense."

Strangely enough, the commission seemed to suggest that journalists should not write about ongoing investigations into their officials' wrongdoing—or if they did so, then the police had a right to intervene. To the commission, therefore, the "efficient pursuit of breaches of professional secrecy" was of the utmost importance.

After some weeks, the police returned most of my files. But they kept an astonishing number of documents—a thousand pages, plus copies of my hard disks, my address books, as well as other papers.

Most of the seized papers had nothing to do with the van Buitenen memoranda. Many of the documents that were kept by the police came from 1999, 2000, 2001, 2003, or 2004—despite the fact that the police claimed to be investigating a case from 2002.

Apparently, the commission was very interested in obtaining access to all of this material. The protection of sources was not its business—the commission wanted to find the officials who had originally leaked the information.

During this time, I had a revealing conversation with police detective Philippe Charlier. "Why do you go through this ordeal?" he asked me. "Why did you not simply reveal to us the name of your source?"

"Because if I had done so, my career as a journalist would have been finished," I explained. "My sources would have dried up. Nobody would have given me any confidential information anymore."

"Why?" Charlier replied. "Okay, you would have burned one source. But that would not have hindered your access to all possible official channels of information."

"What?" I retorted. "What kind of a journalism would that be where you could base your reporting only on official press releases and the words of those who govern us?"

I was not sure whether he got my point. It is not always easy to explain why protection of sources is essential for the work of journalists. Some people seem to believe that journalists are looking for undue privileges.

While I write these words, many questions remain unanswered. Why was the Belgian prosecutor ready to open a case on such a flimsy basis and with such speed? Had OLAF promised something to the Belgians in return? The question has to be asked because, in the past, the commission security service has hired Belgian police in return for services the police have rendered to commission officials, for example, by scrapping speeding fines against them.

And what of the Belgian judicial system! It was obvious that Belgian judges might find it tempting to be employed by OLAF at a salary three or four times as high as that provided by the Belgian authorities. And there was more to explain the good cooperation between OLAF and Belgians. Just prior to Brüner's investigators filing a complaint against me, OLAF had done several favors for local politicians by dropping cases of fraud in which Belgians were involved. (See page 21.)

Belgian judges and the police are notorious among the Belgian people. They have a solid reputation for being slow and ineffective, especially when they are supposed to be investigating members of the Belgian power elite. Nowhere in western Europe do citizens distrust their police and justice system more than in Belgium—at least that is the outcome of a recent commission poll, the so-called Eurobarometer of spring 2004.

I did not have to be paranoid to believe that there was some form of collusion between OLAF and the Belgian forces. Even Raymond Kendall, a former Interpol secretary general and current chairman of the OLAF Supervisory Committee, had the same impression. "There had obviously been some agreement between the magistrate in the OLAF office from Belgium and the magistrate who was going to receive the information from OLAF." Apparently, Kendall told a committee at the House of Lords that they had agreed to issue a search warrant.

They wanted "to get back at [me]," as Kendall put it. But why was I such a danger to the OLAF hierarchy members that they would endanger their own reputations?

The more the public learned about this case, the more embarrassing the story seemed to become for Brüner and his team. First, they claimed that they had nothing to do with the raid—until OLAF admitted the opposite was true. Before the European Parliament, OLAF officials claimed that they had never mentioned a possible "search" when talking to the public prosecutors. Like the others, this statement was soon exposed as a lie.

The Belgian judge and OLAF refused to give me access to the investigative file. But, luckily, the dossier was then leaked to journalists. Even the name of the hearsay witness—former spokesman Joachim Gross—became known. And newspapers like the *Süddeutsche Zeitung* and the *Daily Telegraph* were asking whether OLAF was "abusing its power."

Not surprisingly, that made the OLAF people furious. Obviously, they had hoped to keep their involvement secret. They had even promised Joachim Gross that his testimony would be confidential. When Gross's name came out, OLAF also started an investigation into this leak.

It still chills me to think of what happened. Never in my five years in Brussels had anyone seriously questioned the veracity of what I wrote. But, in this case, people tried to smear my character and put my professional career in jeopardy. OLAF apparently did not act in isolation but received support from the commission and from leading figures in the European Parliament.

Not that I had many illusions left about the character of the Brussels bureaucracy. Indeed, the EU Commission remains an institution that fears nothing more than accountability itself. As Jules Muis—the Dutch accountant and former vice president of the World Bank who left the commission in frustration in March 2004 after three years as chief auditor—once told me, the governing principle of the EU Commission was still "might makes right."

But, for all its weaknesses, the European Union is a club made up of democratic nations. As citizens of a democracy, people tend to place their trust in the rule of law, and they think that they are safe, especially when their breaches of law do not extend beyond the occasional parking ticket. As a result of my experiences, my trust in European democracy has suffered a severe blow.

I felt personally traumatized for weeks. Every time I left my apartment to go jogging—with only the keys to the house in my pocket— I was anxious. What would be left of my possessions when I returned?

The *Washington Post* reported on my case in August 2004 and quoted commission vice president Neil Kinnock: "Those who want to believe that we've got some kind of KGB here bent upon suppressing and, when that fails, penalizing whistle-blowers, are living on Mars." In fact, it is Kinnock who must be living on another planet. My journalistic sources are now possibly exposed to the police and—worse—the EU institutions, which employed many of the people who had leaked information to me. These actions were justified on the basis of an accusation that was completely fictional.

I was lucky because *Stern* is a big media organization. My bosses were ready to defend me and to pay the lawyers' fees. While I am writing this, we have started no fewer than five law suits: one appeal against the Belgian prosecutor, one court case against the commission (representing OLAF), one complaint against Brüner for defamation, and two law suits against Joachim Gross.

At least we were able to deter the Belgian police. Afterward, one of the policemen confided in me that he did not want to handle another case involving journalists during his lifetime. Journalists, he said, were too much of a nuisance.

Chapter 2

IN THE WONDERFUL WORLD OF IZ, IT'S *1984* ALL OVER AGAIN

STEPHEN KIMBER

Stephen Kimber is a professor of journalism at the University of King's College in Halifax, Canada, and an award-winning writer, editor, and broadcaster. He is the author of five nonfiction books, and his writing has appeared in almost all major Canadian publications. He is also a weekly political and general-interest columnist for both the *Sunday Daily News* in Halifax and for the Optipress community newspaper chain in Nova Scotia.

As well as his writing credits, Kimber has won many awards for his journalism, including a Dan McArthur Award for excellence in radio documentary production; a regional Alliance of Canadian Cinema, Television and Radio Artists (ACTRA) award for documentary writing; a Canadian Food Writers' Award for the best magazine article on the Canadian food industry; a National Author's Award for best business magazine article; an honorable mention from the Centre for Investigative Reporting for investigative reporting; and a citation of merit from the Atlantic Journalism Awards for magazine writing. His latest book, *Sailors, Slackers, and Blind Pigs,* a look at life in Halifax during World War II, won the Edith Richardson Nonfiction Prize and the Dartmouth Book Award and was a finalist for the Atlantic Booksellers' Choice Award. His first novel, *Reparations,* was published in 2005.

My fingers hovered over the Send button while I re-read one more time the words I'd just written. I'd been thinking about writing these words for weeks now, chewing over the pros and cons, trying without success to get the phrasing just right, knowing for almost certain the immediate consequences, not knowing what would happen after that.

Would anyone notice?

Would anyone care?

The column was about how CanWest Global Communications Corporation, the owners of the Halifax *Daily News*, the small Canadian daily for which I wrote a weekly column, had been mangling the news and suppressing opinions that didn't suit its worldview. I'd written that CanWest's owners, the Asper family of Winnipeg,

> appear to consider their newspapers not only as profit centres and promotional vehicles for their television network but also as private, personal pulpits from which to express their views. The Aspers support the federal Liberal party. They're pro-Israel. They think rich people like themselves deserve tax breaks. They support privatizing health care delivery. And they believe their newspapers, from Victoria, BC, to St. John's, NF, should agree with them.

If readers were concerned about what was happening at their newspaper, I concluded, they should write to Canada's heritage minister Sheila Copps and demand a public inquiry into the increasing—and increasingly dangerous—concentration of ownership and cross-ownership of Canada's news media.

I knew the *Daily News* would not—would not be allowed to—publish the column. I knew I would then have no choice but to resign. And I knew my resignation—and the reasons for it—would become public. After that . . . well, things couldn't be worse than they had become.

I pressed Send.

I'd been a weekly "whatever" columnist with the *Daily News* for fifteen years. It was a great gig. I could write about whatever I liked. And did. From provincial political chicanery to the wonder of taking my son to his first hockey game, from calling for the federal government to legalize marijuana to lamenting the stupidity of Americans and their obsession with Bill Clinton's sex life.

Whatever.

The column wasn't my day job. In "real" life, I was a professor and director of the School of Journalism at the University of King's College. Sometimes, I got the chance to combine the two callings by writing columns about journalism and journalism-related issues. Occasionally, I'd even take my newspaper bosses to task for some perceived journalistic sin or other.

I got away with that in no small measure because the paper's various owners—at least until the Aspers came along—were willing to let their editors run their papers, and their editors were more interested in offering readers a range of lively opinions than in promoting a particular political agenda or covering their own asses.

The *News* had started life in 1974 as a suburban Halifax weekly founded by David Bentley, a British expatriate journalist; his wife; and another couple. Five years later, it suddenly transformed itself into an urban daily tabloid, puppy-eager to challenge Halifax's venerable (some might say stodgy) newspaper of record, the broadsheet *Chronicle-Herald*. Against the odds, it survived.

Bentley's formula was pure Fleet Street: bold headlines, big photos, and delicious dollops of crime, scandal, and gossip, along with huge helpings of local news and opinion—lots and lots of opinion. I eventually became one of his eclectic stable of columnists. I was considered to be on the left of the political spectrum, as were a few others. But we were well and truly counterbalanced by a small army of right-wing columnists. Bentley didn't care; he was happy enough to have us all stirring the pot.

In 1985, recognizing that he didn't have the resources to take the paper to the next level, Bentley sold out to Harry Steele, a swashbuckling entrepreneur of conservative bent who hired a respected Winnipeg journalist, Doug MacKay, as his editor. MacKay reined in some of the paper's excesses and sharpened its journalism, but he didn't mess with its crazy quilt of column and opinion.

Though Steele must have occasionally spit out his morning coffee over his newspaper—especially when its reporters and columnists not only led the journalistic attack on his politician brother-in-law, who'd gotten favorable treatment on some loans from the banks, but also revealed Steele's own role in helping him out—and though he certainly complained to MacKay from time to time, he never ordered him to publish or not publish a story or an opinion.

Steele, however, was more an investor than a real publisher, and, in 1997, he sold the paper again, this time to the respected Southam chain, which owned many of the major dailies in the country but was then itself almost immediately gobbled up by Conrad Black's voracious Hollinger empire.

Black was a publisher of a different sort. He didn't get into the newspaper business to offer a public service or even simply to make money; he saw his growing newspaper empire—England's *Daily Telegraph*, Chicago's *Sun-Times*, the Jerusalem *Post*, and now thirteen metropolitan dailies in his native Canada—as an ideal vehicle to promote his own conservative agenda as well as serve as his personal entrée into a national and international world of power and influence.

That, in the end, was probably what saved the *Daily News* from Black's often heavy editorial hand. It was too small, too insignificant in the larger scheme of his interests for Black to fret much about anything we wrote. His real concern, it seemed, was how much annual profit the paper could shovel into the fire of his grander ambitions.

Black's grandest plan was to found his own right-wing national daily newspaper to challenge the not-quite-right-wing-enough *Globe and Mail*, which he did in 1998 with the launch of the Toronto-based *National Post.* A vicious newspaper war with its national and Toronto rivals—and the *Post's* ever-mounting losses—kept Black busy enough that he didn't seem to notice or care what people like me were writing in his other newspapers.

What I was writing, among other things, was a column criticizing cuts Hollinger and its local management had made to the *Daily News's* editorial budget—sending what I called "a clear signal that Conrad Black sees the newspaper less as a long-term investment and more as just another profit squeeze"—and another taking Conrad's columnist wife, Barbara Amiel, to task for a "snotty screed" she'd written against the entire profession of journalism and against journalism schools in particular. In it, I suggested one of the problems journalism schools faced was that they are cash strapped: "We don't get a lot of help in improving the teaching of our craft from publishers like your husband, who are happy enough to hire our graduates but not nearly so eager to contribute to their education."

The editors of the *Daily News* published both columns, and, though I know they took some heat for them, no one ever suggested to me that they—or I—could lose our jobs as a result.

Cue the Aspers, stage far right.

On July 31, 2000, Black—squeezed by those huge, continuing, and possibly never-ending losses at the *Post*—sold most of his Canadian newspaper holdings (minus, of course, a 50 percent interest in the *Post;* some dreams die hard) to the Asper family for $3.2 billion in Canadian funds. It was the biggest media transaction in Canadian history.

The buyer was the surprise.

Over the previous twenty-five years, Israel "Izzy" Asper, a flamboyant Winnipeg-born politician-entrepreneur, had built a successful television empire in the highly regulated Canadian broadcasting industry. He accomplished that largely on the strength of his political connections—he was a one-time leader of the Manitoba Liberal Party and a confidant of key Liberals, including Prime Minister Jean Chrétien—and on his company's uncanny ability to identify those new American sitcoms that Canadians would be eager to watch, and then outbid his rivals for the right to broadcast them.

Though his network of eight TV stations made Global Television the smallest of the big three in Canada—the publicly owned Canadian Broadcasting Corporation (CBC) and the private Canadian Television (CTV) were both significantly larger networks—CanWest had the distinction of being the most profitable. Some critics said that was because the Aspers spent less on news and current affairs than any other broadcaster. There was no national newscast and not a single Canadian newsmagazine program anywhere in its TV schedule.

If the company had little experience with news, it had none with newspapers.

The drive to expand the company's reach into newspapers came initially not from Izzy Asper, who was close to retirement, but from his youngest son, Leonard, the company's hard-driving thirty-six-year-old CEO who saw the future, and it spelled "convergence."

Though Izzy would joke that the purchase of Black's newspaper empire was the result of a misunderstanding—Leonard was going out for lunch one day and asked his father if he could bring him anything back, Izzy recalled. "Yeah," he replied, "would you mind getting me a couple of papers?"—the reality was that the acquisition of Hollinger's newspaper chain was just one part of Leonard's much grander plan.

His argument, essentially, was that consumers were about to be inundated with media choices—newspapers, radio, conventional TV networks, specialty channels, movies, DVDs, the Internet—in what was becoming an increasingly unregulated global media world. The only way to succeed in that environment was to take advantage of the "synergies"—"repurposing" content, relentlessly cross-promoting and cross-pollinating its products—

that would be possible if CanWest owned the broad spectrum of media "products."

With the Hollinger acquisition, CanWest went from being a small but successful broadcaster to being the dominant multimedia player in the country. In addition to the *Daily News*, CanWest Global suddenly owned half the *National Post* and thirteen daily newspapers in every major Canadian city except Toronto and Winnipeg. In nine of those markets, including Halifax, CanWest's Global Television Network also owned at least one local television outlet. Not to mention the licenses for four other stations in markets where it didn't have a newspaper, giving its TV network access to 94 percent of Canadian households. Not to forget six digital cable television stations; a television and film production company; Canada.com, the third-most popular Internet destination in Canada; 126 smaller daily and weekly newspapers; and, perhaps as a sign of even larger ambitions to come, broadcast outlets in Australia, New Zealand, Northern Ireland, and the Republic of Ireland.

Whatever their corporate ambitions, the Aspers—who held 45 percent of the equity and 86 percent of the voting rights at CanWest—clearly understood the power and influence that came with such a massive media presence. Very quickly, they began to make their editorial presence felt at their newspapers.

Some of that was simply clumsy—running a front-page puff piece in the *Post* to promote Global's new national newscast, for example—but there were more ominous portents.

In March 2001, David Asper, Leonard's brother and the vice president of CanWest, wrote an opinion piece that was published in all of the company's newspapers. Under the bullyboy title "Put Up or Shut Up," the piece complained that Canada's journalists were too critical of his father's good friend, Prime Minister Jean Chrétien. Ironically, Asper launched his attack at a time when the *National Post* was winning journalism awards for its persistent, groundbreaking investigative coverage of a scandal in which the prime minister was accused of personally intervening to help out a friend get a loan from Ottawa's Federal Business Development Bank.

Four months later, CanWest fired its national affairs columnist, Lawrence Martin, without explanation. Martin, a veteran political journalist who'd already published the first volume of a critical but widely praised biography of Chrétien, later wrote that he'd been told officials in the prime minister's office "pushed for my dismissal."

Two months after that, in September 2001, Michael Goldbloom, the publisher of the CanWest-owned Montreal *Gazette*, resigned, citing "fundamental differences" with the new owners. Though he wouldn't be specific at the time, he would later tell the *New York Times*, "There is no question in my mind the Aspers feel they own the newspapers and the newspapers should reflect their views. It's not just what you see in the paper but what you don't see."*

How fundamental Goldbloom's "fundamental differences" really were quickly became evident at his former paper.

Gazette TV critic Peggy Curran's review of a CBC documentary that criticized the Israeli military for targeting media working on the Palestinian side of the Middle East conflict was held for a day and then altered before being published.

"Usually criticism is criticism and you're allowed to say what you want," Curran explained later. "I can't think of another occasion when this has happened to me." Soon after, Curran gave up her TV critic's job and went on a year's leave of absence. "Whether you know it or not," she added, "you start censoring yourself."

Journalists discovered if they didn't censor themselves, CanWest would do it for them.

During the late fall, word leaked out that CanWest was planning to produce national editorials—up to three a week—which all of its daily papers would be required to run on their editorial pages. Incredibly, the new editorial policy also said that none of

---

*Clifford Krauss, "Canadian Press Freedom Questioned in Publisher's Firing," *New York Times*, June 29, 2002.

the chain's local papers would be allowed to publish an editorial that contradicted the head office slant.

It didn't take a genius to figure out what that slant would be. Earlier in the year, for example, after a terrorist attack in Jerusalem, some Israeli cabinet ministers had called for the Israelis to kill Palestinian leader Yasser Arafat in retaliation. A stand-alone editorial at the time, written at Winnipeg headquarters and published in all CanWest papers, declared, "Howsoever the Israeli government chooses to respond . . . [it] should have the unequivocal support of the Canadian government."

In early December, more than fifty reporters at the *Gazette* protested the company's new national editorial package by removing their bylines from their copy. The paper's editorial page editor asked to be reassigned.

Political columnist Don MacPherson wrote a piece in December 2001 in which he argued that "a policy that forbids a newspaper from deciding for itself where the interests of its readers lie is not only bad journalism, it's also bad business." By the time it was published, the column had been rewritten in Orwellian CanWest newspeak. "A uniquely Canadian policy," began the revised version, "that allows for editorials written from both local and national viewpoints, and occasional lively disagreement between the two, could be good for business."

Terry Mosher, the *Gazette*'s award-winning editorial cartoonist, produced a cartoon spoofing the new homogenization policy. "Imagine," the caption read, "a newspaper that looks just like, ummmm, Global Television." The cartoon was spiked. So was a second that took a similar position.

When fifty-four reporters and other staffers at the *Gazette* signed an open letter criticizing the policy—the letter was published on December 10, 2001, in both the *Globe and Mail* and the French-language *La Presse*, but not in the *Gazette* or any other CanWest paper—David Asper hit back with a public speech in which he described the journalists as "riffraff" and, borrowing

R.E.M. lyrics, boasted, "It's the end of the world as they know it, and I feel fine."

His speech was followed the next day by a "reminder/advisory" to all staff members, informing them of their "obligation of primary loyalty to the employer," and warning that revealing what was described as confidential information or even gossip could lead to nasty consequences. "Case law," the memo explained blandly, "supports sanctions, including suspension or termination."

I watched all of this with growing unease. Unlike Black, the Aspers took a proprietary interest in what any and all of their papers were publishing, including the *Daily News*.

When I wrote a column playfully mocking the *National Post*'s fawning front-page coverage of the launch of what was a relatively pedestrian national newscast on its sister Global Television Network, I got a call from my editor, Bill Turpin. Turpin, who had succeeded Doug MacKay as the paper's editor, was a principled journalist, so it was clear that he was uncomfortable with what he had to say but that he had to say it. Under the dictates of the new ownerships regime, he told me, the paper couldn't run such a column.

I let it go. Partly because it didn't seem like a big deal—it was just a TV show, for God's sake—and partly because Bill was both an editor and also a friend. I didn't want to make his life any more difficult than I realized it already was. I understood—though I didn't understand the half of it at the time—that he and other editors across the chain were fighting a losing battle with head office against the corporate line.

A few weeks later, I smacked up against this official corporate line once again. This time, it was the uncrossable Middle East line. It was just after 9/11 and I, like columnists everywhere, was trying to make sense out of what had happened. I wrote a column in which I cited the failure of Israel's policy of escalating revenge in response to acts of terror as an example of why George W. Bush's single-minded war on terror was also doomed to failure.

In the published version, that argument vaporized. Over the next month or so, I poked and prodded at what I thought might be the edges of what I could write about Israel, the Palestinians, and terrorism and found there wasn't much.

I was far from alone, even at the *Daily News*. But, because I was a freelancer, I didn't know much of what was really happening inside the paper. I knew the paper had suddenly stopped carrying Peter March, a Saint Mary's University philosophy professor who'd been writing a weekly column for the paper for ten years, for example. But I didn't know he'd been dropped because of a column he'd written that criticized Israel. I also didn't know that staff columnist David Swick had been informed he was "no longer allowed to write anything to do with the Middle East," he said much later. "I was not perceived to be adamantly pro-Israel." Or that Parker Barrs Donham, the province's premier investigative journalist and an award-winning columnist for the paper, had decided to abandon journalism for public relations, in part because of the ways in which his columns were also being sliced and diced.

By the time of the brouhaha at the *Gazette*, I was steering clear of those subjects I knew would cause trouble. But the courage of the *Gazette* reporters—and the Aspers' oppressive retaliation—forced me to rethink my all-too-comfortable position.

For starters, of course, I was a journalism professor, which meant not only that I should know better than to acquiesce to such blatant censorship and manipulation but also that I had a tenured job at a university.

Unlike full-time journalists, who would be risking their jobs, houses, and even families if they spoke out, I had the luxury of being able not only to quit my column at the newspaper but also to do so publicly.

I decided to write the column.

I warned Bill Turpin it was coming and turned it in a full day before my weekly deadline so he could try to stickhandle it past Winnipeg. He couldn't. Our phone conversation was brief. We both understood our roles. The paper, he said, wouldn't be running this particular column, but he'd be happy to have me continue as a columnist. I respectfully declined. He said he was sorry, thanked me, and wished me well.

Secretly, I knew, he was hoping my resignation might finally force the nasty story of what was happening inside CanWest papers from coast to coast onto the public consciousness.

It didn't take long for the floodgates to burst. The next morning's *Globe and Mail* carried a story about my resignation, which was quickly picked up by the Toronto *Star* and the CBC, CTV, and private radio talk shows across the country, though not—not surprisingly—by any CanWest outlet.

But I was inundated with messages of support from journalists inside other CanWest papers, including one from Doug Cuthand, an aboriginal columnist for CanWest's Regina *Leader-Post*, who'd just had one of his own columns spiked for daring to compare the plight of Canada's aboriginals with that of the Palestinians. Readers called and e-mailed, too, telling me they were canceling their subscriptions to CanWest papers in protest.

CanWest's Winnipeg head office, for its part, insisted it had played no role in what happened to me. My column, CanWest's vice president of editorial Murdoch Davis claimed, had simply been "declined by management" at the local paper because it was "poorly researched" and contained unspecified "factual inaccuracies."

Intriguingly, there was even more of a response from beyond Canada's borders. I was surprised, but, in retrospect, I shouldn't have been. Globalization had made media concentration and cross-media ownership—well, a global issue. Media outlets from as far away as New Zealand called for interviews. In the United States, the AFL-CIO and the Consumer's Union invited me to be their "canary in the mine shaft" for a campaign they were launching to showcase the dangers of the Federal Communication

Commission's plan to deregulate the broadcast system in that country and allow for cross-media ownership. I also got an e-mail from an Australian journalists' group called Friends of Fairfax, inviting me to tell my story to a parliamentary committee, which was also looking into loosening its media ownership rules.

While all of this provided a welcome boost to my frequent flyer points, it had little, almost no, effect on the Aspers' behavior.

In March 2002, editors at the Regina *Leader-Post* rewrote the lead on one reporter's story. Michelle Lang had been sent to cover a speech to students at the local School of Journalism by the Toronto *Star*'s editorial page editor emeritus, Haroon Siddiqui. Lang dutifully returned to the newsroom, wrote her story, and filed it.

The story began, "CanWest Global performed 'chilling' acts of censorship when it refused to publish several columns containing viewpoints other than those held by the media empire, a Toronto *Star* columnist said Monday." By the time the story appeared in print, the lead read, "A Toronto *Star* columnist says it's OK for CanWest Global to publish its owners' views, as long as the company is prepared to give equal play to opposing opinions."*

Incredibly, the paper's editor-in-chief told Lang her original story had been changed because he wasn't comfortable with her use of the word *censorship*.

In the wonderful world of Iz, it was *1984* all over again.

When ten reporters at the *Leader-Post* withheld their bylines in protest, CanWest handed out suspensions and warned all of its journalists across the country that the company would no longer tolerate such byline protests. CanWest's response to the Regina revolt, coincidentally, helped shed new light on what had really happened to me three months earlier.

In a letter to the editor of the *Leader-Post*, CanWest's top editorial spokesman, Murdoch Davis, defended the decision to change Lang's copy by claiming it had been a local editorial deci-

---

*"Regina Reporters Disciplined after Byline Strike to Protest Changes to Story," *Canadian Press*, March 11, 2002.

sion in the same way that my column had been "declined by management at the *Daily News* in Halifax."

Bill Turpin had had enough. In a letter to the editor of his own in reply in March 2002, Turpin begged to disagree, "I and other [CanWest] editors had been repeatedly urged by Mr. Davis to get his advice on any prospective commentary that might run contrary to [CanWest's] rapidly changing editorial policies. To my profound regret, I did so in Mr. Kimber's case. Mr. Davis told me in colorful terms that publishing the piece would be a career disaster." Davis himself later confirmed that he'd told Turpin to go ahead and publish my column "if you're looking for a hill to die on."

Turpin's courageous letter to the editor did not appear in the *Leader-Post*, of course, but it became required e-mail and bulletin-board reading in newsrooms across the country. He quit a month later.

It only got worse.

On June 1, 2002, during what had been an especially bad week for Prime Minister Jean Chrétien—he'd had to fire one cabinet minister and demote another for ethical breaches—CanWest's *Ottawa Citizen* published a toughly worded feature on how the prime minister had responded to recent parliamentary criticism of his personal business dealings. After laying out the evidence, the *Citizen's* Graham N. Greene wrote, "Our survey of his own words leads to only one logical conclusion: He lied." The feature was accompanied by an equally tough editorial urging Chrétien "to step down for the good of your party and of the country. If you will not, we urge the Liberal party to throw you out."*

Two weeks later, David Asper flew in from Winnipeg and fired the *Citizen's* longtime publisher, Russell Mills. Though Mills himself said he was told it was because he'd allowed the Chrétien editorial to run, CanWest would later insist it was because—wait for it—Mills

---

*Graham N. Greene, "Double Standard: Part Two," *Ottawa Citizen*, June 1, 2002; "Time to Go: Chrétien's Own Behaviour Inspired Government Rot. He Must Leave," *Ottawa Citizen*, June 1, 2002.

didn't display "an openness to all points of view." After the Mills firing became public, more than three thousand *Citizen* readers canceled their subscriptions to add their voice to the growing public protests over CanWest's draconian editorial policies.

Despite the growing controversy, the Aspers' friends in the federal Liberal government did almost nothing about the fact that the Aspers' dominance of the Canadian media marketplace was affecting what Canadians were reading and seeing.

Early in 2001, in fact, Canada's broadcast regulator, the Canadian Radio Television and Telecommunications Commission, tacitly accepted cross-media ownership when it approved TV license renewals for CanWest and CTV. Since both broadcasters had recently acquired key newspaper properties (CTV's new parent company, BCI Inc., bought the *Globe and Mail*), those decisions naturally raised questions about Ottawa's policy on media ownership.

Ostensibly in response to those concerns, Sarmite Bulte, the parliamentary secretary to the federal minister of heritage, told Canadian Press in March 2001 that Ottawa would be appointing a "blue or red-ribbon panel of experts" to examine the impact of media concentration and cross-media ownership. But it seemed she misspoke herself. Within days, her boss, heritage minister Sheila Copps, was backpedaling desperately. The panel of experts suddenly became just a study by the Commons' Heritage Committee. And the promised wide-ranging examination—oops, did not include newspapers.

In the end, the all-party committee bucked its masters and, in a massive 2003 report, concluded that dramatic action was needed to "protect the integrity of editorial independence and journalistic freedom." It recommended, among other things, a moratorium on future acquisitions of broadcast licenses by companies with existing TV or newspaper holdings. But the committee's report received scant attention in CanWest's papers. The Montreal *Gazette* didn't even run a story about it, for example, while the Vancouver *Sun* dismissed it with a seventy-one-word brief. The report's recommendations, perhaps not surprisingly, have not been at the top of any political party's agenda.

Orwell would not have been surprised.

Much has changed since I pressed Send. But more remains the same.

Within a year, CanWest Global, staggering under the weight of the four billion Canadian dollars in debt it had taken on, largely to finance its Hollinger acquisition—and facing continuing losses at the *National Post*, which it now owned totally—began peddling some of its newspapers. In July 2002, Transcontinental Media, a growing printing and publishing company based in Montreal, bought ten of CanWest's small dailies, including the *Daily News*.

The following April, I resumed writing my weekly column. Six months later, Transcon announced plans to acquire Optipress, a smaller regional publisher that owned a chain of seventeen community weeklies in Nova Scotia and Newfoundland. The *Daily News*'s fluffy lead story on the purchase, which appeared under the self-congratulatory headline, "Here We Grow," failed to raise the issue of media concentration even though the new combined company would have a virtual stranglehold on the print media in the region.

I decided I should write about that in my next column. Suggesting that the *News* had "flunked the test" of full disclosure, I wrote that "readers have a right to worry if their newspaper isn't more forthcoming."

The column, I'm pleased to report, ran as I wrote it.

In February 2003, the Aspers' good friend Jean Chrétien retired from politics. His successor was the Aspers' other good friend, former finance minister Paul Martin. CanWest contributed 100,000 Candian dollars to Martin's Liberal leadership campaign. There is no indication that Martin's government is any more eager than its predecessor to tackle the issues of media concentration and cross-media ownership.

In October 2003, Izzy Asper died. His sons, Leonard and David, and daughter, Gail, CanWest's corporate secretary, pledged to continue in their father's corporate and editorial footsteps. And they have.

On September 17, 2004, for example, an intrepid *Ottawa Citizen* reader pointed out in a letter to the editor that the paper had changed a number of words in an Associated Press dispatch from Iraq. The original words were "insurgents" and "fighters." In the *Citizen* version, both words became "terrorists." The word *terrorist* was inserted into the story seven different times. It turned out that editing wire copy from the Associated Press (AP), Reuters, and other international news agencies to conform to the Aspers' narrow worldview was part of a recently instituted CanWest policy for all its papers.

The same day as it published the letter, in fact, the *Citizen* carried another AP dispatch, this one from Jerusalem under the byline of Mark Lavie. The *Citizen* version began, "An Israeli helicopter fired a missile at a car in the West Bank town of Jenin yesterday, killing three terrorists. . . . The three were members of the Al Aqsa Martyrs' Brigades, a violent terror group linked to Yasser Arafat's Fatah movement."*

The original story used "people" where the *Citizen* had inserted "terrorists," and while it confirmed that one of those killed was from the Brigades, which the AP's reporter on the scene called an "armed resistance group," the story added that "two others killed with him were not identified."

Despite protests from the AP and Reuters—"Terrorist is an emotive term that we don't use in the way that they used it," explained a Reuters spokesperson†—and calls from the National Council on Canada-Arab Relations and the Canadian Arab Federation for a provincial press council to investigate CanWest's

---

*Mark Lavie, "Terror Group Threatens to Retaliate after Israel Kills Three Followers," *Ottawa Citizen*, September 14, 2004.

†Nicolaus van Rijn, "Report Biased, Arabs Argue; CanWest Inserts Word 'Terrorist,' Groups Asking for an Inquiry," *Toronto Star*, September 18, 2004.

"biased reporting against Muslims and Arabs," CanWest was defiant. And as Orwellian as ever.

"We're editing for style," Scott Anderson, the editor of the *Citizen* insisted.

In an editorial on the issue, the *National Post* dismissed the news agencies' "misleading gloss of political correctness. . . . We owe it to our readers," the paper said, "to remove it before they see their newspaper every morning."

George himself couldn't have explained it better.

Chapter 3

A LITTLE TROUBLE IN LIBERIA*

TIM LAMBON

Tim Lambon is the senior foreign video producer for Channel 4 News in the United Kingdom. A contributor to the *New Statesman* and the *London Review of Books*, Lambon is also the author of *South of Capricorn*, a photojournalistic look at small-town South Africa from its trains. Starting out as a Special Forces officer, he exchanged his rifle for a camera and has covered almost every war since the start of the 1980s. After the September 11 attacks, it was inevitable that Lambon would cover George W. Bush's wars, starting with the liberation by coalition forces of Kabul. Recipient of the Gold Medal for Editing at the New York Television Awards and a contributor to three Royal Television Society awards and a British Film and Television Society award, Tim was the video producer on the Channel 4 News Baghdad team that won the International Emmy in 2003 for coverage of the most recent war in Iraq. A second International Emmy was won by the team for its coverage of the 2004 Madrid train bombings.

---

*Those parts of the text set in block quotations are taken either from the original documentary treatment or the diary Tim Lambon kept during his stay in Liberia.

Stretched out half asleep on the floor, I heard the noise of men shouting, heavy footfalls, and the rattle of rifles, which awoke me instantly. Rule number one—never remove your boots. I just managed to pull mine on before the flimsy door burst open, slamming against the wall. A braying mob of black-uniformed thugs streamed through the door, shouting and brandishing their Kalashnikovs. There was hardly a moment to grab possessions and clothes as hands reached out for us.

My colleagues Sorious Samura, David Barrie, and Gugu Radebe were already being roughly forced out the door as I managed to snatch up my shirt and waist pouch. A huge hand slapped the small of my back, grabbing my trousers and belt, dragging me toward the door. I swiveled to provide the least resistance and started running, harried by the last two goons.

Ahead of me, I could see the others being forced to run across the concrete parking lot of the compound toward the vehicle entrance. In my memory, it's a silent movie in tones of sodium pink and brown. I see the faces of our assailants twisted with apparent anger, but I can't hear what they are shouting. The tall metal gates are open, and, at first glance, the street is one-in-the-morning deserted. Terrified, I imagine four bodies lying in the road, blood pooling darkly across to the gutter and a headline proclaiming "Spies shot trying to escape." Immediately, I shut down the image, suppressing the fear and working on tactics for the immediate reality.

Was this the moment to run? I knew where the US Embassy was—not too far. I'd planned such a run in the days that led up to this. I weighed my chances.

Then, we were turning left up the hill, and half the fear subsided. Toyota pickup trucks waited with engines running. It wasn't to be a death, framed by the government, on the streets outside the National Security Agency headquarters. Not here, not yet. But the remaining fear formed the next question, "Where are they taking us?" We were hustled up to the vehicles, and searching hands were thrust into our pockets to steal precious possessions. I gave a grim smile. I had left my veteran Swiss Army knife back at the hotel, so no rich pickings in my pockets!

The shouting and gesticulation indicated we should climb into one of the vehicles. It didn't take many threats before Gugu, my big Zulu soundman, and I vaulted into the truck. We were forced to sit on the floor of the truck under an A-frame section of back-to-back seats. I was pulling on my shirt when one of the goons noticed my waist pouch. Good-bye to all that.

There was much shouting and gunning of engines. More troops or policemen or whatever they were climbed aboard. "Hands on the seat!" We complied. Then, the trucks were turning clumsily in the narrow street. Up on the pavement. Down again and, with a lurch, we roared away. I saw the black-bereted bruiser standing on the tow bar look at my watch.

"What's that?" he demanded with a sneer that said he knew very well what it was. Lunging for the watch, he almost fell off as the vehicle sped around a corner. Momentarily recovering his balance, he ripped the old Casio from my wrist. Something at the back of my mind smiled at the slapstick. The watch was the least of my worries.

Such experiences were very different from the original negotiations for the venture.

"If I do this doco, Ron, I want to meet the director, and he has to give me a one-sheet treatment of how he's going to shoot it." I was adamant, and Ron McCullogh, owner of Insight News Television and producer of the documentary series for Britain's Channel 4 and America's CNN, acquiesced.

"He's going on Monday, but we'll meet for breakfast on Sunday and David will show you his ideas," Ron assured me. It was the continuation of a discussion about the suitability of the director assigned to the documentary. David Barrie was a neophyte. With no experience in Africa, he was being sent to make a film in one of the continent's most dangerous countries. A film about subjects that in west Africa are valued in lives: diamonds, timber, and guns.

I was prepared to forego my worries about the documentary's style as long as I was sure the journalism was sound. At the break-fast meeting on a bright summer's morning in Islington in the United Kingdom, the journalism became a security issue for me. I was presented not with a single-page treatment about the film's style but with six sheets of the most extraordinary creative writing.

> Eight o'clock at night. Monrovia, Liberia. The streets are deserted. . . . Sorious Samura awkwardly checks his bow tie in the bathroom mirror of his decrepit hotel bedroom. He is about to meet Africa's first mafia head of state, a fugitive from American justice, known for his Rolls Royces, endless dating of beauty queens and $110m annual earnings from the illicit trade in diamonds and marijuana—Dr. Charles Taylor, President of Liberia—a man who also happens to have won a thumping majority in national elections in 1997. A presidential limo scoops Sorious up from outside his hotel.
>
> Sorious has been invited to the Executive Mansion to hear about Taylor's peace plan for the region and strategy for recon-struction of the country.
>
> Sorious challenges Taylor. The encounter is dramatic. The debonair mafia boss meets the troubled, sincere Sierra Leonean, desperate to find a solution to Africa's trouble.
>
> Why did Taylor recently execute fourteen top security men supposedly loyal to him? Forty others remain unaccounted for—where have they gone? How is it that the Antwerp dia-mond council records $300m worth of diamonds sourced in Liberia, while the Government budget says it is just $30m? How could Taylor reject the British and American allegation that he supports the RUF,* when refugees in camps talk openly about

---

*Revolutionary United Front. A guerrilla force that fought a ten-year civil war to seize control of diamond production in Sierra Leone. The RUF was virtually disbanded with the arrest of its leader Foday Sankoh.

rebel soldiers living in camps, going about their business and trading diamonds with dealers in Monrovia? Eighty-five percent of the Liberian population is unemployed. The Government cannot afford to keep the lights on and water running in Monrovia. There is little evidence throughout the country of public spending. And yet, Taylor runs a fleet of Rolls Royces and earns an annual income, estimated by the US Ambassador to Liberia four years ago, and the Interim Government seven years ago, of $100m upward. Couldn't a fraction of that wealth be invested in improving the lot of ordinary Liberians, say keeping the lights on in Monrovia? Perhaps even sowing the seeds of a political system which would allow an individual without a private army to win power?

Ron gave me the document and poured coffee as I glanced through it. Right from the first paragraph my jaw dropped. As a film treatment, it was a fantasy, one that I immediately realized would be very dangerous.

"What on Earth do you think this is?" I asked, slapping the pages down on the table.

"Yes, well, it is a bit hyped, but it's just the selling treatment David put together," Ron huffed. They tried to mollify me with assurances that it was only a few ideas David had thrown together after surfing the Web, that it was written solely for the commissioning editors, "And you know what they're like. They love all that hyped stuff," they said. "Shows them pictures they can get off on."

"Well, that had better not go anywhere near Liberia while I'm there," I replied vehemently, emphasizing that if I were to look after the security of the team, I did not want the document in any form to be taken with us. I was assured it was only for marketing purposes.

None of this answered my question about how David wanted to shoot the documentary. As we talked, it became clear that he had no real idea of what the film would look like. The whole thing appeared to hinge on not one but two interviews that my companions assured me David had set up with President Charles Taylor. I laughed at them, and I remember betting my fee for the shoot that we wouldn't get anywhere near, much less speak to, Taylor.

In the end, much against my better judgment, I agreed to continue with the project because it was a production of such narrow margins that my late withdrawal would jeopardize Ron's whole business. Back home, I showed the offending document to my partner, the diplomatic correspondent at Channel 4 News, Lindsey Hilsum. She wasted no time in getting on the phone to Ron to ask exactly what he thought he was doing.

Sorious Samura is a Sierra Leonean cameraman who woke up one day to find that RUF rebels had occupied his neighborhood in Freetown. Taking his camera, he shot award-winning material first aired by the BBC in a news broadcast some weeks later. Moving to London from Sierra Leone, Sorious became an eloquent spokesman for the ordinary and oppressed in Africa. Ron McCullogh was commissioned by David Lloyd of Channel 4 to produce a documentary series, including the Liberia film, to be fronted by Sorious.

The director, who was David Barrie, and Sorious flew to Liberia the day after our Islington meeting and spent the week setting up appointments and working out a schedule for the documentary. I flew to Abidjan, Côte d'Ivoire, the following Sunday. There, I met up with my old friend and colleague Gugu Radebe. A son of the South African struggle, Gugu started as a runner* for Britain's Independent Television News in the early 1980s; later, he followed the well-trodden path from soundman to cameraman. The next day, we caught a Ghana Airlines flight to Monrovia.

Collected from Monrovia airport by Wellington Smith, the shoot's local fixer†, Gugu and I arrived at the Mamba Point Hotel to find David and Sorious in a bit of a funk. They were still optimistic but grappling with a government that appeared to be

---

*A runner's duty is to fetch and carry, as well as undertake other small jobs in the production department of a film or television company.

†A fixer is usually a native of the country where the documentary team is filming who is responsible for "fixing" local difficulties.

retreating after what initially had seemed like enthusiasm for the project. My diary entry on August 9, 2000, written the next morning, observed,

> It seems that despite the much vaunted "access" . . . David and Sorious haven't made much headway in getting this thing off the ground. Interview with the Boss (Charles Taylor) hasn't been . . . mentioned, so may or may not be off. Other players seem to be the Minister of Defense and the Party Chairman, aside from some former combatant, now amputee, who dances on his crutches and a bunch of guys who make gravel by hand. . . . Three different away days are possible. . . . Whether any of this will actually happen, we'll have to wait and see.

Obviously, I was skeptical.

It didn't get much better. Tropical downpours disrupted the filming of what few sequences had been set up. One that worked out was an interview with Sam Bokry, a vicious Sierra Leonean rebel commander who had been semiretired by Taylor. He claimed that all the blood he'd shed was on behalf of his fellow countrymen. By contrast, the impoverished workers crushing rocks by hand at a defunct gravel quarry provided a stark illustration of what west Africa's wars have visited upon its people. Later, hopes were initially raised by an evening shoot at a hangout appropriately named "Sharks." There I filmed the minister of defense thrashing Sorious at pool, but we later came to realize that he was not part of the inner cabal actually running the country and was powerless to help with any of our requests.

By Friday, five days into the project, we had shot very little footage. An expedition to a diamond-mining village had come off, but the story was soft. There was no edge to this thing. We arrived back at the hotel to find David was "one worried puppy," according to my diary. After dinner I was writing in my diary and reading when David came to discuss the way the project was going. Afterward I wrote,

Just had David in here, quarter past eleven at night, scrambling to try and make sense of this thing. . . . Gone the TWO interviews with Taylor, gone the "everything's set up and they've been encouraged by African-American leaders in the States," gone even the Party Chairman so much a part of the scene when we arrived. In fact, the whole ridiculous proposal (the treatment I'd been shown) not only has no legs to stand on, it is probably a document which could be held up in the court which may have to judge whether the production money for the series was procured under false pretences!

But having said all that, we'll go back with enough footage to create an extended news piece and it will work, but it'll have been cobbled together around a slightly fuzzy central theme of "oh isn't Liberia fucked up and aren't these African leaders shitty and this is all because of our colonial masters." David, however, has already realized that he'll not be making the solid piece of arty documentary he thought he was coming here to do.

Two days later, with just one week of filming left before we were scheduled to leave, we had failed to film a sequence with the dancing amputee and things were looking bleaker. As my diary suggested on August 13, 2000,

It wasn't a good feeling in the car on the way back to the hotel this evening. Everything they've tried to set up this week has turned to dust. People who initially appeared enthusiastic have backed off and gone to ground. . . . The doco is in serious trouble if they don't lock onto a hard story line and fast. The Minister of Defense was supposed to let us know about accompanying him on a tour of some place up North by eight this evening, but nothing has happened yet (23h00).

More worrying for me from a security perspective was "A report in the President's own newspaper yesterday alleged that the US government has made funding to the tune of US$2 million available for a hit on Taylor. It alleges that US and UK missionaries and diplomats are roaming the streets of Monrovia spying out the best places to do the deed. . . . The article is really worrying because it's playing with the sort of mob hysteria that gets people killed."

I met with various diplomats on the security situation, which was rather succinctly put by "Roger Arsenault, UN Security Chief for the country. His advice? Don't stay overnight outside Monrovia. His opinion? Pieces of paper don't mean shit and even having a Minister along, unless he's a big hitter, is more likely to endanger the minister than get you through. 'It's the Wild West out there man. Frontiersville and Monrovia's authority stops just beyond the airport.'"

David was almost in despair. We had a strategy meeting with Smith and Pius, the local co-coordinator for a human rights organization, the Justice and Peace Commission. I approached the thing the way I would a news shoot, suggesting we

> find out who has integrity in the society. Who is the Desmond Tutu of Liberia? Immediately, Pius and Smith came up with three names—two human rights lawyers and a man who started Susuku, an "education-for-weapons" program, which has processed and tried to rehabilitate over 19,000 of the estimated [23,000 to] 25,000 ex-combatants."
>
> In an attempt to get at the "have-nots," I suggested that we get hold of some of the local NGOs I felt must be operating in West Point (the shanty town on a spit of sand sticking out into the lagoon—25% of which has disappeared to the waves over the years). It turned out that Pius has a man who works there permanently and who could take Gugu and Sorious around to meet people.

We decided to try and lower the team's visibility by sending only the black members out onto the streets. Two white people in public merely drew attention to the camera, something we needed to avoid.

It was during this discussion that David came up with the

idea of filming at the port of Bucanan, the second-largest town in Liberia. Filming at any port is usually a bureaucratic process of permissions and minders, so sneak filming at a harbor reputedly owned by the president himself was a very bad idea. As security adviser, I absolutely forbade it. I also warned David that no attempt should be made to film the illegal hardwood logging that constituted a major part of the traffic at the port. We were too high profile in a very small country. After being so open about what we were doing, we could not start filming surreptitiously.

However, another story in Bucanan illustrated not only the country's state of decay but also the ingenuity of its people. Although no rolling stock survived the war, the tracks of the railway into the interior were still more or less intact. People still needed to move themselves and their goods backward and forward, so inventive operators had built wooden trolleys that ran on the tracks. Charging a modest fare, the operators manually pushed passengers and their luggage to destinations up and down the line. I agreed to let Gugu and Sorious go to Bucanan the next day to film the story.

My diary is mute about that day. The entry finishes just before lunch because I later went back and excised the part that described what happened for fear it would be found by the authorities and used against us. It was at lunch that David admitted to me that he had told Sorious to pursue both the logging and port sequences. I was furious and insisted that he immediately try and reach the team members by radio to recall them. The radio was not working. The wait began. Sunset faded into the dense tropical night. The team was long overdue. I had expressly forbidden travel on the roads after dark, and David and I were so concerned by nine o'clock that evening that we contacted Brian Brewer, the British honorary consul, and our friend Roger Arsenault, the UN security chief.

Eventually the team rumbled into the parking lot around ten o'clock. The relief I felt was short-lived as the team revealed how successful it had been in filming both the logging and the port. Brewer, who was with us at the time, concurred that these activities would not have gone unnoticed and that the authorities would probably come looking for the footage.

Sure enough, the next afternoon, we were summoned to see Joe Mulba, the minister of information. His boss, the minister of public affairs, and Mulba berated us roundly. He claimed that we had been filming without permission from the president and beyond the bounds of our accreditation. Although no mention was made of the filming in the port at Bucanan, it was obviously implied. Initially, we thought we might get away with the reprimand, but Mulba demanded VHS copies of all our tapes and banned any further filming. According to my diary, "we filed out like a string of whipped dogs and went back to the hotel having agreed to make copies of the footage. . . . 'In the interests of fair play and objectivity' said the Minister, 'we don't want to censor anyone, just to have a record.'"

We called London to tell Ron about the situation. I knew we had to do a sweep of our possessions for anything that could be misconstrued by the government, should our rooms be searched. I instructed the film crew members to bring me absolutely anything they thought might endanger us if found by the paranoid authorities. Each of us did his own "housekeeping," and the gathered effects were spirited to a friendly African embassy via a secure conduit. I rewound and relabeled all the tapes we had shot, creating a bogus set of appropriately doctored surrogates that could be surrendered if necessary.

The team was nervous and, according to my diary, Sorious, who went to gather information from the hotel staff came back,

> freaking out about the Anti-Terrorist Unit [ATU—Taylor's squad of private thugs] being about to attack—"there's a truck load just down the road . . ."—and about how someone had told him that the team had only just missed being done by the ATU last night on their way back from Buchanan.

"They were there at the last check point and they were arguing with the police as we went through and just kept on driving. . . ." he reported . . . this sort of talk makes everyone jumpy, but on reflection, although it's good to take precautions, the likelihood of anyone attacking foreign journalists in the only operational hotel in Monrovia is unlikely.

Brian Brewer . . . came straight over. We discussed strategy and he confirmed the things I suspected—attack unlikely, port incriminating, confiscation of tapes possible even probable.

The machinery of the state had kicked into gear, and those who knew it well were worried. I wrote,

Poor Smith [our local fixer] has now flipped out completely. He was already windy about the repercussions even if everything had gone well, but now he's lost it completely, moving his family into hiding and not sleeping in the same place twice in a row. Seldom do we realize what a major upheaval our short trips to these places cause our fixers. I bet that Smith will now have to leave this country altogether whilst this administration is still in power—and what does he get for that? US$150 a day for two weeks and goodbye!

But my "housekeeping" was not thorough enough. I should have personally inspected everyone's gear, but I didn't, fearing that this would indicate that I doubted their professionalism. It was a mistake that came back to haunt us.

Before lunch the next day, the deputy justice minister (in charge of national security) held a meeting with Ziad, the Lebanese manager of the hotel. Our pulses raced in anticipation. Sure enough, at around four o'clock, a crew of uniformed Clerks of the Court and various hangers-on arrived. Having shown a search warrant to Ziad, they went through our possessions and equipment. The British Honorary Consul was there as a precaution. By sleight of hand, I managed to swap the crucial tapes from a room that had not been searched to one that had while the delegation searched a third. The searchers left with the bogus tapes I'd created and a pile of documents from Sorious's room. What I did not know was that among those documents was the expressly forbidden "treatment."

But, being ignorant, I was still reasonably optimistic at that stage. A discussion with Brian Brewer concluded that at worst, now that they thought they had the footage, they would probably detain us for a short period and then deport us. I felt we might just get away with it, but no, at about eleven that evening, Paul Mulba, the director of police, arrived.

> Mulba said he had come to ask if we would accompany him to the Police Station to make statements about our activities in the light of the things confiscated during the raid. We asked if we were being arrested and he said no, but he wished to ask us some questions.
>
> We acquiesced with good grace to accompany him to the Station. Everyone except Gugu had brought their passports and when Gugu offered to go and get his, Mulba said there was no need, as we would be coming back later anyway. It was a comment that lulled us into a false sense of security and we filed down to two waiting vehicles. In retrospect, I realize how devious this man was, but at the time we were unaware of the severity of the situation because of what they'd found.

We were taken to the National Security Agency headquarters. The NSA was Taylor's secret police. After a while it became clear that we were being detained. When four mattresses appeared, we accepted our fate and prepared for the night. It was about an hour later that the terrifying snatch occurred.

The Anti-Terrorist Unit thugs took us to the Monrovia Central Police Station, where we were detained in the "officers' cell," which meant we were saved the indignity of being stripped to our underwear and thrust into an inner sanctum called the "sweats."

That was a fate afforded other unfortunates guilty of such heinous crimes as leaving a nightclub drunk or arguing with a police officer. The officers' cell had a single sixty-watt bulb and a wobbly ceiling fan. The only piece of furniture was a counter, now turned on its side and used as an impromptu bed, supplementing a filthy foam mattress covering much of the floor.

The problem with being assigned to the officers' cell is just that—the officers. The worst of the psychos in black uniforms who transgress their own brutal code end up marking time in that fetid hole. Six of them sprawled on the floor on the Friday night we arrived. We were snapped from our adrenaline stupors at five the next morning when they woke up and immediately started fighting. The struggle flared from punches to cracking heads on the floor. As suddenly as it started, it was all over amid shouts and laughter.

Throughout the weekend, the population of demented and drugged-up policemen ebbed and flowed, culminating with an influx of fifteen or so on Monday morning. Violence was always there, a mean and capricious spirit hovering just beneath the ceiling, waiting to drop into someone's crazy head and send him into a froth over nothing.

After being arrested in more vile places than I care to recall, I've learned that the best policy is to "present no edges." Stand with your shoulders drooping, head forward, hands held like a penitent Presbyterian. Never sit or lie down while there is a threat or when anyone new walks into the cell. Be alert to the mood swings and currents in the cell, always listening, but never overtly paying attention. Avoid eye contact and move quickly but unobtrusively away from any aggressive activity.

I quickly tutored the others in these tactics, and we managed to avoid much of the unfocused aggravation that engulfed the place. Reminded of eighteenth-century woodcuts depicting the chaos of Bedlam, I knew there was a similar element of malicious insanity in the cell, which had to be avoided.

After a few days among the policemen in detention, we realized that it was a safe area for drug transactions to take place. The brutal mobs of black-suited policemen who maraud the streets of Monrovia often appear to be high. What we saw in the jail confirmed that large amounts of cannabis and alcohol are probably to blame.

Before our detention, the warrant to search our hotel rooms had listed "marijuana, cocaine, and heroin" among the things the searchers were looking for. I found it ironic that it was in the police station that narcotics came into their own. The loudest and most aggressive of the Monday morning miscreants, having staked their places on the fallen counter, loosened their uniforms and took off their boots. Then they smoked their way through at least three huge spliffs each before falling soundly asleep. The dope was a blessing, suppressing the noise and aggression during our last few hours in the officers' cell.

Our counsel visited us on Monday afternoon. He insisted it was highly likely we would never be charged and anticipated our release the next day. We were heartened, but I had a sneaking suspicion he was underestimating his opponents' resolve. Sure enough, less than twenty minutes after our counsel left, we were taken to the steps of the Liberian High Court, summarily arrested, and charged with the capital crime of espionage.

Now on remand, our residence changed to the Monrovia Central Prison. It was late in the afternoon when we arrived, and, after perfunctory processing, we were marched into a long, low, and very dark building. The walls were painted boot brown to seven feet, with the remainder and ceilings a bright yellow. There was a desultory selection of graffiti on the walls of the cell into which Sorious and I were ushered. I took a scratchy drawing of an old-fashioned helicopter on the west wall to be a good omen for our release. The Sierra Leonean ambassador had hinted that they might use one to fly us from the country should we be freed.

High on the east wall was the single word *Victor*, which, for the first few days, I failed to recognize as a name. So set was I on encouragement that I thought it was the result of someone being disturbed before he had been able to add the letter Y. Although I never underestimated the seriousness of the charges and accepted that the duration of our imprisonment might be extended, I never lost faith in the UK team of people I knew who were working for the victory of our release.

As soon as the news of our apprehension had reached London, Ron and Lindsey kicked into high gear. Channel 4 seemed at a loss as to what to do, and it was with the extraordinary help of Independent Television News (ITN), for whom Gugu and I have been long-standing freelancers, that Ron was on an aircraft to Monrovia by Sunday morning. Lindsey started calling everyone she knew, from journalists to African heads of state. Former antiapartheid activist and friend of South Africa Peter Hain was minister in charge of African affairs at the time. Lindsey managed to get through to him. "Listen, Peter, about the Channel 4 crew that's been locked up in Liberia. These are not just any old hacks. One of them is my partner—get the message?" The resulting effort and cooperation from the Foreign and Commonwealth Office was exemplary.

The reaction from friends and colleagues in the industry was immediate and sustained, as witnessed by the number of articles that kept the case high on the news agenda. Luckily, it was August, traditionally the month when news slows down in Britain, so maintaining the editorial pressure was easier. Lindsey managed to secure two audiences with President Olusegun Obasanjo of Nigeria, who by chance was in London to discuss the Sierra Leone/Liberia problem with the British government. He became instrumental in applying diplomatic pressure on Taylor, along with the gravity of the personal intervention of Nelson Mandela, whom David's family contacted. Mandela knew Gugu and me from all the years we'd worked in South Africa during the struggle, and he took a personal interest in our case.

Life in Monrovia's jail was remarkably structured. The building was clean; the ablutions block, though old and destroyed in places, was clean, and the population was viceless. Smoking was not allowed, and if drugs were in use, they were out of sight. This regime was maintained, not by the six or eight venerable wardens who wandered around with plastic nightsticks during the day, but by an internal mafia of inmates who called themselves the "Government." With the cellblock as their realm, they ruled by night the plausibly named "Republic of You-Go-Sober."

Their "commander in chief" or "C in C," was a mestizo of medium build, innocuously named Russell. He headed up the fifteen-man Government, which included a "cabinet" with ministers of finance, foreign affairs, justice, and defense, among others. His lieutenants were a six-and-half-foot Nigerian called the Godfather and Hassan, a wiry Sierra Leonean.

We became aware of the Government on our first night when an hour after lights out, someone started drumming energetically on an oilcan and the clamor of the cells instantly stopped.

"This is a news flash from Radio 'You-Go-Sober,'" announced the newsreader several times from the far end of the corridor. What followed was an impeccable parody of a 1950s news bulletin informing the silent inmates that because a cabinet member had been transferred, another had been appointed after a vote within the Government. There followed a series of "sound bites" as to the new incumbent's attributes and abilities from several of the senior ministers before the news flash ended with another drum roll on the oilcan.

It seemed that the Government was a self-perpetuating organism, deciding its own hierarchy through which the prison authorities worked. After six at night, the whole block was locked, and the keys to all the cells passed into the Government's hands. They were in charge until six the next morning, when the uniformed officers nominally took over again. In charge of not only security but also the economy, Russell and his team supplied us with toothbrushes and toothpaste (welcome after four days), candles, and matches at prices that had, surprisingly, not been inflated because we were foreigners who would ultimately have access to dollars.

After supplying our Earthly needs, the "Church of You-Go-Sober" kicked in. Brother Tobias, a constantly sunny character on crutches with round, John Lennon–style glasses, handed out Billy Graham magazines of encouraging stories and supplied David with a Bible. David read Exodus with zeal, no doubt dreaming of parting the Red Sea to escape the prison. With little else to do and the African mania for Pentecostal Christianity, church services with much singing and chanting were a daily feature of prison life.

As a result of the experience, I learned that fear is not a constant. But, given that its level is continually rising or falling, I could dissect fear into two distinct categories—that of bodily harm engendered by perceptions of immediate physical danger and that of how serious one understands the general situation to be.

The fear of physical danger brings a metallic taste to the mouth and makes it difficult to keep control of a pen afterward. The nightmarish ride from the NSA to the Monrovia Central Police Station on the first night was probably the biggest spike in that fear quotient. The holding cells of the police station, with their unpredictable sense of imminent violence, then kept that dread at a high level. But the structured environment of the central prison, after an initial peak from the apprehension of something unknown, came pretty low on the scariness list.

The second type of fear is always in the background in addition to the dread of bodily harm, even when there is no threat to one's person. The fear level fluctuates with news from home, articles in the press, or the prognoses of one's counsel, feeding on thoughts of years being wasted while serving an unwarranted sentence.

This fear is the pulse of a prisoner's morale. Our states of mind were always influenced by the pronouncements from individuals, whether or not they came true. It led us, after the first few days and several disappointments, to almost write off the Sierra Leonean ambassador as a genial but overoptimistic buffoon. Initially, our counsel, Liberian lawyer Varney Sherman, looked like he had it nailed down. Ultimately, although he had a great deal of panache, the system ran him—not, as he claimed, the reverse. The British consul Brian Brewer, however, was always straight, and like us all, he initially underestimated the severity of the predicament. But he never spun a line that ended in disappointment.

At a low ebb for much of the time, morale plummeted the night that counsel was surprised with our formal arrest on charges of espionage. Morale clawed its way back up slightly with counsel's optimism about the applicability of bail, only to plunge when bail was denied. It was only after these reverses that I think the others started to learn the trick of hoping without counting on the outcome.

When rumors of our release started to circulate, we had hope, but we dared not count on the whispers being true. The disappointment would have been unbearable. Through that long last morning and into the afternoon, we told ourselves that nothing was happening until finally the call came—"Bring your things, you're going home." Only then did we dare to hope.

In the end, the diplomatic pressure on Taylor and his hoods became too much.* They started seeking a way out, which turned out to be the very instrument that had caused us to be jailed in the first place: the treatment document. I believe we would probably have just been deported once the government thought it had the incriminating footage of Bucanan. Instead, while searching Sorious's room, the clerk of the court had picked up the damning document. Sorious had not gone through his papers as I had asked. The pages of marketing hype and bad journalism sent the paranoid regime into a complete rage and us into jail.

Seeking a face-saving exit from the situation, Channel 4's chairman apologized for the existence and content of the treat-

---

*President Charles Taylor left office hurriedly on August 11, 2003, after losing a bloody civil war. He accepted political asylum in Nigeria.

ment and promised to shelve the project in order to secure our release. It was a matter of bureaucracy, and within twenty-four hours, our liberty was imminent. In the care of the British ambassador to the region, we went from cramped cells in Monrovia Central Prison to a private jet in a couple of hours. The long haul for Lindsey's release committee and an extended ordeal for our families and friends were both avoided.

At that moment in South Africa, friends and journalist colleagues of ours, led by the BBC's indomitable Alan Little, were able to end the shortest and most successful protest ever held outside the Liberian Embassy in Pretoria. Alan had just finished a short speech on the evils of locking up journalists when his mobile phone rang. After a moment, he gleefully announced that as a result of their protest, Charles Taylor had relented, and we were on our way home.

Chapter 4

"PATRIOTISM" VS. INDEPENDENCE

STACEY WOELFEL

Stacey Woelfel has been part of the faculty at the University of Missouri and in the KOMU-TV newsroom since 1986, where he has been news director for more than fourteen years. Under his leadership, the newsroom has moved into the twenty-first century of digital television newsgathering, picking up numerous awards along the way, including a national Edward R. Murrow Award for Overall Excellence and a Payne Award for Ethics in Jour-

nalism. Before joining the Missouri School of Journalism faculty, Stacey began his career as a news photographer and assignment editor for WESH-TV in Orlando, Florida, where he covered stories ranging from the opening of EPCOT Center in Disney World to the *Challenger* disaster. Stacey has a Bachelor of Journalism degree from the Missouri School of Journalism and a Master of Arts degree in political science from the University of Missouri.

mmediately following the events of September 11, 2001, I began to see a surge of patriotic displays by television newsrooms around the country. These were not totally unanticipated, as I had seen similar ones during the first Gulf War. At that time, some anchors and reporters had donned red, white, and blue ribbons to show some sort of support. The movement was not widespread, and it came and went in the course of a few months. But it did foretell the conflict ahead between newsroom ethics, public opinion, and political pressure.

As news director at KOMU-TV in Columbia, Missouri, I lead a unique newsroom that bridges the gulf between the academic and professional worlds. KOMU-TV is the commercial, NBC affiliate for central Missouri, but it also serves as the teaching lab for students learning television news techniques at the University of Missouri School of Journalism. Despite the state ownership and the academic mission, the newsroom runs as much like a commercial, professional operation as possible. A small staff of faculty editors runs the newsroom. The faculty members are assisted by a dozen or so full-time staff members. Students do the rest of the work—reporting, photographing, producing, editing, and writing.

The station is managed by a local general manager, who answers to the chancellor of the Columbia campus. As a faculty member as well as a news director, I answer to both the general manager and the dean of the School of Journalism. Daily management is left to me, and so are most long-term policies. In general, the campus is not involved in the operations of the station.

In late September 2001, we were obviously very busy with the 9/11 aftermath and all the coverage it had generated. The newsroom had done well on the day of the attack and in the days that followed. We had set the local standard not only for covering the events in New York, Washington, and Pennsylvania but also for giving local viewers the information they needed to see what in their lives had changed since the attacks. I had worked a lot of long days overseeing the coverage and had allowed much of my everyday work to pile up. Among my necessary tasks was an e-mail memo to the faculty, staff, and students reminding them of our unwritten policy about not wearing any adornments that would send personal messages or express personal opinions.

The policy was one that had been in place—in unwritten fashion—for as long as I had been news director. (I took that position in 1990.) Simply stated, we did not wear ribbons, pins, buttons, or other items that would be used to send a message. The ethical principles at stake were simple enough. First, such items were out of place on our newscasts because they put our anchors and reporters in the position of injecting their personal opinions into the news presentations. No matter how universally accepted or seemingly noble those opinions might be, they do not belong on the newscast. Second, the ribbons and such serve the purpose of making the anchor or reporter wearing them somehow newsworthy or noticeable for their own sakes. This is not their role.

On September 17, after seeing the proliferation of patriotic pins and ribbons that had been springing up on network and other local newscasts, I stopped and typed a brief e-mail:

> This probably won't be a popular decision for some of you, but I need to remind everyone that our news broadcasts are not the place for personal statements of support for any cause—no matter how deserving the cause seems to be. This includes the little red, white, and blue ribbons that a lot of people are sporting these days. Our job is to deliver the news as free from outside influences as possible. And while it seems that there could be no one who would object to us wearing such symbols, you might be surprised. And it also sets a precedent where countless other causes would want us to wear their symbols as well.
>
> I could go on with more reasons, but let me just say this. Leave the ribbons at home when reporting or anchoring for KOMU News. What you do on your own time is up to you,

though I would urge you to consider the fact that you are always "on the clock" in terms of being known as a reporter and representative of the station.

The e-mail went to approximately three hundred faculty and staff members and students, all with ties to the KOMU-TV newsroom. The instant response I received after sending it—nothing. With the exception of one weathercaster who agreed to follow the principles of the memo even though he disagreed with them, most I spoke with said the notion of not displaying personal opinions on air was nothing new to them. I think that consensus arose from some consistency in teaching within the journalism school. While not so plainly stated there, our curriculum provides students with the ethical framework from which they can draw their own conclusions about the proper actions to take when faced with pressure to conform. This memo did not conflict with that ethical framework.

But it was soon to become apparent that it did conflict with what many outside the newsroom thought our role should be during times of national crisis—particularly those in political positions in the state of Missouri. Shortly after the e-mail went out to the KOMU group, it ended up in the electronic in-boxes of a number of Missouri state legislators. I received my first e-mail inquiring about the memo on September 21. A state senator wrote to see if I had indeed written what was forwarded to him. I wrote back confirming that I had and never heard another thing from that particular senator. But, by the following Monday, September 24, the legislators who were writing had become much more aggressive in their approach with me. A Republican state representative from Kansas City, Matt Bartle, was the first to issue a threat to the funding of the University of Missouri:

> It is more than a little troubling that in your rush not to offend that you would ban the wearing of a symbol of compassion for those who have suffered immense tragedy. This is not a matter

of journalistic even-handedness. This is a matter of simple decency and respect for our fellow human beings.

As a member of the state legislature in Missouri, I am going to [evaluate] far more carefully state funding that goes to the school of journalism. If this is what you are teaching the next generation of journalists, I question whether the taxpayers of this state will support it.

By [copying] this e-mail to the Governmental Relations office for the University, I am hoping that the administration will look into this matter.

By this time, one week after writing the original memo, much of my day was consumed by answering e-mails, phone calls, and letters regarding the policy. I decided it was important to respond to each correspondent as quickly as possible—particularly when I believed the person had some mistaken impression regarding the purpose of the memo. Representative Bartle was among a growing number of people who misconstrued the policy to be for the purpose of avoiding any offense to viewers. That was never part of its intent. I wrote my first reply to him within an hour of receiving his e-mail:

As a Columbia native and Mizzou graduate, I'm sure you are aware of the School of Journalism's worldwide reputation for excellence. For nearly one hundred years, we have been teaching what we as a faculty believe to be the proper skills and knowledge for the working journalist—including training in ethics. The memo you cite is one of those lessons. Not all ethical decisions are popular with either the public or those who must exercise them. But it is a measure of the strength of the ethical position and the person who holds it to see if it can remain intact against prevailing sentiment. I'm sure you have encountered similar conflicts with the many ethical decisions one must make as an attorney—perhaps more than in any other profession.

I encourage you to do your research and find out how the School of Journalism actually does use the portion of its budget that comes from state appropriations. I think you'll be pleased with most of the lessons taught—even if you aren't in total agreement with the ethical responsibilities a journalist must carry. I think you'll also realize that the Governmental Affairs office at the University has no input into the academic freedom of the Journalism School faculty, or the editorial decisions made at KOMU-TV, KBIA-FM, or the Columbia Missourian.

Bartle wrote back almost immediately. He questioned whether reporters were allowed to wear school colors, and if running advertising on the station should be considered as showing "allegiance" to capitalism. He concluded his e-mail with this:

When questioned on matters like this, it is not uncommon for journalists to sound the high tones of journalistic integrity. It sounds good and in many cases it is appropriate. In this case, however, journalistic integrity cannot conceal simple foolishness. Decisions like yours do immense harm to your profession. Decisions like yours cause the public to question the reliability and intelligence of journalists.

Like it or not, recipients of public monies must answer to the public. If the public disapproves of what is being done with their money, they have the right to direct funds elsewhere. I am sure that we will find that the KOMU news department is a recipient of public money.

In fact, the KOMU-TV operation as a whole does not receive any public money. As a commercial television station, it is expected to earn enough each year to operate profitably and without state appropriations. In most years, the station profit is enough to fund other university programs, thereby actually reducing the need for some state expenditures. I wrote back to Bartle, addressing the additional concerns he outlined in his last e-mail and inviting him to see how we operate and earn our own operating funds:

I would welcome you to come see our facility to find out the real lessons being taught within these walls. We have been voted again and again as the school that best prepares young journalists for television news careers. That success is something of which I am very proud. And the station's commercial success is something in which the University and state can also take pride. Our success in the market helps keep us financially self-sufficient and free from the need for any state appropriations that might leave the perception of having to answer editorially to state government. Heck, we even give some extra back to the University to pay its bills.

It would be unfair, however, to expect every state legislator to know the internal funding methods of each department the state operates. So I was ready to pass on the funding formula to each who wrote to question the policy. And soon, I had many such e-mails to answer. Representative Bartle passed his exchange with me to a number of his colleagues. I soon began to hear from them. Representative Chuck Purgason, a Republican from Caulfield, wrote, "Could you please let me know if the information that I have received is correct when it comes to your station and it's [sic] policy on the American Flag? As a member of the budget committee in the state, I will certainly look into this policy when it comes to funding in the next legislative cycle if this information is shown to be true."

I wrote back to Representative Purgason outlining the same funding scenario I had given Representative Bartle. I then received this e-mail from Rep. Carl Bearden, a St. Charles Republican:

I have read your response to Representative Bartle's e-mail regarding the display of patriotic symbols by journalists working at the various University media outlets. The response fails to indicate any basis for invoking Journalistic Ethics. In fact, the decision appears to be based more on someone's percieved [sic] political correctness than journalistic ethics.

If the School of Journalism is in fact more focused on political correctness issues than on true journalistic ethics, then I
would contend that the well earned reputation of the program
is in jeopardy. While the Governmental Affairs office may not
have any input, the University Curators and Administration
must guard the reputation of the University and the School of
Journalism from actions such as this one. I trust that as a result
of this errant application of journalistic integrity, they will
indeed review the decision.

Representative Bearden was the first to threaten going to the university's governing board, the Board of Curators. It was no empty
threat. The curators would indeed consider the policy soon.

By Tuesday, September 25, the e-mails were coming in large
numbers—and not only from state legislators. The memo had
been posted by an unknown party on a number of bulletin
boards and other Web sites frequented by journalists. This set up
a nationwide discussion on the pros and cons of my position. So
e-mail was pouring in from journalists as well as from the state
leaders. Many of the e-mails I received were less than polite.
Some called for my firing, while others suggested I look for work
in Afghanistan. I answered every single message as politely as
possible. At the same time, the letters from legislators were also
taking on a less professional and more aggressive tone. Republican representative Martin "Bubs" Hohulin from Lamar did not
see any reason to mince words:

Add me to the list of legislators appalled by your memo and the
arrogant reply you sent to Rep. Bartle. The bulk of funding for
the University comes from the taxpayers, of which we are their
representatives. I would suggest you come down from your
ivory tower in the make believe world of academia and sample
the real world. We have no obligation to fund your part of the
University, or any part for that matter. I too will be in contact
with the Government Affairs office. They do not control your

"academic freedom," but with no money, you could be a little less free.

In fact, state appropriations make up 17 percent of the total university budget.

More legislators added their voices to the fray, mostly after reading the ongoing e-mail exchange between Representative Bartle and me. Representative Rod Jetton, a Republican from Marble Hill, wrote a long letter extolling his service in the Marine Corps, the need for patriotism at that time, and, of course, his plan to look into university operations: "I hope you will change the policy and I too am going to use what little influence I can to see that our state college students are free to show their support for the very nation that has given them the opportunity to be all that they want to be."

All through this period, I had been sharing the correspondences I was receiving from the legislators with my students via the same e-mail group to which I had sent the original e-mail. On nearly a daily basis, I would copy and paste the e-mails I was receiving, along with my replies, and send them out to the group. These digests of all the activity provided excellent material for classroom and informal discussions. But, much as the original memo had found a wider audience, these e-mails soon made it into a story in the Columbia *Missourian*, the School of Journalism's daily laboratory newspaper. The story ran on the morning of September 27, prompting local radio stations to make it the topic of conversation. Upon my arrival in the newsroom, I was flooded with phone calls and e-mails from angry viewers demanding I change the policy. Many of them also announced plans to ask their state legislators to seek some sort of retribution against the television station. This sort of message was typical:

> I was shocked when I heard of your e-mail to your staff. News people usually scream free speach [sic] but now you are

restricting speach. As a veteran I feel that every American has a right to show their support for our country. You claim that it is an ethical issue. Your station is the most biased station I have ever watched. You take positions against the death penalty. You speak out against pro-lifers. How can you say that you are trying not to take a position. I am glad companies are pulling their advertising from your station. I will encourage any company I do business with to do the same. I will also ask my representative to pull all funding from the school of journalism until major changes are made to your station. I will also encourage my friends and family to do the same.

Many of these viewers did follow through and speak to legislators about the issue. That was evident in the e-mails I was continuing to receive from those legislators, mixed in with all the mail from the general public. Representative Carl Bearden, in response to a School of Journalism alumnus writing in support of the policy, invoked his constituency:

> I continue to maintain the decision is a bad one. Feedback from a number of my constituents who pay the taxes that support the University system confirm that view.
>   Decisions have consequences. Although it is not my intent to call for an investigation of the issue, if the result of the errant decision made by station management is that closer scrutiny is applied to University funding, so be it. It is neither blackmail nor is it unreasonable.

Not all the feedback sent to legislators opposed the KOMU policy. I received copies of a few letters sent to legislators by either their constituents or members of the university or journalism communities. These letters called on legislators not to punish the school for proper ethical actions. According to one,

> [For] Mr. Bartle, to call state funding into question because you disagree with an inner-office ethical decision made by a semi-

private media institution is in direct conflict with the principle of freedom of the press. You called the decision "censorship of journalists," yet I find the threat of press-coercion by the state a much more menacing possibility than a TV station that is missing a few red-white-and-blue ribbons.

Which brings us to Mr. Purgason's statement about the need for the state to review the policy: Do you really think that the state has any right to question the ethical judgments of a news station that is funded by private advertising, not the state? Would you suggest that the United States Congress review ABC for making the same policy decision? (Which the national network did after the terrorist attacks.) I would argue that in order for the press to maintain its roles as a governmental watchdog and public informant, it must be free from review by the state. The suggestion of state-review is decidedly against the press's First Amendment rights.

But my mail and calls were running about nine to one against the policy, and I imagine the correspondence from constituents to legislators was running at an even higher negative ratio.

The flurry of complaints I received following the September 27 publicity surrounding the decision took my mind off the state legislators for a short time. But soon it returned in the form of a two-sentence threat on September 30 from Rep. Bubs Hohulin: "So am I to take it that you aren't going to rescind your memo? Failure to do so will result in problems for KOMU and MU."

I replied that I had no intention of doing my job any differently than I had on September 10 or before and the policy would stand. Hohulin replied that I must not be doing my job very well and should do it better. But he and the other legislators turned their attention toward the university administration to see what could be done there. The School of Journalism and the chancellor's offices began drafting their own responses to the criticism.

At the School of Journalism, that action came in the form of a resolution of faculty support for me and KOMU. The decision to pass the resolution was not an easy one. Some members of the faculty disagreed completely with the decision I had made; others found it to be the correct policy for commercial newsrooms but worried about limiting the academic freedom of students in a teaching environment. Nearly all faculty members agreed the threat of political and budgetary sanctions was wrong. After one meeting and some e-mail balloting, the school's faculty passed this resolution on October 2:

> A recent editorial decision made at KOMU-TV that prohibited journalists from wearing red, white and blue ribbons during their reporting and on-air appearances has ignited an important public debate.
>
> The action at KOMU was taken as an effort to preserve a fundamental principle of journalism—editorial independence. The faculty of the Missouri School of Journalism supports the action and supports the right of faculty editors to make policy decisions in our newsrooms.
>
> Preserving editorial independence is essential. Journalists best serve the people of this country by reporting independently and neutrally. It is a principle almost universally shared among those in the nation's press corps, and it is something the public should expect and demand.
>
> Such a principle is relatively easy to uphold in most circumstances and in most news coverage. The events of Sept. 11, however, are unprecedented in the working careers of our faculty and most of the nation's press corps. Not since Pearl Harbor has our nation been directly attacked, and not since the War of 1812 has our mainland been attacked by foreign forces.
>
> As journalists and journalism educators, we have struggled since Sept. 11 with how best to uphold the fundamental principle of editorial independence in the face of an attack on our nation. We are a diverse group of people with the same range of feelings and the same degree of patriotism present in the community and nation.
>
> Many journalism organizations have taken the course

KOMU has taken—striving to maintain complete independence even in such trying times. Others have openly displayed
their colors by displaying the American flag on television
screens hour after hour.

History fails to help us resolve this dilemma. Some of
American journalism's most revered figures, including Edward
R. Murrow and Ernie Pyle, were open advocates of the Allied
cause during World War II. Others of that era merely reported
independently on the events of the day.

This debate provides an excellent opportunity for all of us—
faculty, students and members of the public—to debate the fundamental role of journalists when their nation is under attack.
Accordingly, we call on our Dean to convene one or more public
forums so the serious issues involved can be adequately and
openly debated. Topics to be discussed should include:

- The value of journalistic independence.
- The role of journalists when their nation is under attack.
- The relationship between professional journalistic
  activity and citizenship.
- The role of journalists in creating a civil and ultimately
  peaceful political society.

We believe it is important for journalists and the public to
engage in a discussion of the issue of editorial independence
and its importance in a free society.

We believe it is important that students, particularly those
who disagree with decisions made in our newsrooms, feel
empowered to voice their views.

We also believe that our many international students, some
of whom have expressed concerns about our coverage and our
"Americanized" view of the current worldwide problem, need a
forum in which to explore those issues.

Finally, we urge that the forum include an examination of
the scholarship of our field, particularly a critical examination
of media performance during times of war, media coverage of
international issues, and media coverage of conflict and crisis.

Meanwhile, across campus, the Office of the Chancellor had been drafting its own statement of position on the matter. The office had been flooded with calls, letters, and e-mails from politicians, alumni, and supporters of the university. Like the feedback I was receiving, most people who contacted the chancellor were vehemently opposed to the policy. Faced with either pleasing important constituents or the possibility of compromising the reputation of its exemplary School of Journalism, the office issued a statement that tried to do neither. In part it said:

> During this time of national distress, the news director of KOMU-TV, the University's television station, asked members of the on-air news team to continue to observe station policy that bars the wearing of any special insignia during a news broadcast including red, white and blue ribbons. This policy has been in effect for many years and is a common practice in broadcast journalism throughout this country to assure editorial independence. The University administration and the station manager were unaware of the directive. The station news operation, which is separate from KOMU's business operations, is responsible to our School of Journalism, and is charged with teaching skills and knowledge for working journalists, which also includes training in journalism ethics. In this regard, the station is a teaching laboratory. Other national news operations, including those of major TV networks, have currently carried out a similar policy of not permitting personal insignia to be worn on air. The journalism faculty has voiced its support of the action and the "rights of faculty editors to make policy decisions in their newsrooms" and further stated "it is important for journalists and the public to engage in a discussion of the issue of editorial independence and its importance in a free society."
>
> The station's news policy, when made public, has resulted in a number of letters, e-mails and calls to the University protesting it. MU deeply regrets that this policy has caused offense to KOMU viewers and other citizens. This was an action taken in the TV newsroom to assure editorial independence

that did not in any way reflect a policy of the University. We are proud to be a state university—proud to represent our state at the national level in so many ways, and even more proud to represent the United States of America in international circles.

The chancellor's statement did not end the conflict. Instead, it angered some on both sides. Legislators were unhappy the chancellor did not take a stronger stand to change the policy. Representative David Levin, a Republican from St. Louis County, wrote to the university system president (the chancellor's superior) and continued to threaten action: "Apparently you're suggesting Mr. Woelfel and the University are not accountable to the taxpayers and their elected representatives. I will support efforts to hold the University and Mr. Woelfel accountable. Accountability includes consequence for actions."

It is important to note that the state legislature in Missouri meets from January to May each year. Legislators had actually been in a brief special session when the attacks of September 11 took place but had adjourned shortly thereafter. The ongoing correspondences took place while the lawmakers were not meeting, but many had begun to refer to action they would take when the session resumed in January, and university budget talks began.

Journalism alumni were also unhappy with the statement from the chancellor. Most felt the wording said little to support the KOMU policy or me personally. Many told me they had wished for the chancellor to have issued a strongly worded message of support rather than one designed to placate the larger constituencies of the university. A few took time to write the chancellor with their complaints. This letter was typical:

> The decision by KOMU's news director not to allow its folks to wear patriotic ribbons on air was both brave and laudable. I am deeply disappointed that you could not stand in support of that decision.
>
> I understand that you are facing political pressure from

politicians who found the policy objectionable, and that you need to stay in good graces with those folks to keep the university financially sound. But you owe it to the journalists you are training to stand up for sound ethical policies when they are enacted and not bow to what is politically correct.

As Disney and other large corporations continue to buy up our news outlets and the line between journalism and entertainment continues to blur, I was very proud to see Mizzou take the hard stand on behalf of good old-fashioned ethics. I was a political reporter for a decade and as such gave up the right to attend political rallies for my chosen party or to put signs in my yard for any candidates. It's just part of the job. KOMU's reporters can wear ribbons off the air. They aren't being deprived of any rights of citizenship.

The question of just what official position the university would take on the matter reached the highest levels on October 10. The university's board of curators met by conference call to vote on a resolution concerning the use of patriotic symbols by university students and employees. The board comprises nine members appointed by the governor of Missouri. No more than five can be from one political party. Several members of that board were very unhappy with the KOMU policy and had complained to the dean of the journalism school and the chancellor for some time. But the resolution passed that day was fairly vague in its wording:

> WHEREAS, the extraordinary events of September 11 have forever changed the United States of America and the international community; and
>
> WHEREAS, the University of Missouri community is profoundly saddened by the loss of so many lives to acts of terrorism and has responded with spontaneous and heartwarming expressions of personal support for those who have suffered the loss of loved ones and friends; and
>
> WHEREAS, the American people have united in their com-

mitment to uphold the principles of individual freedom and justice for all; and

WHEREAS, the University of Missouri remains committed to the free and open expression of ideas, and to the preservation of individual liberty, academic freedom and freedom of the press; and

WHEREAS, the Board of Curators has received numerous communications indicating the need to clarify and articulate University policy with respect to the display of patriotic symbols during a time of national concern over acts of terrorism against the United States of America; and

WHEREAS, the Collected Rules and Regulations of the University of Missouri do not preclude individuals from displaying patriotic symbols that express individual support for the United States of America, nor does the Board of Curators see any necessity to make such a modification in the Collected Rules and Regulations:

NOW, THEREFORE, BE IT RESOLVED, that the Board of Curators encourages administrators and supervisors to extend wide latitude to individuals in the University community who desire to display symbols of their sympathy for those directly affected by acts of terrorism, or who desire to express their patriotism and love of the United States of America in appropriate ways, consistent with concerns for health and safety in the work environment; and

BE IT FURTHER RESOLVED, that the Board of Curators further encourages members of the University of Missouri community to demonstrate the utmost respect for members of all cultures, religions and nationalities in keeping with the University's commitment to tolerance and understanding of divergent viewpoints; and

BE IT FURTHER RESOLVED, that the Secretary to the Board of Curators cause this resolution to be spread upon the minutes of this meeting.

The resolution had little effect on ending the controversy. Some of the legislators saw it as a statement calling on the chancellor to fire me if I did not change the policy. But the spokesman for the curators said the board believed the resolution would have no effect on the newsroom policy or me. And it did not.

Legislators were unhappy with the outcome of the curators' resolution. But their pressure subsided at that point, though angry e-mails from viewers and others around the country just hearing about the policy did not. But the legislators were not gone for good. Their next full session in Jefferson City began in January 2002, and as soon as budget matters were taken up, the attacks on me, KOMU, and the University of Missouri resumed. In April, in the midst of approving the $400 million appropriation the university would receive in the upcoming fiscal year, the subject of KOMU's ribbon ban was discussed on the floors of the Missouri House and Senate. Members of both chambers recalled the events of the previous fall and pointed to my actions and those of the university administration, calling both of us unworthy of funding. One legislator even went so far as to say—while in session on the House floor—that he would like to punch me in the nose. That prompted long-time capitol regulars to announce that I was only the second person in modern times to be threatened with physical violence from the floor of the general assembly. Adolf Hitler was the other.

The actions on the floor brought a new round of attention—local and national—on our policy and the furor it had created. Some, like this journalist from California, were astonished by the actions underway in Jefferson City:

> I read with horror this evening about the "punishment" Missouri legislators have leveled upon KOMU and the University of Missouri for what they consider an unpatriotic decision last fall. While I believe, personally, cases may be made for and against your policy (regarding the wearing of American flag pins by your staff), I find the actions of your state's legislature to be 100 percent outrageous. Unfortunately, it appears KOMU cannot effectively act as an independent voice of journalism, nor as a training ground for those studying our craft—at least, not

without the threat of retribution. The people of Missouri should be ashamed of their elected leaders.

I hope you will continue your best efforts, there or elsewhere, to objectively inform your viewers.

But others—mainly local viewers just hearing about the policy for the first time as the budget battle played out in the local papers—renewed their complaints:

Is it possible [*sic*] that Patriotism is not out of style and that the problem with your readers and viewers is the very fact that the horendus [*sic*] threat to our nation seems to be burried [*sic*] in the Politically correct mind of those who might be out of touch with what is most important to us, our freedom.

Is it possible [*sic*] that in retrospect, a policy made by one individual reflects poorly on the majority of those in the School of Journalism, yet no one has the courage to correct the error for fear of being accused of not supporting the School? Could some in the legislature be correct in referring to the attitude of the school as aggogant [*sic*] to a fault?

Speechmaking over, it became time for legislators to decide if they would actually cut funding over the policy. Representative Bubs Hohulin called for a $5 million cut. Those writing the appropriations measures deemed that figure too high, but they allowed a $500,000 figure to be added by amendment, which received early approval and stayed a part of the appropriations legislation until the waning days of the session. As the statutory deadline approached to approve the budget, senators cut the budget reduction aimed at the KOMU policy to $50,000. Many in the room decided the half-million-dollar figure was too high and would hurt too many programs at the university. And all acknowledged the cuts would not affect KOMU at all, due to its self-supported status, and most likely would have no impact on the School of Journalism.

In the end, the cost of the entire episode was some lost ad revenue at the television station (quickly made up by other advertisers) and a lot of my time and that of my supporters around the university. But ratings that November (the first ratings period following the ribbon debate) showed no decrease in our audience. The legislators would have liked to see the whole ordeal cost more—both financially and in the independence of our news operation. Instead, we actually gained quite a bit from the episode. Journalism professionals around the country and the world saw that the University of Missouri School of Journalism was still the leader for the ethical teaching of our craft. We received the 2002 Payne Award for Ethics in Journalism, a national award that goes to those in the profession who take a strong ethical stand and hold it—no matter what the costs. And more than anything else, our students and faculty and staff members came through the episode feeling good about what we had accomplished.

Since 2002, I have actually heard almost nothing from the legislature about the policy. A few of our reporters faced some hostile sources in the capitol for the next session. One legislator, Bubs Hohulin, refused to do interviews or even speak to KOMU reporters. But most relations went back to normal levels. And Missouri constitutional term limits meant that many of those legislators involved in the original conflict were eventually forced out of the general assembly.

Chapter 5

THE PROHIBITED IMMIGRANT

ANDREW MELDRUM

Andrew Meldrum has worked as a journalist since 1974, first on newspapers in Ohio and California. In 1980, he went to newly independent Zimbabwe, where he reported on the country's transformation from minority-ruled Rhodesia to majority-ruled Zimbabwe. From 1983 he covered events in Zimbabwe and other southern African countries for the British newspaper the *Guardian*, and the *Economist*. In May 2003, he was illegally expelled from Zimbabwe for reporting on state torture. Since then he has been based in South Africa, where he writes for the *Guardian* about Zimbabwe and South Africa. In October 2004, Meldrum received Columbia University's Kurt Schork award for freelance international journalism.

In May 2003, I was just finishing an article about how harsh and chaotic life had become in Zimbabwe when someone rang at our front gate. My wife, Dolores, answered it and, surprised, said, "It's some men from immigration. They want to see you."

It was after dark and well past business hours. I knew they were not coming for a friendly chat. Months earlier I was nearly deported by government security agents purporting to be immigration officials, but the courts ruled I had every right to stay and work in Zimbabwe.

In any case, I needed to write only two more paragraphs to finish my story, and I was not going to let the men at my gate stop me. In fact, their menacing presence added urgency to my writing, and I rattled off the final sentences with a flourish. I quickly e-mailed the story to the *Guardian* in London.

My wife went to the gate, where several men waited in four vehicles, including a large van with blacked-out windows. They refused to show her any identification or to tell her why they wanted to see me. My lawyer had informed us that by refusing to give that information, the government agents were acting illegally. I had interviewed many people, including journalists, who were taken away by government agents at night to be beaten and tortured and illegally detained. I was not about to give myself up to those men.

Dolores told the men that I was not at home—and she was telling the truth. I had gone out the back door, scaled a wall, and jumped into the neighboring yard. As nonchalantly as possible, I walked down the street and away from the men at my gate. I knew my lawyer, Beatrice Mtetwa, and fellow journalists were already on the way to our house to support Dolores.

In the previous two years, I had been hit with truncheons by police, threatened by cabinet ministers, vilified in the state press, jailed for two days, and charged with a crime carrying a two-year jail sentence. After a two-month trial, I was acquitted and

declared by the magistrate to have acted as a responsible journalist. Almost as soon as I had received the not-guilty verdict, the
government agents tried to deport me, but the courts once again
ruled in my favor, finding that I had the legal right to live and
work in Zimbabwe.

Now, the agents were trying to get rid of me outside the law.
I knew very well that my best defense was to evade the security
agents and work with my lawyer to get things on a legal footing.

For ten days, I did not go home and stayed at different places
each night. My lawyer tried to get officials at the immigration
department to say why they wanted to see me. They simply
insisted they had to see me without giving a reason. In the end,
we decided to stop the cat-and-mouse game by going to the
immigration offices. We met the chief immigration officer, Elasto
Mugwadi, who was pleasant and said that a few details on my residence permit needed to be clarified. He requested that I bring in
some articles I had written about Zimbabwe's economy and its
tourism. Then, somewhat nervously, he said he had to leave and
told me to go across the hall to see Evans Siziba, one of the immigration officers who had come to my gate.

As soon as we entered Siziba's office, the atmosphere
changed. Siziba, tall and burly, leaned across his desk and glow-
ered at me. "You are writing bad things about Zimbabwe," he
said. I denied his charge, saying that my articles may criticize the
government, but they supported democracy and human rights for
all Zimbabweans.

Siziba was not interested in debating the merits of my
reporting. He said that I was declared a prohibited immigrant
and I would be expelled from the country immediately.

"This action is completely illegal," said Beatrice, holding up
the court order that stated I was working in the country legally.
Siziba shrugged and stomped out of the room. Beatrice and I
spoke briefly in his office. She told me that she anticipated this
action and had already prepared papers to get an urgent court

hearing to stop my expulsion. As soon as we walked out of Siziba's office, Beatrice and I were surrounded by eight policemen who herded us into an elevator, which took us to the ground floor.

I was pleased to see a hardy band of journalists from both the foreign and domestic press. Beatrice advised me to notify the press of my meeting with immigration. "The press is our best protection," she said. "If they record what happens to you, it is less likely you will be mistreated. Whatever you do, don't say you are being deported because deportation is a legal procedure and this is not a legal action."

I knew all the reporters, photographers, and cameramen and began to fill them in on what had happened.

"I have been declared a prohibited immigrant and am to be expelled from Zimbabwe. This is not the action—" At that, the police began to pull me away from the crowd of journalists, but I continued, raising my voice, "of a government that is confident of its own legitimacy. It is afraid—" The police wrestled with me and I temporarily lost my balance. "It is afraid of a free press. It is afraid of independent and critical reporting!"

By that time, they had dragged me to a nearby car and, though I struggled, they kicked and punched me and forced me into the back seat. Plainclothesmen jumped in on either side of me, and the car sped off. One man threw a coat over my head so that I was hooded. I was held in the basement of Harare International Airport for ten hours and then forced on an Air Zimbabwe flight to London.

Beatrice valiantly tried to stop the security agents from forcing me on the plane, running through airport security waving a new court order. But the agents ignored her and pushed me onto the plane and slammed the door shut. After twenty-three years living and working as a journalist in Zimbabwe, I had been thrown out of the land that I loved.

I was no stranger to difficulties with Zimbabwean authorities. My work as a journalist led me to several run-ins with President

Robert Mugabe's government. But I was not the government's only target. Since 2000 it had pursued a concerted campaign to muzzle the press, both domestic and foreign. By the time I was illegally expelled from Zimbabwe, more than seventy journalists had been charged with crimes by the Mugabe government, two had been tortured, and several had been beaten. In the year following my expulsion, the government closed three newspapers. Through repressive legislation, intimidation, arrests, and brute force, the Mugabe government worked to prevent the press from drawing attention to its human rights abuses, corruption, and stifling of democracy.

I had been working in Zimbabwe since 1980, shortly after the country transformed from white minority–ruled Rhodesia to become majority–ruled Zimbabwe. I was excited about how the country had moved from a bitter, bloody war to peace and racial reconciliation. In the first years, I wrote about how life improved for black Zimbabweans, especially in health and education. But, by 1983, I was covering the gross human rights abuses perpetrated by the army in Zimbabwe's southern Matabeleland provinces. Some two hundred thousand rural people from Zimbabwe's Ndebele minority were killed by the army's Fifth Brigade, according to human rights groups. My articles on what became known as the "Matabeleland Massacres" brought government authorities to reprimand me for what it called "exaggerated" reports. I was warned to stop writing such false stories.

I knew these were not idle threats. Nick Worrall had been expelled from Zimbabwe in 1983 for his reports about the Matabeleland killings for the *Guardian* in London. I had been working for the French news agency Agence France-Presse (AFP), and, when Nick left, he asked me to take over writing for the *Guardian*. It was a great opportunity for me as a journalist and a daunting challenge.

Although I once respected the Mugabe government, I was convinced it was responsible for the gross human rights abuses in Matabeleland, and I could not heed its warnings. International press reports exposing the atrocities had put considerable pressure on the Mugabe government to eventually curb the army's horrific campaign. I knew my journalistic responsibility was to report all the information I could gather and confirm on the Matabeleland killings.

The Matabeleland violence finally ended in December 1987, when Mugabe's Zanu-PF party swallowed the opposition Zapu party, which had been supported by the minority Ndebele people. The ethnic violence abated, but by then considerable corruption and misgovernance were evident throughout Zimbabwe. Once again, I felt a professional duty to expose those wrongs wherever I found them, in the hope that they would be righted. I also wrote about the many positive aspects of rural development and the improvement in the standards of living of the majority of black Zimbabweans.

But, by the end of the 1990s, those positive stories became increasingly difficult to find. In August 1998, Mugabe sent the Zimbabwe army into a war in the Democratic Republic of Congo (formerly Zaire), more than a thousand kilometers (621 miles) away. The government claimed the deployment of 12,000 troops to Congo would cost very little. But within a year, the country plunged into an economic crisis and a drastic shortage of gasoline, diesel, and jet fuel. Despite the government's denials, it was clear to the thousands of people waiting in long lines for gas that the shortages resulted from the Congo war.

Zimbabwe had a few privately owned weekly newspapers that countered the government's rosy reports about the Congo war with stories about fatalities, soaring costs, and corrupt business deals in which army generals had companies delivering supplies to the troops. These weekly papers did not reach the mass of the population, so, to a certain extent, the government was content to denounce their reports on the state-controlled television and radio broadcasts and the state's daily newspapers. The state has a legislated monopoly on all broadcast media. At that time, there were only two daily newspapers, and the state controlled them both. So the Mugabe government was confident that its version of events reached the mass of the population.

But in January 1999, the *Standard* newspaper reported that army officers were so unhappy with the Congo war that some were talking of a revolt. The minister of defense denounced the report and vowed that those who wrote it would be punished. Within days, the *Standard*'s editor, Mark Chavunduka, and its reporter, Ray Choto, were abducted by army officers. They were missing for several days but were eventually turned over to the police and appeared in court and were released. Their swollen hands and feet and bruised faces made it obvious they had been tortured.

Mark and Ray had been warned by their torturers not to tell anyone of the abuse they suffered. But the two brave journalists decided to go public. They held a press conference to detail how they were taken to a basement in the Goromonzi police station and how they endured days and nights of beatings, electric shocks to the point of convulsions, and other harrowing torture. Doctors' examinations confirmed injuries consistent with their testimony. Robert Mugabe appeared on state television and warned that any journalists who angered the army should expect such treatment. It chilled the journalists in Zimbabwe and many ordinary people to see how little the government respected press freedom and human rights.

By the year 2000, Mugabe had been in power for twenty years. His policies to improve the health, education, and general welfare of the majority of the population had the opposite effect, and standards of living declined to such an extent that they were below preindependence levels. Instead of trying to improve general social welfare, however, the Mugabe government responded to growing unrest with an emphasis on the military, police, security network, and control of all aspects of power. The government used the state-owned press to put forward its assertions that it was the country's only valid political movement. The small, privately owned press supplied the only critical view.

Far from preparing to retire and allow others to lead Zimbabwe, Robert Mugabe entrenched himself for continued rule and ruthlessly suppressed any challengers that emerged, either within his Zanu-PF party or outside it. The press was part of this battle. Mugabe began to further tighten his control of the state media. He was angered by the privately owned press, even though it was small, because it questioned the legitimacy of his rule.

By 2000 Mugabe had found a henchman to help him pursue his campaign to control the press: Jonathan Moyo. At first glance, Moyo was an unlikely recruit to Mugabe's camp. He had never been a member of Zanu-PF or active in the liberation struggle against Rhodesian rule. He pursued graduate studies in the United States. Eventually, he became a lecturer in political science at the University of Zimbabwe in the late 1980s. Moyo became a prominent critic of Mugabe's rule. He wrote a book detailing how Mugabe and Zanu-PF had frustrated free and democratic elections in 1990. I often interviewed him for his outspokenly critical views of Mugabe. In fact, I once commissioned him to write an opinion piece for the *Guardian* in which he forcefully argued that Mugabe had strangled Zimbabwe's democracy.

Moyo went to Kenya, where he worked for the Ford Foundation, but he ran into trouble and was eventually charged with embezzling from the aid organization. Then, Moyo went to South Africa, where he directed a project for Witwatersrand University, which eventually collapsed amid charges that he had milked it for funds.

In 2000, Jonathan Moyo was looking for something new. Robert Mugabe, recognizing that Moyo was ambitious, tempted him with access to power that he could not refuse. Jonathan Moyo became the director of Mugabe's campaign to win national support for a new constitution that would have increased Mugabe's already considerable power. Moyo launched a slick and sophisticated multimedia campaign the likes of which Zimbabwe had never seen before. The state media, both broadcast and newspaper, promoted the proposed constitution with saturation coverage. The radio played a catchy song that Moyo had commissioned, which featured many of Zimbabwe's top musicians. "Vote Yes" T-shirts were widely circulated. Moyo masterminded all of this.

But, in February 2000, the population shocked Mugabe by voting against his proposed constitution. Despite Jonathan Moyo's persuasive press blitz, people said they voted against the draft constitution because they wanted to see Mugabe's powers reduced, but the constitution increased presidential powers. The defeat of Mugabe's constitutional referendum came just four months before parliamentary elections. It appeared that Mugabe's Zanu-PF faced certain defeat in the polls.

Mugabe reacted with fury. Rather than accept that the majority of Zimbabweans had enough of his twenty years of rule, Mugabe blamed the country's white minority, who, by that time, made up less than 1 percent of the country's 12 million people.

Within weeks of the defeat of Mugabe's constitution, the invasions of white-owned farms began. War veterans and other supporters of Mugabe occupied farms across the country. Police refused to stop the trespassing. The occupations were often violent. Twelve white farmers were killed during the period, and at least one black farm manager was also murdered. Hundreds of black farm laborers were beaten and their belongings burned. Zimbabwe's political and economic assault had begun.

Reporters of the local weekly newspaper, the *Zimbabwe Independent*, found that agents of the state's Central Intelligence Organization (CIO) and other government officials were involved in coordinating the farm invasions. Foreign correspondents based in Harare, especially those writing for the British press, extensively covered the chaos and violence of the farm occupations.

But Mugabe's farm occupations were only part of his campaign for the June 2000 parliamentary elections. Across the country, his supporters launched vicious attacks against the opposition party, the Movement for Democratic Change (MDC). More than three hundred MDC supporters were killed by government supporters, which showed that Mugabe and his Zanu-PF party were attacking black Zimbabweans, not just white farmers. I remember one case where the black leader of Zimbabwe Lawyers for Human Rights went to a rural area to investigate reports of beatings. He was beaten by the police, and, once released, he went to doctors who documented his injuries. That case became a widely used story to illustrate the abuse perpetrated by the Mugabe government.

It was not just foreign correspondents who were writing about the election violence. Leading the pack was Zimbabwe's own new independent daily newspaper, the *Daily News*. The privately owned newspaper was launched in 1999 to provide independent news coverage as opposed to the state-owned and increasingly strident government mouthpiece, the *Herald*.

Very quickly the *Daily News* captured the public imagination and overtook the long-established *Herald* in circulation. The *Herald*'s news had become stiff government propaganda that bore little relation to what was actually happening on the ground. For instance, when nurses went on strike for higher pay, the *Herald* announced the strike was over when, in fact, it lasted for several more days. Similarly, when the country was confronted with serious fuel shortages, the *Herald* proclaimed the shortages had ended. But a week later, cars were still waiting in lines that stretched a kilometer in the hope of getting even a half tank of petrol.

In contrast, readers welcomed the *Daily News* reports, which won a reputation for reporting the situation accurately and exposing corruption and human rights abuses. People enjoyed its cheeky, irreverent cartoons. At one point, the paper ran a serialized version of George Orwell's *Animal Farm*, and the parallels between the story of how the oppressed can become the oppressor were not lost on the public.

During the feverish campaigning for the June 2000 parliamentary elections, Jonathan Moyo was again leading Zanu-PF's media management. He wrote vitriolic attacks on the opposition in the state newspapers and appeared almost daily on the state television. More catchy pro-government jingles appeared on the radio.

But despite Moyo's efforts, the government's violence, and evidence of massive rigging, the opposition came very close to winning the elections, taking fifty-eight seats to Zanu-PF's sixty-two. With so much weighted against it, the opposition came tantalizingly close to victory and showed that it commanded support of a significant proportion of the population. The independent press highlighted the blatant perversions of democracy that the government had indulged in to manage a victory. The privately owned press argued persuasively that if the parliamentary elections had been at all free and fair, the Mugabe regime would have been voted out of power.

A major part of Mugabe's effort to bend Zimbabwe to his will was to subdue the press. And his lieutenant in the battle against the press was Jonathan Moyo, who was appointed minister of information.

Moyo's main target was the *Daily News*. A hand grenade was thrown into the paper's offices, but there were no arrests. Reporters and photographers were repeatedly arrested and frequently beaten. When street vendors selling the popular paper were beaten by Mugabe's youth militia, *Daily News* editor Geoff Nyarota went out onto street corners to show solidarity with the hawkers. Nyarota received death threats over the telephone, and one call was traced directly back to the headquarters of Mugabe's Zanu-PF party. In a separate incident, a man confessed to being contracted to assassinate Nyarota, but he decided not to go through with it because Nyarota had been friendly with him in the elevator.

Moyo's fulminations against the *Daily News* grew more threatening. In January 2001, Moyo said about the paper's criticism of the government, "It is now only a matter of time until Zimbabweans put a final stop to this madness in defence of their cultural interest and national security." Within forty-eight hours, a massive explosion rocked Harare. The printing presses of the *Daily News* had been destroyed by three anti-tank landmines detonated by dynamite sticks. It was an expert job, and private forensic investigators said only Zimbabwe's military would have had the expertise and access to the explosives. Police investigators came to the scene of the explosion only long after reporters, photographers, and camera people had recorded the mangled wreckage of what had been a modern printing plant with newly purchased Swedish equipment.

It was a devastating blow, but the *Daily News* was not knocked out. Even as journalists were witnessing the destruction caused by the explosion, *Daily News* executives were striking a deal with a privately owned weekly newspaper to share their printing press. The *Daily News* continued publishing and did not miss a day.

But the Mugabe regime's security network across the country prevented the *Daily News* from circulating outside the main cities of Harare and Bulawayo. In many small towns and rural areas Mugabe's youth militia beat up anyone caught selling the *Daily News*, and the militia seized and burned the papers. In one tragic incident, a rural schoolteacher caught reading a copy of the *Daily News* was beaten to death.

And yet the *Daily News* continued publishing and its circulation continued to grow, selling more than one hundred thousand copies every day. Because of Zimbabwe's economic crisis, people share newspapers, and it is estimated that nine to ten people read every copy of the *Daily News*. That means that nearly a million people read each edition of the paper.

Under the direction of minister of information Jonathan Moyo, the government turned on the foreign press. In quick succession, it expelled Mercedes Sayagues of South Africa's *Mail and Guardian*, Jo Winter of the BBC, David Blair of the *Daily Telegraph*, and Griffin Shea of Agence France-Presse. Sayagues had exposed brutal torture and murder by Zanu-PF agents during and after the 2000 parliamentary elections. The government responded by branding her a spy and declaring her a "prohibited immigrant" and throwing her, and her nine-year-old daughter, out of the country.

Jo Winter's expulsion was more frightening. Immigration authorities told him to leave the country within twenty-four hours. His lawyer, the tenacious upholder of press freedom Beatrice Mtetwa, won a court order stating that he could take a week to wind up his affairs in Zimbabwe. But that was not fast enough for security agents from the notorious CIO. A gang of thugs came to the Winter house and started to bash the door down. Jo called Beatrice and several journalists, and we all rushed to his place at 2 a.m. Our presence, and particularly the light generated by the camera of Reuters photographer Howard Burditt, caused the attackers to flee. Jo and his wife and baby daughter fled their home and quickly left Zimbabwe.

In comparison, the expulsions of David Blair and Griffin Shea were relatively straightforward. Their immigration permits had expired and the government refused to renew them and ordered the journalists to leave the country. I found myself the last foreign journalist in Zimbabwe, but the government could not get rid of me so easily because I held a permit of permanent residence, which gave me the right to stay and work in Zimbabwe indefinitely. The government would have to use other methods to get rid of me.

The government turned its attention back to the domestic press. Seeing that the *Daily News* could not be silenced by bombs, violence, and threats, Moyo turned to the government's strongest weapon: legislation. Moyo and his lawyer drafted a piece of legislation, the Access to Information and Protection of Privacy Act (AIPPA). The name of the law may have sounded innocuous, but the effect on Zimbabwe's press was diabolical. The law required all journalists and editors and newspapers to get a license from the government-controlled Media and Information Commission. To work without the permit was illegal and punishable by a jail term. In addition, any journalist convicted of "publishing a falsehood" would be liable for a two-year jail term. Even members of Mugabe's own Zanu-PF party balked at the repressive nature of the bill. Former justice minister Eddison Zvobgo said the bill was "the most pernicious assault on Zimbabwe's constitutional freedoms since independence." Nevertheless, Parliament passed the bill.

In March 2002, Mugabe was reelected as president in polls that were just as violent and unfair as the parliamentary elections in 2000. International observers condemned the elections, and eventually Zimbabwe was expelled from the Commonwealth, the esteemed organization of former British colonies, for holding such undemocratic elections.

The first action that Robert Mugabe took after being sworn into his new term was to sign the new press bill into law. The screws on the press were tightening.

On May 1, 2002, police came to my house at 7 a.m., and I was arrested and thrown in jail for thirty-two hours. I and two *Daily News* reporters were accused of "publishing a falsehood." We had written stories quoting a man who said his wife had been beheaded by Mugabe's supporters. I had written the story as the most dramatic of several incidents in which twelve opposition supporters had been killed in a wave of political violence following Mugabe's reelection. Eleven people had indeed been killed, but it turned out the husband interviewed had lied and his wife had actually died of AIDS. He had tricked the local newspapers and the entire foreign press corps. But, I was the one put on trial, the first journalist to be tried under the new AIPPA law.

The trial lasted for two months, and I was ably defended by Beatrice Mtetwa. After having seen her in action, ably defending the rights of Jo Winter and Mercedes Sayagues, I was absolutely certain that I wanted her to represent me. Beatrice handled the case brilliantly through several twists and turns. In the end, I was acquitted, as the magistrate ruled I had "acted as a responsible journalist" by trying to confirm the story with the police, who refused to give me any information.

My celebrations lasted about two minutes before the tall, lurking figure of Evans Siziba issued me with a deportation order that gave me twenty-four hours to leave the country. I was so discouraged that I said maybe it would be best to be deported. "I would be very uncomfortable representing you in that situation," said Beatrice. "As a permanent resident, you have every legal right to stay in the country. If the government gets away with deporting you so easily, then it will set a precedent that will reduce the rights of more than a million people who are also permanent residents here. We must take this to the courts."

Beatrice strengthened my resolve, and we immediately went back to the courts. Within two days, we had won a court order stating that I had the right to stay and work as a journalist in Zimbabwe.

I continued my work, writing about political rapes, torture by police, corruption, and growing famine. I felt I had a responsibility as a journalist to report on all these issues. Although the Mugabe government painted me and other journalists as "enemies of the state" and "supporters of terrorism," I believed I was reporting on the best of Zimbabwe, those brave people who were standing up for their basic freedoms. The warm and enthusiastic support I received from ordinary Zimbabweans wherever I went boosted my spirits. People frequently told me I was representing them.

I continued my work, especially chronicling the many incidents of torture and rape carried out by the police, the CIO, the youth militia and the army. In May 2003, the government agents came for me again. They dragged me away from the pack of journalists as I shouted, "This is a government that is afraid of a free press and of independent and critical reporting!" It was an unceremonious scuffle, but I wanted to get my message across.

Once they got rid of me, the government set about using its press legislation, AIPPA, to silence its main target, the *Daily News*. By the end of September 2003, the paper was closed because it was not registered by the government's media commission. Two months later, a positive court verdict emboldened the paper to print again, with a front page headline proclaiming "We're Back!" But the next day, armed police storm-trooped onto the newsroom of the *Daily News* and closed the paper. The sister paper, the *Daily News on Sunday*, was also closed.

Information minister Jonathan Moyo crowed over his "victory" in shutting down the *Daily News* and said that his next target would be the weekly newspaper the *Zimbabwe Independent*.

Instead Moyo shut down a different newspaper, the *Tribune*. And journalists continued to be arrested and charged with crimes. But no journalist has yet been convicted of a crime under AIPPA, which Beatrice tells me is largely the result of the strong legal precedent we set when we won acquittal of the charge against me.

Moyo continued harassing the press and passed an amendment to AIPPA, which stiffened the bill's already restrictive measures. The amendment, which became law in January 2005, states that any journalist caught working without a state license can be sentenced to a two-year jail sentence.

An even more repressive bill, the Criminal Law (Codification and Reform) Act, was passed by parliament. That bill carries a twenty-year jail sentence if a journalist is convicted of publishing or communicating to another person false information deemed to be detrimental to the state.

"The codification act is the really scary one," a veteran Zimbabwean journalist told me. "The courts could deem almost anything to be prejudicial to the state. And then it's in the slammer for a long spell." The new act threatens not only journalists but also anyone who is a source for journalists. It would become risky for sources to speak to foreign journalists working outside Zimbabwe.

The New York–based Committee to Protect Journalists said it was "deeply troubled" by the new measures. "They will have a further chilling effect on independent journalism in Zimbabwe," said Ann Cooper, the committee's executive director. "We call on Zimbabwe's government to reject all repressive media legislation and to ensure a free media climate for the March elections." The committee named Zimbabwe as one of the ten worst countries in which to work as a journalist in 2004.

But Moyo's ambitions appear to have cut short his reign as Mugabe's press czar. Throughout 2004 he was angling to run for parliament in his home constituency of Tsholotsho in the Matabeleland north province. But Moyo made the mistake of questioning Mugabe's choice of Joyce Mujuru to be one of Zimbabwe's two vice presidents. He went so far as to hold a secret meeting in which he urged a number of Zanu-PF officials to refuse to support Mujuru. When Mugabe found out, he was furious. Moyo was publicly reprimanded, and he quickly lost his positions on the Central Committee and the Polituro of Zanu-PF. Mugabe punished Moyo further by making it impossible for him to run for parliament in Tsholotsho by stating that all candidates in that constituency must be women. Moyo appealed the all-female ruling but was rejected. Because Mugabe said that he would appoint only elected members of parliament to his cabinet, it appeared that Moyo's days of wielding power over Zimbabwe's media were numbered.

Although many rejoiced over Moyo's downfall, it is not clear that his repressive measures over Zimbabwe's press will be reversed. Much more than just Jonathan Moyo's downfall is needed for press freedom to be restored to Zimbabwe: The *Daily News* would have to be re-opened, charges dropped against more than seventy journalists, the AIPPA bill scrapped, and foreign journalists permitted to report freely.

There have been many casualties in Zimbabwe's battle for press freedom. Mark Chavunduka, the editor of the *Standard,* eventually died after his torture, and there is no doubt that the trauma contributed to a deterioration in his health. Ray Choto, Geoff Nyarota, and many other journalists left Zimbabwe and are working in South Africa, Britain, the United States, and all over the world.

But, despite the Mugabe government's calculated efforts to silence the press, it has not succeeded. Dedicated Zimbabwean journalists continue, against frightening odds, to write about events in the country for the *Standard* and the *Zimbabwe Independent.* A hardy band of hardened Zimbabwean journalists continues to write for the British newspapers the *Times* and the *Daily Telegraph* and the international news agencies the Associated Press, Agence France-Presse, and Reuters, although in some cases their reports have been watered down because of political interference.

A particularly encouraging phenomenon has been the growth of Zimbabwean journalism on the Internet. Several new agencies and news digests have sprung up, using the Internet and e-mail for wide dispersal. Even as the government tries to shut down newspapers, new publications on the new technology are growing and proving more difficult to control.

Beatrice Mtetwa has continued to take up every legal challenge to press freedom, in addition to fighting for human rights and the rule of law in Zimbabwe. It has not been easy for her. At one point, she was badly beaten by police at the Borrowdale police station. After documenting her injuries and recovering for two days, she typed up assault charges and went back to the police station and served the papers on her assailants. Beatrice was named "Human Rights Lawyer of the Year" in 2004 by the British organizations Liberty and Justice.

Government agents succeeded in throwing me out of Zimbabwe, but they did not manage to shut me up. I have continued to write about Zimbabwe and the growing body of evidence of human rights abuses for the *Guardian*. Indeed, the government's policy may have backfired, as its action against me has given me more prominence and the opportunity to write a book about my twenty-three years in Zimbabwe.

It was a traumatic exit, but my problems were small compared to the sufferings of thousands of Zimbabweans. I lost my home and contact with colleagues and friends, yet I consider myself to be a very lucky journalist. The gratification of being able to report on the compelling issues of Zimbabwe's struggle for democracy, human rights, and press freedom far outweigh the troubles I've encountered. The Mugabe government has won a few rounds, but the press is tenacious, and I am convinced it will triumph.

Chapter 6

AT THE BORDER BETWEEN LIFE AND DEATH

AARON BERHANE

Aaron Berhane Tesfazghi was born on October 6, 1969, in Asmara, Eritrea, in northeastern Africa. He received his BA degree in journalism and mass communication from the University of Asmara and cofounded the first independent newspaper in Eritrea—*Setit*—in 1997. He worked at *Setit* as editor-in-chief until it closed in September 2001.

During his time as a journalist in Eritrea, Berhane wrote several critical editorials and articles that convinced the Eritrean government to implement the 1997 constitution. He also wrote articles on a number of other subjects, such as Eritrean land policy, corruption in the administration, and the poverty of the justice system. As a consequence of his writing, Berhane was often summoned before the authorities—and received threats over the telephone.

In September 2001, Berhane was forced to flee Eritrea. Although hunted by the security forces, he managed to escape the country, but, as a reprisal, officers arrested his brother and cousin. They were released after being held in prison for two years and one year, respectively. Berhane was granted political asylum by the Canadian government in August 2002. In recognition of the suffering he had undergone, the New York–based Human Rights Watch awarded him a Hellman/Hammett grant in 2003. He currently lives in Canada, where he runs a newspaper in Tigrigna and in English. Aside from journalism, Berhane has written a screenplay in Tigrigna, which is waiting for a producer.

That was my last one-way trip from my country, Eritrea. It wasn't of my own volition. I was forced out. I had to flee—hunted like an antelope by the security forces. I traveled a long way with my colleague to Eritrea's border with Sudan. Death was opening its mouth to swallow us. An alarm sounded in our direction. A voice ordered us to stop in our tracks. Noisy guns and the sounds of soldiers shouting overwhelmed us. We had no opportunity to discuss the direction in which we should run. The soldiers were only twenty meters (sixty-five feet) away. I had only one choice—to make a mad dash for the Sudan border. My capture meant death.

I cofounded the first independent newspaper in Eritrea, *Setit*, in August 1997 to express my beliefs and to provide a public forum for discussion. The unhealthy situation after Eritrea secured independence in 1993 triggered my response. I had written articles criticizing the government and sent them to the state-owned newspaper, *Hadas Eritrea*. Not one was published.

I wrote my first critical piece when the government ordered all former fighters who had enrolled at the University of Asmara to give up their studies. About three hundred former fighters had passed the strict university entrance exam. What a blessing it was for them to get back to school after years in the thirty-year armed liberation struggle. Of course, being forced to leave the university was very painful. Such a measure affected their futures, slapping them in the face and denying their basic right to an education.

Former fighters deserved more than that! They had shed their blood to win peace and to further their education. Instead, their hopes were dashed. I was shocked—I was one of those former combatants. I couldn't imagine why such a ridiculous order had been given. The government gave a very feeble excuse: "We need the former soldiers to join the workforce because important offices no longer function."

I was in my early twenties at the time, forced to quit my studies in 1994 after having enrolled for only one year. Nevertheless, I had some hope of returning because government officials said that we would be back at the university the following year. I was determined to get a formal statement from the Ministry of Education saying that I used to work so that I could return to my studies. I begged and pleaded to continue my education; however, the ministry and the Office of the President were determined to deny me, like so many others, my basic right to higher education.

The government did allow some former fighters to study at the university. One of the senior government officials told me in a private conversation, "The government gives releases only to those who have no qualifications or to those who are not able to support themselves and always looks for the help of the government." Why? Because this minimizes the government's load! If the government knows someone has some potential, it prefers to keep him within its realm—not so he can serve the country but to restrict his individual growth. As a result, this individual would never be a threat to the government. The reason President Isaias Afewerki's regime decided to kick all former fighters out of the university was the government considered university-educated former combatants a potential threat. If former fighters enriched their experience with a university education, they would not allow their country to be run by a dictator. The president was wary of those former fighters influencing the young who attended the university with them. The ruling party simply did not care whether or not this amounted to a loss for the country. My first critical piece was really very mild, even though it included all of the previously mentioned issues, but it was never published in the country's only newspaper.

I didn't give up. I kept on writing. In April 1994, a brother of a friend of mine was arrested and jailed for two weeks. He was suspected of stealing a spare car part from the auto-parts store where he used to work. He fought to prove his innocence, but the police refused to listen to him, finally setting him free when the real thief was caught. According to Eritrean law, a police officer doesn't have the right to detain anyone for more than seventy-two hours without a trial. But this law exists only on paper. Unfortunately, such violations of basic rights are quite common. The government does not have a policy to educate the people about their rights via the media, simply forcing people "to do their duty." I wrote about this situation and sent it to *Hadas Eritrea*—but my article ended up on the floor!

It is really difficult to bring issues to the attention of the people or the government when the media are neither free nor accessible. The single newspaper—published in Tigrigna, Arabic, and English—the one radio station, and the sole TV station are all owned by the government. No letter with any critical comments had ever been published. Without alternative voices, people had to send letters to the government-owned media, even though they knew that their letter would end up in the garbage bag.

My dissatisfaction increased. I dreamed of a free press in Eritrea, but as long as the country was run without a constitution, my dream was impossible. In June 1996, the government passed a press law that allowed print media to be privately owned. The regime issued the press law to satisfy the loan requirements of the International Monetary Fund (IMF) and the World Bank, including the introduction of democracy and the freedom of the press. The vague press law, unfortunately, was deliberately drafted to allow the government to control the journalists. But this did not stop me from launching my own newspaper, the first independent newspaper in Eritrea: the newspaper that caused me to flee my country.

"You've got to watch what you write; I don't think this government is ready to be criticized," my late father said when I told him about my plans. He was right. Every public office was unwilling to provide my newspaper with information. When asked, government officials were not prepared to be interviewed, so obtaining information was extremely difficult. Even though the press law gave journalists the right to information, practically speaking, all doors were closed to independent journalists. Nevertheless, due to popular support, the content and the paper's circulation increased steadily.

Setit started as a paper published every other week, with a circulation of about five thousand copies; it reached a circulation of forty thousand by printing twice a week. Simret Seyoum, Habtom Mihreteab, and I were the cofounders and only staff members in the beginning, but we increased to ten by including Dawit Issak, Fessehaye Yohannes (Joshua), and others after about three months. The paper's large circulation made *Setit* the most widely read newspaper. Some months later, at the end of 1997, a number of other newspapers were launched following my example. At one time, eighteen weekly or biweekly private newspapers were in the market. However, eleven of them disappeared within a very short time because of the fierce competition. Seven private newspapers (*Setit, Tsigienay, Kestedebena, Mekalih, Hadas Admas, Wintana,* and *Zemen*) remained and overcame a variety of political and financial obstacles until they were finally closed in September 2001.

We had experienced several difficult challenges before our paper's death. One of my frequent problems was obtaining information from senior government officials, who were not willing to cooperate with the private newspapers. They made themselves unavailable or ignored phone calls. Their defiance encouraged us to look for alternative sources of information and to work with international reporters. The officials preferred to give information to international media rather than to local private media, so we used to share information with them. Sometimes, we used to write news about what had happened in Eritrea quoting the BBC or the Voice of America (VOA) because senior officials refused to provide us with information. Whenever the Ethiopian media said something against Eritrea, I used to call the Eritrean government spokesman to confirm the claim. He usually refused to make himself available. However, if a BBC or other foreign media correspondent contacted him, he rushed to respond. That technique could be good for international news consumption, but it appeared to be disrespectful to Eritrea's own people. Eritrean officials didn't care whether the information was delivered to their own public at the same time. That's why we used to hear about our own issues and what had happened in our own capital from the outside media.

Refusing to provide information to local journalists could also be seen as the government forgetting its responsibilities. But government officials did not seem to understand, not wanting to be blamed by the international media. The local media are under their control, and they can easily silence the criticism or impose censorship. That was another challenge we journalists faced.

I went to the battlefield of Zalambesa in July 1998, right after the border war with Ethiopia erupted (in May). I stayed three days on the front line and interviewed a wounded young man who was doing his national service. I wrote an interesting piece that showed the courage of young Eritreans in defending their country and the experiences they had in battle. However, the minister of information, Beraki Ghebresilassie (he is now in jail along with the other reformists), personally censored my piece and refused his permission to publish it. "We don't want you to publish such a story. You are going to terrify the people by mentioning youths who do national service and get wounded," he said.

The people already know what can happen to their sons and daughters on the front, but the ministry censored my article because the ministry was not ready to talk about the war. Government media barely mentioned the battle and did their best to cover it up. My newspaper provided the only reporting of the battle. The government was not only sensitive to news from the battlefield but also wary of any information that had some news value.

The Anadarko Petroleum Corporation and the government of Eritrea signed a US$28 million deal in 1995 and another US$23 million oil and natural gas exploration agreement in 1997 in the Zula and Edd Blocks. Drilling began in early 1998, and many rumors soon surfaced about their successful drilling activities. I interviewed a manager of Anadarko in Eritrea to learn more about the drilling. He gave me a considerable amount of information that our readers deserved to know, though he was circumspect about answering many questions due to the agreement his company had with the Eritrean government.

For example, he mentioned that the first well his company drilled after a completion of a five-thousand-square-kilometer (310,700-square-mile), two-dimensional seismic survey over the twenty-seven-thousand-square-kilometer (16,778-square-mile) Zula Block was unsuccessful. In contrast, at the Bulissar No. 1 well, the company found source rock at multiple levels, good seals, and quality reservoir oil sands, which meant the well could have produced millions of barrels of oil. However, the reserve was not economically viable, so there was no reason to continue digging. Hence, Anadarko was looking to explore the Edd Block and the other parts of Zula Block.

My interview subsequently went to the censor. The Ministry of Information's censorship committee did not block the interview but instead edited it by removing information that interpreted the data. Then, the Ministry of Energy and Mines reevaluated it and cut out important elements of the story. Finally, in parts of the article, only my questions remained. I wish I had not published it because it provided very little information. To my surprise, the information removed by the ministries had already been published in the *Oil Journal*, which meant that the government was not worried about leaking information to neighboring countries. The government officials just did not want their own people to know. Why not? I still do not know. Perhaps the people in charge lacked confidence as a result of the weak political structure of the government.

The government system has always been problematic. Most of the time, officials decline to cooperate with independent journalists not because they were ordered to do so but because they lack confidence in their own positions. They always wanted journalists to check with their superior rather than just provide the needed information. Superiors always brushed off journalists: "This order came from above; you had better ask them." The chances of reaching a minister or the president were slim, which discouraged many journalists from writing some articles. This common, deliberate technique obstructed journalists who wanted to report on burning issues—such as the article I wrote about land distribution.

The Land Proclamation in 1994 introduced a nationwide land reform program, vesting ownership of all land with the government and granting limited rights to Eritrean individuals. There were land leases for domestic and foreign investors. The land bill introduced a dynamic new system that replaced the former system of land tenure. However, many villagers, particularly in Asmara and its vicinity, were not happy. Their lands were the first target of the new policy, as many investors applied to get land leases in the suburbs of Asmara. There was some corruption in distributing the leases, so some villagers revolted and prevented their land from being distributed. The government reacted by jailing the elders who openly opposed it.

Years later I tried to interview the department heads of land and investments to find the roots of the problem after I published several critical letters and people's complaints. Government officials always made themselves unavailable, and finally I gave up trying to contact them. But I conveyed a clear message to the people—the corruption that they experienced was rooted among not only their immediate bosses but also those at the top. The land redistribution problem was raised in several issues of my newspaper. Sadly, there was never any adequate response from the people in charge. A journalist is always restricted; there is no way to move beyond government control. Those who try to do so face the inevitable severe intimidation.

In mid-2000, the price of sugar increased rapidly, and people were complaining. I decided to write an investigative piece to find the reasons behind the daily price increase. I collected important information by interviewing several merchants and officials from the Trade Department in the Ministry of Trade and Industry. It turned out that there were three main reasons for the skyrocketing sugar price. First, the government secretly imposed regulations on the exchange rate of the dollar, which was previously free. Merchants were having difficulties in obtaining a hard currency and were not motivated to import sugar into the country. Second, the Red Sea Corporation, the biggest sugar supplier, a corporation of the ruling party, concentrated on giving sugar to the Eritrean Defense Force and slowed supply to the civilian market. And the third reason was the poor supply from sugar-producing countries—sugar prices were rising in the world market as well.

I concluded that the first cause was the core of the problem. Later, I received a telephone call from a senior official of the ruling party, the People's Front for Democracy and Justice (PFDJ): "I learned that you are writing about sugar. It is a very sensitive issue. Our country is at war, so drop it. Don't write anything about it." I tried to reach a compromise, but he was adamant. "I said, don't write [about sugar] if you want to stay in business." I had no alternative but to focus on the other reasons, though their impact on the sugar market was insignificant in comparison.

Telephone threats were the first tool the ruling party used to intimidate independent journalists. It was part of my daily experience when encountering intolerant officials who would complain about the editorial section. I used to write every editorial, and I received warnings all the time—especially when the editorial carried some criticism of official government policy. The adviser and spokesperson of the president, Yemane Ghebremeskel, was angry with me when I criticized some elements of the Comprehensive Peace Agreement signed by Eritrea and Ethiopia in Algiers in December 2000.

Eritrea and Ethiopia signed this agreement to end their border conflict by accepting the decision of a boundary commission, and a UN cartographic unit carried out the actual demarcation. I was afraid this agreement might benefit Ethiopia more than Eritrea. Ethiopia was trying to insert its new boundary map prepared in 1997. This violated the legal borders, established by treaties signed with Italy (Eritrea's former colonizer) in 1900, 1902, and 1908. The Ethiopian government, however, wanted to change these treaties because the border had not been demarcated.

The Eritrean government was aware of this and insisted that a demarcation of the border, based on the treaties of 1900, 1902, 1908, be carried out by a UN cartographic unit as a technical matter. When the Comprehensive Peace Agreement was signed, I assumed the issue would pass beyond Eritrea's control. However, the technical issue of border demarcation was opening the way for other political influences, changing the former treaties between Italy and Ethiopia.

I criticized the Eritrean government for coming up with such an agreement, which was more beneficial to Ethiopia because of its diplomatic influence in the world arena. Ghebremeskel was upset and called me twice early in the morning before I got to my office. He had used uncomfortable words with my secretary, who was extremely worried by the time I arrived in the office. She ran toward me: "Oh, Aaron, Yemane is going to kill you today. He is really angry about today's editorial. He wants you to call him." Even after I comforted her, she continued to shake.

That is also one of the government's tactics. Everyone who worked for the paper had to feel threatened. I sat in my office and scanned the editorial once again before I called him. I knew exactly what he would say. I was used to his complaints. He or another official called at least every two weeks to give stern warnings when I wrote a line indicating the weakness of the government or leaking some secrets.

"Don't confuse the people," said Yemane before he greeted

me. "There is nothing changed in our stance; you have to watch what you write." I asked him if he would give me an interview since nothing had changed. He refused, sternly warned me, and ended the telephone call.

His argument simply did not stand up. The Boundary Commission was established to delimit and demarcate the line between the two states through binding arbitration in accordance with the relevant colonial treaties and applicable international law. The commission issued its decision on April 13, 2002, and awarded a lot of the Eritrean land to Ethiopia, even though the focal point of the conflict, Badme, was awarded to Eritrea. My editorial was right, but I was blamed as an irresponsible journalist.

In the Eritrean government's view, there is an unwritten rule for a "well-qualified" journalist, who must always highlight the positive aspects of government and undermine the negative. A journalist who always tries to serve the people and criticize the government, however, is considered irresponsible. This was seen clearly in 2001. The criticism of private newspapers sharpened after Eritrea and Ethiopia signed the secession of hostility agreement.

Journalists called for the implementation of a constitution ratified in 1997, aggressively attacking the weaknesses of the government officials. They brought to light the complaints of the people who were continuously ignored. Journalists made citizens aware of the exploitation of military officers under the compulsory national service scheme, who were forced to build their private houses using government equipment and labor. Newspapers revealed the absence of justice and good administration as the cause of Eritrea's slow transition to democracy. The papers became a true mirror of the government's actions. The government, however, was never able to tolerate its ugly reflection. This was particularly true when some senior leaders of the People's Front for Democratic Justice criticized the president in the columns of the private newspapers.

A group of influential PFDJ leaders wrote an open letter to the president in May 2001. There was nothing new in the letter. The criticism had already been printed in the columns of most private newspapers. But the government was shocked when the cumulative complaints of the people were presented in an organized way. This was a great boon to the private newspapers, as it helped them to win public trust. The people wanted to see changes in the political system, and they deserved to know what was at the bottom of the conflict between the president and the reformers. That's why I rushed to print the open letter in my paper.

This was unlike the G-13, a group of Eritrean academics and professionals who wrote a letter to President Isaias Afewerki on October 2000, calling for a critical review of post-independence development and the nature of Eritrea's leadership. This letter didn't have a chance of being printed in the private presses because of the prompt action of Isaias's regime. At that time, the government arrested eight journalists right after the letter appeared on the Internet. To justify the arrests, the government said the journalists had evaded national service, which was a complete lie. Some of them were students at the university while others were carrying out their duties.

In any case, due to the absence of their editors, all seven papers failed to go to press for a week. I was not arrested at that time. I was away when security officers came to my office to arrest me. However, two journalists at my paper were thrown in jail for a week. I went into hiding until it was safe. Finally, the government released everyone following some criticism from the international community, or perhaps the government was merely satisfied with the reign of terror inflicted on the journalists and the campaign mounted against the G-13. The people didn't know what the G-13 said; they only heard the accusations against it from the government-owned media. Since at least 99 percent of the population didn't have access to the Internet, the truth about the G-13 failed to gain popular support. The story was different, however, with the case of the G-15—the new group of dissidents composed of the influential PFDJ leaders.

The general population learned about the positive things the G-15 wanted to implement from its letter printed in my newspaper, *Setit*. The interviews the G-15 members gave to several private newspapers helped them fight the accusations coming from the government media.

The role the private newspapers played was really quite tremendous. But the senior leaders of the G-15 appreciated this when only they found themselves caught in the war of words. Some dissidents had refused to give interviews to private newspapers while they were in office. Later, when they were forced to resign or were frozen out, they came to the papers to be heard. Even the president and his group, who used to undermine the private media and acted as if no one read them, changed their opinion after they found out about the private press's rocketing circulation and felt the sting of criticism. However, they still declined to provide information—perhaps not the best media technique.

We sharpened our criticism to bring the government to its senses. We kept publishing stories about the arrest of two thousand Asmara University students who were detained at a deserted camp for refusing to sign up for a government-organized compulsory work program, and we demanded the release of their president, Semere Kesete. The deaths of two students from heat stroke and the complaints of the students' worried mothers were printed in our columns daily. Unfortunately, the reporting failed to force the government to provide adequate answers to its critics. Instead, the security officers blatantly started to intimidate us. The police summoned editors to the station every now and then, even for very trivial matters.

I was summoned several times and asked to reveal my sources or the name of a person who had criticized a branch of the government in the paper's opinion column. This was understandable. Those articles had a very strong message and wounded the government. One thing, however, that made me sick and delayed the paper's publication for hours was the case of a former senior military officer. It was an isolated case, but the police pressured me greatly to reveal my source. I was being summoned once or twice a week for questioning in August 2001. I wrote a news story about a former senior military officer who was released from prison after serving ten years for molesting male teenagers. I didn't mention that he had been arrested for his homosexual acts—which are illegal in Eritrea. Instead, I wrote that a senior military officer was in jail for practicing things that our culture and ethics do not permit. Even though my report was true, I was summoned by a police officer and told it was false. He asked me to tell him the source of my information. I refused: "If what I have written is not true, file a case against me in court." I was sent away with a stern warning, and I assumed the matter was over. But it was not. I was summoned six more times and asked the same question. Each time, I gave the same answer.

I was not angry because of the summonses and the threats; I got used to them. I was mad because each time the police asked me to show up, it was on the eve of the newspaper being printed. My newspaper came out on Tuesdays and Fridays, and an officer would summon me on a Monday or Thursday, the busiest days of my week. "Why do you always want me to come on those days when you know I am busy?" I asked him one day. He didn't even bother to reply; he just told me to come. I found it very stressful to work under such conditions.

It was particularly stressful when pressure also came from my parents. My mother and brothers always advised me to tone down the paper's criticism—particularly when they had been advised by people who seemed to have better access to the executive branch of the government than I did. Whenever there was time to talk at lunch or dinner, this issue was raised. My family members feared that my activity would disrupt their lives.

One day, my mother came home from a funeral with a long

face because of the news that she had heard from a distant relative: A government informant was determined to pressure me to listen to his poor advice. I had never seen my mom so terrified. She didn't want to lose me. She had lost three sons in the thirty-year war of independence. "Please, son, stop writing; they are after your life!" She was crying. "I don't want to see any bad thing happen to you while I'm alive. I have seen enough."

It was really hard. I love my mother, and I have always respected her wishes. But I could not drop my profession. I was committed. I wanted to become a significant player in the shaping of my country's future. I wanted to push the plate of constructive criticism into the middle of the discussion table. I was committed to disclosing the dirty game that had caused so much damage to Eritrean society. If I got into trouble because of my positive contributions, let it be. I didn't listen to my mother. I kept writing and publishing letters critical of the government. But there was a heavy cost. The executive branch of the government tried every means possible to silence me and the other editors. Telephone threats, accusations, and intimidation followed, but none were effective. That's when the threats became physical.

At the beginning of September 2001, two security officers visited my home around 10 p.m., waiting outside for me. I drove home rehearsing the conversation I had had with a gentleman about that day's editorial about how the fight of two elephants damages the grass. I was trying to show that the fight between the president and the G-15 would hurt the people who were already suffering from a shortage of medical supplies, administrative services, and justice. The gentleman had appreciated the editorial and suggested that it might bring both parties to their senses. I wish the president had thought that way.

I arrived home and got out to open the gate. Two security guys rushed from the shadows and blocked my path, standing three inches away from me. Their hats half covered their faces, making it difficult to recognize them.

"Hey, we just came to give you a final piece of advice," said a short guy as he pushed a gun hidden in his jacket into my ribs. "If your paper contains any further criticism of the government, that will be your final byline."

I could feel the tip of the gun against my ribs. I didn't dare to say anything until he removed the gun. "Who are you?"

They didn't answer directly: "Just concern yourself with the advice we are giving you."

The government did not cross the line until the events of September 11, 2001—the attacks on the World Trade Center and the Pentagon. With world attention deflected, President Isaias arrested eleven dissidents one week later and closed down all seven private newspapers—*Setit, Mekalih, Kestedebena, Tsigienay, Hadas Admas, Zemen,* and *Wintana.* The newspaper of the National Union of Eritrean Youth—*Tirgita*—also closed, even though it was the government's mouthpiece.

What amazed me were the accusations made against us. The government media blamed us for violating the press law, collaborating with the enemy, evading national service, and getting funds from foreigners. All these were baseless accusations. We didn't have any means to respond to such defamations. So we had to do something to defend ourselves. There were no newspapers or journalists' associations. We had tried several times to establish one, but we were refused. I took the initiative and organized the journalists to make a formal request. I wrote a letter demanding that the government give us some adequate explanation for the closure of our papers and for the accusations against us.

Between September 19 and 20, I invited each editor-in-chief of the private newspapers to sign the letter. In the end, Amanuel Asrat, the editor of *Zemen,* and I submitted the letter to the Ministry of Information on September 21, 2001. While we were waiting for a reply, security officers came to pick us up from our homes.

I now remember this unfortunate date with contradictory feelings—sad because my colleagues went through hell and good because I escaped from that hell. September 23, 2001, was my luckiest day, but not for my colleagues. The security officers started to hunt for journalists at their homes. Most of them were picked up that morning—except Joshua, Simret, Seyoum, Dawit, Habtemichael (Mekalih), and me.

We stayed where we were when we learned of the round up of journalists. It didn't take them much time to get Dawit and Joshua. They arrested them on September 26 and 27, respectively. Since the security forces controlled the checkpoints with great caution, they were also sure to find me soon. It was then that the battle for my survival began.

Thanks to Almighty God, I heard about the search for me. To prevent my crossing into Sudan, my photo was distributed to fourteen checkpoints from Asmara to the border. At the same time, the armed forces tackled a potential threat from G-15 supporters in the city. A number of people sympathizing with the G-15 were taken to prison after being picked up on the street or in their homes. I restricted my movements to a thirty-square-meter (98-square-foot) room. It was like a prison without guards. I tried to read and to relax, but my mind was preoccupied with what to do next. Should I flee to Sudan or to Ethiopia?

Knowing that my photos were posted at every checkpoint on the way to Sudan, it was hard to select that escape route. However, I made it my first choice. The Ethiopian government blamed us journalists for plotting to overthrow the president. That was the funniest joke of the year. Had my grandma been alive, she would have opened her toothless mouth to laugh.

I had to be careful that this complete lie did not confuse naive people. That's why I decided to risk escaping through Sudan. After hiding in Asmara for 103 days, I planned my escape with my colleague Simret. I let my beard and my hair grow wildly to change my appearance, so much so that I barely recognized myself. I looked not only much older but also like I belonged to one of the ethnic groups that live on the Eritrean/Sudanese border.

The first precaution that we took was very helpful for our escape. We got counterfeit IDs to show the authorities if asked. The four-wheel-drive Mitsubishi that we rented was our other tool to freedom. We departed on January 6, 2002, at 5:30 a.m. from Asmara, determined to flee the country. It was a long drive from my home city of Asmara to Ghirmaika, a small town located near the Sudan border. We had to reach Ghirmaika by dusk; we got there at 7:15 p.m. without difficulty. We could not take the car across the border, so we left it in Ghirmaika and set off on foot guided by our "fixer." (A "fixer" was one who provided accurate information about army patrols.)

The Eritrean army tried to make things difficult for anybody trying to flee to Sudan, which may be a sign of insecurity for a government that has still to mature. Our "fixer" did his best to get the latest information for that evening. Unfortunately, he was wrong. The army didn't leave the area at the supposed time, and we were trapped.

An alarm echoed in our direction—a voice ordered us to stop where we were. The sound of guns and shouts overwhelmed us, leaving no chance to discuss in which direction to run. As the soldiers were only a few steps away, I made a mad dash to the Sudan border under a moonless sky. Simret and our "fixer" followed. When the troops realized we were not ready to give up, they started firing. We did not know if our lives would end right there on the flat lands of the border, the line between life and death. Everything was terrifying, but I never thought of surrendering. I believed that if I were captured, that would be the end of my history. So I persuaded myself to run without hesitation, to prolong my life as long as possible.

Although the dark night made it very hard to see what was in front of me, I was able to penetrate the thick bushes without a problem. I don't know how I managed to jump the big bushes and to run with miraculous speed. I ran like an antelope for about two hours. I didn't stop until I stumbled and fell. My body and my bag went in different directions. I wasted no time getting my bag. I just kept on going, leaving my belongings behind. I kept hearing gunfire from where I had last seen Simret and our fixer. When the shooting stopped, I thought they were dead.

To my delight, two months later, I learned they had been captured but were still alive. I was the only one who had managed to escape to safety. In reprisal, the government arrested my brother and my cousin. My brother Amanuel remained in custody for two years, and my cousin Petros Tsegay, for one. They may blame me for being the cause of their misery or for not listening to their advice when I knew the government would punish any member of the family for my action. Neither of them had been involved in the field of journalism, nor had either of them cooperated with me in my work. But the Eritrean government usually carries out such arrests to intimidate parents. Journalists and their relatives were perceived with just one eye in that dark period. The Committee to Protect Journalists (CPJ) has, in fact, named Eritrea as the worst place in the world to be a journalist! I would add that Eritrea is also the worst place to be related to a journalist. Relatives still live in fear even if they are not in jail.

The bittersweet periods of my life were the times that I worked in journalism in Asmara. It is painful to suffer for upholding the truth. It is tough to be dumped in prison for advocating openness and calling for justice. Yes, it is a threat to your life to criticize the government's abuse of power. It is a challenge to ignore the pressure of your parents. However, it is also rewarding to see that some changes have occurred as a result of one's own contribution, though it is small.

My journalist colleagues, except Simret Seyoum, who was released a year ago, are still in prison as far as I know. The winner of a press freedom award and the very talented documentary filmmaker, Seyoum Tsehaye, and the bravest and most brilliant journalists, Yosuf Mohammed, Dawit Issak, Seid Abdelkadir, Medhanie Haile, Mathewos Habteab, Dawit Habtemichael,

Amanuel Asrat, Ghebrehiwet Keleta, and Temesghen, are all incommunicado. I have had no news of their whereabouts. Their only sin is that they are journalists. My brother's sin is that he is my sibling.

Once again, those contradictory feelings for September 23, 2001, return. I don't know how to mark it. However, I know one thing, my colleagues' and family's three years' misery is my misery too. I may live happily in a democratic country, but it is in the flesh only; my soul is always with them in their confinement and shares the pain they suffer. This will forever remain my driving force as I pursue my career.

Chapter 7
SWIMMING IN THE GREAT LATRINE
IMPUNITY AND IMPRISONMENT IN CHIHUAHUA

ISABEL ARVIDE

Isabel Arvide has been a journalist for more than thirty years. She began her career at the popular Mexican newspaper *Excelsior* in 1976 and later moved to become part of the editorial staff at the *El Sol de Mexico*, where she developed a solid reputation for writing on political issues in the editorial pages. In this period, she also worked for the *Ovaciones* newspaper.

During the 1980s, she reported on the Iran/Iraq conflict before returning home to cover the political campaign of Miguel de la Madrid, who was president of Mexico from 1982 to 1988. Arvide's articles on de la Madrid were subsequently turned into a book titled *The End of the Tunnel*. In 1984, Arvide was the first woman to win the National Journalism Prize.

Aside from her journalism, Arvide was a 1979 finalist in the National Poetry Competition and has written a number of books, including *The War of Mirrors*, about the war in Chiapas, and *Death in Juarez*, which documents serial murders and corruption in and around the town of Juarez.

eing in prison is like the slow fall toward the abyss experienced by those who commit suicide: That fall provides time to reflect on past errors and on how we went down the wrong path.

I was behind a heavy metal door sealed by a big lock. I had called out my name when the list of inmates was read. I waited in the darkness, terrified and staring at a dirty toilet, as I curled up on the urine of others.

Those who had brought me here and placed me behind bars without allowing me to see my arrest warrant are the main characters in a thousand other stories of deaths and disappearances. I was as certain as can be that they would not be satisfied until they had taken their vengeance and destroyed me.

After all, I had challenged them with the most effective of weapons: Bricks in the form of words had constructed a solid public history of corruption. My fate had been determined by an article of mine, published by various daily newspapers, that had detailed conspiracies as big as a house and as invisible as the power of money. For many years, I had written newspaper articles about the complicity of public officials in the disappearances of men and women in the border state of Chihuahua in Mexico and about their links with criminals.

I knew my time had come when those disgusting men, who claimed to be policemen, grabbed me in the waiting area of the Chihuahua airport, when they shoved me into a station wagon that cruised the deserted streets of the city, and when they denied me a phone call in the sinister offices where uniformed police mocked my solitude. I knew I had lost all the battles. Sometimes I think that there is a signed contract on my life that one day will be put into effect against me.

Still today, two years later, my body gets a chill when I lose sight, even for a moment, of the federal agents who "protect" me day and night. My enemies, who that day ordered my arrest by uniformed police officers, are like ghosts who live like parasites in my mind and body each minute of the time I still have left. They have power and a first and last name. They have countless deaths in their personal resume. I exposed them for the murderers they are. They know that I sentenced them publicly.

Female paranoia? On the contrary, those who know me accuse me of overconfidence and near reckless behavior. As if I did not know reality. Even so, I must admit that my fear concerning what I have published about illicit activities in Chihuahua is constant and has sources that are certain, even if not verifiable.

That is the price to be paid: The terror that grips my home and denies me the comfort of turning the lights out every night. This is the price beyond the pending sentences I received as a result of two sham court cases on the charge of defamation (which, according to the outdated law in my country, defines even truth as "irrelevant").

These sentences can impose upon me a maximum of two years for each "crime." That is to say, this very day, I can receive four years of prison for having written the truth. Fear is even a greater price than the hundreds of trips I have taken to the court in Chihuahua. Upon my arrival, in obedience to the orders of a judge whom they have bought, I must sign a register meant for murderers free on bond, as if I were those killers' equal.

I am a journalist who one day chose to write that the democracy that so many extol in song in my country does not exist in fact.

Chihuahua is not my only topic or obsession, though it has been a reference point for years. The fact is that the more one knows and writes about the reality of this area of the country, the more one finds testimonies, proofs, and confidential communications on one's desk.

And it becomes impossible to accept that the official version is the truth. That is to say, what exists are hundreds of deaths, disappearances, loads of cocaine, violence, corruption at the highest official levels, and collusion between law enforcement officials and the heads of the drug cartels. This is a world where drug traffickers give orders, and the ones that follow them are police officers, constables, government attorneys, and government officials themselves.

Chihuahua borders the state of Texas, where the drugs that originated in South America finally cross the bridges into the United States after traversing all of Mexico in order to satisfy the vices of millions of Americans.

Ciudad Juarez, whose fame is known throughout the world, continues to be the the entry point for more than 70 percent of the cocaine that comes into the United States. The city bears an avalanche of men and women from further south who look for work and want to go to "the other side" in order to earn dollars and a better living for their families. The rich, the powerful, and the local lords live right next to the hundreds of thousands of "outsiders" who have built temporary cities and who bury their dreams under cardboard ceilings.

Chihuahua is also the name for the state's capital, where one finds the state government offices, restaurants where a slice of meat costs thirty dollars, universities, and dress codes that require gentlemen to wear ties.

The capital is where members of families of "old lineage" continue to preserve the fortunes and surnames of their grandfathers. They sometimes live in homes that signal their economic power in former centuries. They are like tourists who come to enforce their rules in the large businesses that they own, to collect their earnings in dollars, and to look down upon the poor. They are the ones who decide who governs, and they alternate between political parties in order to hedge their bets on both sides. What matters to them is the protection of their interests rather than the certification of voting ballots.

Here is where the Mexican Revolution of 1910 began, precisely because of the vast differences between landowners and peasants. This is the place from where Pancho Villa raided the United States in the only recognized invasion of that country.

This is how Chihuahua has been governed by such barons. In order to be more precise, I will restrict my analysis to the twelve years ending in 2004. One of these barons comes from the National Action Party (PAN), which represents the right, and the other baron comes from the Institutional Revolutionary Party (PRI), which is supposed to represent the center-left.

Two men, Francisco Barrio and Patricio Martinez, have, as part of their sad resume, the honor of having sponsored the murder of more than three hundred women who are known to the world as "The dead women of Juarez." These men are responsible for the disappearance of more than two hundred citizens and the execution of more than one thousand persons in the clear light of day. Add to their resume unsanitary conditions, unemployment, assaults, vehicle theft, and the lack of schools.

Each man has leveled charges at the other about the protection of drug traffickers, as if such accusations were simply part of a political campaign to smear each other instead of accusations worthy of investigation by the authorities.

What do I mean by "sponsoring" these crimes? In simple terms, according to Mexican law, those who do not fulfill their responsibility to respect and enforce respect for the law commit the crime of "omission," thereby making themselves accomplices of criminals worthy of imprisonment.

In that entity, the norm is death, violence, and, consequently, wanton disregard for the law. There is not a single criminal act that cannot be credited to the complicity of local, state, and federal law enforcement. There is a chain of corruption that reaches to the desks of the chiefs of these law enforcement organizations. There is more than ample documentation for these charges.

Without going too far afield, in January 2004, a special prosecutor, María Luisa López Urbina, was named by President Vicente Fox to address the hundreds of complaints and inquiries from human rights organizations concerning the murders of young women in Ciudad Juarez. Mexican law requires that all

murders, regardless of number, be prosecuted under the juris-
diction of state authorities. The special prosecutor issued a
recommendation that more than one hundred officials, both
upper-level and low-level agents of both administrations, be reprimanded for the crime of "negligence" in the relevant murder
investigations. This recommendation derives from looking at
about forty cases of young women who were first reported as
"missing" but who then became statistics.

That is to say, the federal prosecutor "discovered" that, in the
cases of more than forty murdered women, the local authorities
had not even fulfilled the most basic tasks of investigation as
required by law. For over five years, the Association of Disappeared Family Members, headed by Jaime Hervella in El Paso,
Texas, has amply documented the same sort of intentional official neglect in the cases of almost two hundred people who have
"disappeared."

This negligence cannot be classified as anything other than
"complicity." International courts regard as complicity those
human rights violations cases in which local authorities knowingly permit or encourage murders.

Obviously, since I am speaking of Chihuahua and of the local
authorities who continue to be on the payroll, the special prosecutor's recommendation came to naught. No one was, or will be,
punished. No one was punished under the administration of
governor Patricio Martinez, a PRI member of around age fifty
who served as mayor of the capital city and who established
numerous businesses during his administration.

Without these facts, one cannot understand the journalistic
activities that can take one to prison and live in the custody of
federal agents. Because what exists all around is the appalling
reality of corruption.

The journalist who writes about the reality of Chihuahua
(and I have done this for eight long years and published a book
on it) has no recourse except to denounce corruption. Such

denunciations always definitely affect the highest powers as well as local political authorities.

And so, on that long first night in prison, the big question to be answered was not why I was there but rather what had made me stubbornly write about what I had seen. Time and again I had filled entire pages and computer screens with complaints sent by citizens and even by some officials who felt ashamed of what was happening. They thought that I, as a journalist, had the power to change reality solely by exposing complaints through the media.

I knew then what I know now: Writing about the links between local authorities and drug traffickers was dangerous. But I also knew that remaining silent was equivalent to a grievous defeat whose pain even death could not console. And I innocently believed it was possible.

Each time that I traveled to Chihuahua to meet my confidential sources in the last eight years, and before I was accused of defamation and imprisoned twice, I had encountered the growing participation of local authorities in drug trafficking.

The same thing may be said of both previous governorships. One previous administration was headed by Francisco Barrio, who now leads the PAN congressional caucus and enjoys such impunity that he could become that party's presidential candidate, despite the sharp criticisms of the debts he owed to the dead women during his administration. Patricio Martinez of the PRI party had the governorship during the six years prior to 2004.

To understand who these men are, it is sufficient to visit any newspaper archive. Barrio will be remembered for the illicit businesses, never examined legally, run by his late brother. He will also be remembered for his unfortunate remark that the murdered Juarez women, whose corpses appeared for the first time during his constitutional mandate, had sought their own death by dressing provocatively.

His successor, Patricio Martinez, experienced an assassination attempt as he exited his government offices. The attempt was understood to be the work of drug traffickers who wanted to send a message as they do with their own associates who do not follow their rules.

As a journalist who has exercised my profession for nearly thirty uninterrupted years, I have elected not to write on subjects with which I have no deep familiarity. It certainly does not seem very pleasant or very interesting to probe into the insides of criminal mafias. I declare myself to be, therefore, ignorant of the internal workings of the large drug cartels. I have no informants among them, nor would I recognize them except by the photographs published when they are captured. I do not yearn to read their biographies, and I am even less prone to make them characters in my novels. This is not my issue, nor is it very satisfying to investigate something that necessarily requires depth and a large investment of time.

This is why I have avoided this topic when I could by writing a daily opinion column instead in a country where "red-letter articles" are in the front pages. Among my many other conclusions, I believe that drug traffickers are murderers who do not deserve any space for public glorification.

This way, no one can accuse me of being a mental patient in search of nothing, or accuse me of being some sort of idiot who, through some sick love of danger, places herself in the path of galloping horses. On the contrary, I see my job as foreign to all of this.

Nonetheless, during these thirty years, I have expressed publicly my disgust, and I have swum in the great latrine that is the corruption of public office. Moreover, I have done this conscientiously, considering it as the only mountain worth climbing. I have been obsessed with matters in which politicians, from the president of the country to the lowest bureaucrat who charges bribes in a post office window, use their positions to steal, extort, and murder.

And much of this exists in Mexico, even in 2005. Witness the massive report, published at the beginning of the administration of President Vicente Fox, that exposed the purchase, with taxpayer money, of $400 towels in the presidential palace. A news story that every one of my colleagues wished we had written.

Over twenty years ago, one of my articles triggered the public anger of Miguel de la Madrid because I spoke of his purchase of household furniture as a bridal gift for his daughter (a purchase in the United States he eventually canceled) at a time when Mexico was experiencing great economic austerity, with an inflation rate above 150 percent.

Not much has changed. In my country, we have an excess of corruption related to the exercise of public office. For a political analyst, which is what I am, there is no way of avoiding writing about it if one is to keep any sense of self-respect.

So I eventually ended up writing about "narcopolitics," or the relations between public officials and drug traffickers. These relations have superseded a nation of law and now form a basic rule of social life.

Let me explain. In Chihuahua it is normal for a person to enter a restaurant and murder a person eating his soup in the full view of other diners. This is just as normal as the so-called big lift, wherein a vehicle is blocked by another, while police block all local traffic, so that a victim might be "lifted" off the streets, never to be seen again. Authorities care little for investigating something well known to be part and parcel of local police complicity. They know that the payroll of criminals includes hundreds of police officers and local and federal officials. That is why the great flow of drugs into our neighboring country has not been able to stop.

In 1995, I wrote a book titled *Death in Juarez,* now out of print, where I recounted the impossibility of investigating the disappearance of a woman at the Ciudad Juarez airport in front of dozens of witnesses as she rode in a taxi, whose driver was murdered the next day. In the book I had named corrupt police officials and authorities and the existence of corruption and neglect in the middle of the country.

These testimonies led, years later (at the end of August 2000), to the discovery of the so-called FBI trenches. More recently, in 2004 in a residential neighborhood of Ciudad Juarez, "narco-trenches" were discovered, which are nothing more than burial sites for those "lifted" by the police on behalf of local drug traffickers. Such persons are usually murdered after being tortured for some act of betrayal related to drug trafficking.

Still pending are the arrest warrants issued by federal authorities against local police chiefs that I stubbornly chronicled. Likewise, available are the identifications, through DNA of family members, of many of the murder victims whom I had mentioned in my reports. The discovery of these hidden graves confirmed what I had already written long ago, naming both the murderers and their victims.

Can one think of a greater punishment than the discovery of secret burial trenches, even years later, because of something one writes? If one searches for a cinematographic analogy, one may think of a horror movie. Afterward I was cursed by reality, by truths so unacceptable that all one can do is to close one's eyes and wish they would go away. But closing one's eyes is the same as being an accomplice to these crimes. That is not my case.

I have been asked to write about the difficulties of exposing official corruption and the complicity between officials and drug traffickers in Chihuahua. I must admit that such a difficulty does not exist or ever existed because it is enough to go to this part of Mexico and to just talk, listen, and open one's eyes a bit to document what is repeatedly found in the inside pages of the newspapers. There is no merit in investigation because crime and violence are like daily bread. For this topic, and especially in this part of the country, one does not need some special training in investigative journalism. It is enough to want to know.

When I arrived in Chihuahua at the beginning of June 2001, I intended to document, confirm, and develop information that had already reached my desk. All I had to do was ask, and, in a few days, I had confirmed the existence of an investigation into the relationship between Patricio Martinez and drug trafficking. I confirmed this on the basis of sources in the highest levels of the military, in the attorney general's office of the country, and even in the American FBI at El Paso, Texas.

These sources provided detailed information concerning a shipment of cocaine that had been intercepted a few weeks earlier by federal police. The case brought the intervention of Jesus "Chito" Solis, the brother of the secretary of public safety for the state, in an attempt to prevent that interception. The drugs belonged to a cartel that identifies its shipments by using packages weighed in ounces rather than in kilos, as is usually the case.

Journalistically, the topic was priceless, and my sources were and continue to be irreproachable. Fortunately, at that time, between 2000 and 2001, I usually collaborated with *Milenio*, a journal with a national circulation and managed by a professional journalist—Raymundo Riva Palacio—known for his keen sense of smell and honesty. He trusted his reporters and knew me for a long time. Likewise, the area newspapers, fourteen of them, published this article without flinching about its magnitude.

In page after page, the friends, associates, and "godfathers" of the governor, Patricio Martinez, tell of the corruption in that administration, perhaps the most important of which concerns the chief of public security, who, in an even greater act of cynicism, appointed as the attorney general Jesus "Chito" Solis, an old policeman linked to drug trafficking by sheer virtue of his involvement in a large plantation of marijuana, which roused even public indignation. No one could be surprised. There in Chihuahua a new criminal mafia was emerging, and, above all, a new kind of impunity for organized crime.

On Sunday, June 3, the front page bore my byline under prominent headlines as well as the names of the "untouchables." The next day some of those named in that report protested with incredible anger, but not one public complaint could produce any proof or evidence to contradict the obvious truth in my report.

And so came the messages, and veiled threats, from local powerbrokers who insisted that my audacity was a sin to be punished. I did not believe it, and I did not take it seriously, in order to preserve my mental health and a free conscience.

Then came, in the following months, assassinations as stupid as the murder of an attorney of a supposed "lady killer" who was literally shredded by bullets from the police acting on the orders of the prosecutor, "Chito" Solis. This murder received the explanation that, since it was a mistake, the police were not liable from the very moment that they fired. As is the case with many other violent acts in Chihuahua, this murder received a brief note in the inside pages—but I wrote many indignant pages. And I became known as one of a few Mexican journalists who spoke about things that others preferred to keep quiet.

That is to say, my articles became a standard reference about the impunity and official sponsorship of violence in this part of the country. I was so well known that I thought there was no danger when I received an official invitation from the national leader of the PRI party (which governed Mexico until 2000) to accompany him, in July 2002, on a campaign tour of Chihuahua. It was a trap.

Without respecting my constitutional right to be informed about any accusation against me, an arrest warrant was issued that was executed by governor Patricio Martinez's own aides. I spent the night in a small cell of a prison known as Aquiles Serdán, located on the outskirts of Ciudad Juarez. I expected to be assassinated, and I would have become a statistic if it had not been for the outpouring of publicity in the media—principally in the nightly television news and various radio programs—that immediately rejected and protested my incarceration.

The great publicity offensive launched by my own son, Bruno, who knew the danger I was in after hours of being held in isolation, allowed my detention to become official and proceed to what should have been automatic: my delivery to the appropriate judge. The judge, in fact, placed a bond upon me that was five times as high as what a murderer should pay for provisional liberty. It was the equivalent of $10 million, which was paid in cash.

Eight months later, at the beginning of March 2003, and during one of many trips that I have had to make to Chihuahua (trips that have cost me much more than my income as a journalist), I was detained a second time in a scene reminiscent of the movie *Traffic*. With the luxury of the most unjustified force, I was detained as I exited a downtown restaurant in plain sight of about a hundred people, only a few hours after being in the court office of the same judge. At 4 p.m., the same police officer—who currently has a pending arrest warrant against him for murder and who is a member of a special unit—approached to notify me of a new arrest warrant for the crime of defamation that I committed in my article. After his disrespectful address, he asked me whether I remembered who he was because he would come for me again.

The federal agents who, by the recommendation of the National Commission of Human Rights, were protecting me pulled out their weapons. Dozens of police officers, in some twenty-eight vehicles, as I was later informed, participated in my arrest. Once again, the very police officers who, in the light of day, murdered an attorney "by mistake" without paying any penalty, insisted that I had to be booked, placed in isolation, and humiliated while being denied my constitutional right to know the charges against me.

Can anyone imagine a more vulnerable position than being locked in a cell that did not even have toilet paper and guarded around the clock by five guards and by the chief of prison security, all employed by the very same man who accused me?

The next day, I had the honor of setting the record for the largest bond, approximately $20,000, compared to the $2,000 that a criminal usually pays, imposed on anyone for a misdemeanor. And, obviously, it had to be paid in cash. The prosecutor's office, also under the orders of my accuser, urged that I be denied my constitutional right to provisional liberty.

Three years later, the same judge, Octavio Rodríguez Gaytan of the Second Criminal Court of the judicial district of Morelos, had learned, through the mass media, about deaths through public execution. This was the same judge who would sentence me on account of two criminal complaints, based on my article, that are historic in their lack of adherence to the law. Because of foreign petitions, he had also learned about imprisonments and about removals from public office because of suspected drug trafficking. He knew about the arrest warrants for various local figures I mentioned in my article.

What do I want to say about all of this? Something as simple as this is unacceptable: That a judge is about to sentence me for the crime of "defamation" for an article where I spoke about criminal links that are today the motive for arrest warrants. In June 2001, I wrote what today is an irrefutable truth, as confirmed by federal judges and authorities. Those I named as accomplices to drug traffickers have arrest warrants pending against them, except for the ones who have been murdered. The same official who could be promoted to state prosecutor of Chihuahua can go to prison at any moment. And he remains my accuser.

By November 2004, Patricio Martinez had left his post as governor. By 2005, his attorney general, Jesus "Chito" Solis, has seen his own properties raided in search of drugs. At the same time, he has been questioned several times by federal authorities on the basis of information provided by the FBI. The truth that I published has continued to be just that, the truth.

Many journalists come to ask me about Chihuahua. Without even wanting to be, I have become a "source of information" for both foreign reporters and for scholars of drug trafficking. And fear also remains ever present in my life.

In addition, I must live in the "custody" of federal agents. And it is not as in the movies, where the bodyguards are handsome and friendly. The federal agents who guard me have been removed from time to time because of complaints about their own gross misconduct, as, for example, urinating in the elevator of the building in which I live, stealing the keys to my apartment and entering it without authorization, and being arrested during one of my trips to Veracruz because of rowdiness and shooting their weapons in their hotel room.

I am not speaking of people who can perform their duties professionally or with enthusiasm especially because I do not have the resources to pay them "bonuses." I also do not have a living standard or the income that corresponds to the status of someone who may otherwise require bodyguards.

These guards must accompany me to the grocery store, to coffee shops, to the theater, and just to walk down any street. I don't have the space in my apartment so that they can wait for me until I leave, and so they wait by the street door. I don't give them gifts or buy them clothes. One of the ways that the guards can be relieved of their duties is if they show up unwashed and unkempt, something that causes embarrassment in any environment in which I have to be. In short, all of this stops me from doing many activities, and I think twice about going to any public place. The guards must accompany me to the bathroom door, but even that is no guarantee that they are capable of protecting me or that I can trust them. They take offense at the mere fact of having to protect a woman, an inferior being in their hierarchy of personhood, which is permeated by machismo.

This is an uncomfortable situation. If I asked that my escort be removed, then the criminals and former police officers, who are now fugitives from the law and who undoubtedly think that my articles contributed to their official persecution, would think that the federal government no longer cares if I am killed. And then they would kill me.

The reason is that, while the corrupt local officials may lose their power, the web of complicity that sustained them at the federal level has not changed. The wanton disregard of the law continues to be the norm in crimes against women and against journalists. It is routine in my country to hear about a journalist murdered in front of his or her children or about a corpse found in a neighborhood street or about the applause for these crimes from officials who deserve to be in prison.

When I am sentenced by the judge of the Second Criminal Court in the Chihuahua justice system and when I have exhausted all the legal options available in the Mexican justice system, then my case will be heard in international court. I will keep on fighting for the revocation of the law of defamation, or at least for its modification, so that the legal standard becomes the truth of what is published and the journalistic endeavor does not become the object of retaliation on the part of spurious authorities.

Was I wrong to write about Chihuahua? Would I do it again? At night I have questions without answers. In the morning, and without even thinking about it, I again begin to type stubbornly about the same truths as if it were possible to change them.

Chapter 8
UNITED WE FALL
THE RISKS OF MARGINALIZING DISSENT

TOM GUTTING

George Ramirez

Tom Gutting graduated from the Johns Hopkins University in Baltimore in 2001. After holding internships at the *South Bend* (Indiana) *Tribune, Frederick* (Maryland) *News-Post,* and *Baltimore Sun,* he began his professional journalism career as city editor of the *Texas City Sun* in June 2001. That career came to an abrupt end in September 2001, when he was fired after writing an opinion column criticizing George W. Bush's response to the September 11, 2001, terrorist attacks. After writing a follow-up op/ed that appeared in the *Houston Chronicle, Dallas Morning News, San Antonio Express-News,* and *Austin American Statesman,* among others, he appeared on ABC's *Nightline* and NPR. His efforts to find another newspaper job proved unsuccessful, and he began working as a grant writer, which he remains today. He works and writes fiction and lives in Houston, Texas.

I woke up the morning of Tuesday, September 11, 2001, to the unexpected sound of a telephone ringing. My wife and I had been engaged in a month-long battle trying to get a phone service connected in our new apartment, but the surprise of learning our phone worked was swamped by the absolute shock of the news the call brought. Turn on your TV, the caller said, the World Trade Center is on fire.

You know how the rest of the morning developed.

At the time, fresh out of college and with my first real job, I was a city editor working the night shift at the *Texas City Sun*, a small daily newspaper thirty-five miles southeast of Houston. I immediately called the office and said I would be in before lunch. For journalists, the challenge this presented is ultimate. I didn't relish the work that lay ahead. Like so many others, I grappled with the disbelief and sadness of what had happened, but I was excited to be part of a big national story and was moved by ideals of what the press could do for the public in a crisis. With a fledgling naïveté, I told myself that even two thousand miles away in Texas City, a blue-collar town of forty-five thousand dominated by refineries and chemical companies like BP, the residents expected and deserved the best coverage we had to offer.

In the days after September 11, I believe the *Texas City Sun* gave its readers just that. Time went by in a blur. I worked ten out of eleven days. We devoted roughly half of the paper to the disasters, with the stories—mostly from the Associated Press but with as many local angles and as much local reaction as possible—grouped under the common header "A Nation's Heart Torn." The news came fast and furious:

> Fire put out at Pentagon
> Air traffic restarts; New York, D.C. airports shut down
> Reserves called up
> Hijackers' identities revealed; first arrest made

Bush puts government on highest alert
As shock subsides, American anger builds[1]

Journalists weren't immune to the flurry of emotions that came with all these developments. Since I wrote an opinion column once a week under the title "From the Gutt," I had an outlet for my feelings, which made it easy to separate my opinions from the news coverage we provided our readers.

During my time in Texas City, both the publisher, Les Daughtry Jr., and Dale Dimitri, the managing editor, encouraged me to take on tough issues with my column. Over the years, the *Sun* took pride in its local reputation for writing thought-provoking opinion pieces. Daughtry made a point of not reviewing any op/ed content prior to publication. He preferred, he often said, to stay out of the newsroom unless absolutely necessary. So I wrote my columns with confidence, knowing I had the full support of superiors who believed in publishing a wide range of views.

My first post–September 11 column criticized the decision of Texas high schools to play their full slate of scheduled football games on September 14. I had feared a negative reaction taking on a famous Texas sacred cow, but I never heard anything other than from a couple readers who told me they thought my sentiments were right on the money—those games should not have been played.

The following week, I decided to write something that would fill an obvious void in the September 11 coverage. The press, filled with emotion and patriotism, had lost its critical eye. I wanted to take a hard look at what George W. Bush's leadership had been like.

It was clear that, in the first moments after the attacks, he appeared weak. From the seemingly dazed and uncomprehending stare of the president continuing to read to schoolchildren after he had received the news to his first public remarks, with his all-too-characteristic deer-in-headlights look, gave no comfort to a stunned nation. Bush then disappeared for a few hours, resurfacing at Barksdale Air Force Base in Louisiana. Upon arrival, he gave a short, shockingly unsettled speech, appearing frightened. According to the *Washington Post*, "Reporters in the room noted that his eyes were red-rimmed. It had been more than three hours since Bush or any senior official had said anything publicly. . . . He spoke haltingly, mispronouncing several words as he looked down at his notes."[2]

My evaluation of Bush's behavior closely mirrored that of conservative commentator Tucker Carlson, former co-host of CNN's *Crossfire*. He was embarrassed that the president had chosen not to return to Washington, instead disappearing "in a bunker on some faraway military base" while Carlson's family "sat unprotected" in their house near the Pentagon.[3] Bush's behavior "initially made me sorry I'd voted for him," Carlson wrote, adding, "Leaders must take risks, sometimes physical ones. Bush should have elbowed his Secret Service detail out of the way and returned in a display of fearlessness to his nation's capital."[4]

In the opinion of Carlson and other pundits, Bush righted the ship in the days following September 11, especially in his joint address to Congress on September 20. When Bush made the speech, he faced a nation reeling domestically, internationally, and economically. I found his words dominated by generalities and vague plans, and the war on terrorism sounded distressingly like the amorphous and endless war on drugs. The biggest weakness stood out in the line, "Americans are asking: What is expected of us? I ask you to live your lives, and hug your children."[5] Wars and crises of years past in our country have forced the population to make great sacrifices of money, material, and life. The war on terrorism? Bush was asking for nothing more than the status quo, except for mourning and maybe a little extra vigilance.

Bush's speech cemented my decision to write a strong, forthright column about leadership during the war on terrorism. Obviously, that was a more serious undertaking than criticizing high school football in Texas, and my opening paragraph probably should have tried to do a bit more to diffuse readers' natural defensiveness: "I'm aware of the American custom not to criticize our country's leaders in times of crisis. But after George W. Bush's vague, trite speech Thursday night, it's time we snapped out of the 'support our president' trance and start to be vigilant citizens, as our Constitution demands."[6]

I took Bush to task for his leadership and judgment on September 11 and its immediate aftermath. "When Dick Cheney went on 'Meet the Press,' last week, it became abundantly clear W. hadn't done the one thing he promised—lead," I wrote. "Cheney was making all the calls while Bush ran scared, thereby fulfilling the terrorists' wishes to make the most powerful man in the world fear them."[7]

Bush's behavior stood in stark contrast to that of New York City mayor Rudolph Giuliani, who was out on the streets that morning. "He never hesitated or made his personal well-being a top priority," I observed. ". . . In addition, Giuliani makes a point to show terrorists he isn't afraid to continue doing everyday business. He's highly visible, not hiding underground in Nebraska."[8]

The lack of leadership Bush demonstrated made me extremely nervous about our newly declared war. "He has dropped no hints, however, about what the objectives are. . . . He makes broad, sweeping statements about ridding the world of evil and delivering 'infinite justice,'" my column read. "I feel like we're being led by the pied piper. We have pledged our full resources to something, and our citizens are frothing at the mouth to get involved, but we have no idea what lies ahead."[9]

Looking back on it, I believe I was one of the first people in the country to hit on a lot of points about Bush and the war on terrorism that have become centrally debated issues. I freely admit that it wasn't a perfect piece. The tone may have been a little off. I wince myself at a phrase or two, particularly, "So last Tuesday, there was W. flying around the country like a scared child seeking refuge in his mother's bed after having a nightmare."[10] But the core message of the column was important and worth bringing to my readers' attention.

The day my column appeared was the first I had off in more than a week. I actually had a three-day weekend coming to me, and our coverage had gotten back to normal so that Dale Dimitri told me to take it. As it happened, my in-laws were in town, and we planned to spend some time in Galveston, south of Texas City, on Saturday. On the way, we stopped at the *Sun* offices.

Later, I realized I should have known something was amiss when I saw Les Daughtry's car in the parking lot. As I walked in the building, the lady working the phones that morning said they had gotten a lot of angry calls about my column. I was shocked. After giving my in-laws a quick tour of the office, I went to see Daughtry. We talked about a lot of things, but what I remember most is telling him, first, that I didn't realize the column would cause such an uproar and, second, that I hoped he wasn't going to fire me. I'll never forget his response. He told me unequivocally there was no chance he would fire me. He said he would never fire someone because of his or her opinion.

Our discussion covered much the same ground this chapter does. I explained my rationale for writing the column, while Daughtry made it clear he disagreed with my opinion. At the same time, we talked about *Texas City Sun* policy about op/ed content. I told him I respected that, as publisher of the newspaper, he could decide what got printed and would continue to adhere to the editorial policies he had laid out. Daughtry said twice that he thought our September 11 coverage had been outstanding and that I, in particular, had done a "fucking incredible" job since joining the *Sun*'s staff. He also said he might write something giving our readers a counterpoint to my column. With that, our meeting ended. I offered to stay and help field phone calls—I told Daughtry I would stand behind my words and talk to our readers if he wanted me to—but he declined.

I was somewhat upset with the apparent level of anger with my column. One woman wrote that, "at a time like this, you're not allowed to have an opinion." Others told me I should move to Afghanistan to be with bin Laden or be tried for treason. Dale Dimitri reassured me that it would all blow over soon. The *Sun* was no stranger to storms over opinion pieces. He said not to worry about my job security, and he let me know Daughtry planned to write a letter to our readers for the September 23 edition.

Daughtry's letter, however, turned out to be a front-page apology. He wrote of my column, "[It was] not appropriate to publish it during this time our country and our leaders find ourselves in." He called the decision to publish it "ill-advised," describing my piece as "mean-spirited and inappropriate."[11] But that didn't hurt the most. I felt punched in the stomach when I read Daughtry's second piece in that day's paper, an editorial under the headline "Bush's leadership has been superb." In addition to his responding to me, he encouraged "others to do so as well."[12] His op/ed appeared as a staff editorial. Mine had run with a column header and picture.

"Tom's column was so offensive to me personally that I had a hard time getting all the way through it, and in fact, still feel ill from its effects as I write this," Daughtry wrote.[13] Reading the editorial, I had a hard time believing it was written by a man who had guaranteed he wouldn't fire me.

When I arrived at work on Tuesday, September 25, I found a letter from Daughtry at my desk. In it, he detailed the new policy he had determined for our op/ed page. Effective immediately, the content would have to be approved each day by Daughtry. In addition, for an unspecified period of time, every column I wrote would have to be reviewed ahead of time. As I had told him at our Saturday meeting, I respected Daughtry's role as publisher and would abide by his editorial policies. Upon reading his letter, dated September 25, I sighed with relief—obviously, my job was safe.

So I went about my business, getting ready to put together the day's paper. I pulled photos from the AP wire to accompany our national stories and began correcting them. That's when Daughtry appeared and asked me to come to his office. I sat down, assuming we would talk about the new editorial page policy. We didn't. Daughtry didn't beat around the bush. He told me he had done a lot of thinking over the weekend and concluded that we couldn't "work productively together" anymore. It took a brief moment to sink in. Daughtry said he would give me two weeks' pay, and he made it clear that I couldn't change his mind. I was fired and dumbstruck. In this same chair, seventy-two hours before, he had promised me he wouldn't fire me and had praised my work ethic and ability. Not unexpectedly, anger boiled in me, but I swallowed it. I calmly told Daughtry he was making an enormous mistake because I had a lot to offer the *Texas City Sun*. And that was it. I walked out and went home.

Survival instinct kicked in next. There I was, twenty-three, recently married, and had just lost my first job out of college. I hadn't worked anywhere except newspapers, but I knew that Southern Newspapers, Inc., the parent company of the *Texas City Sun*, owned every other daily paper in the surrounding area, except the *Houston Chronicle*. I called my wife and left what must have seemed like a cryptic message, asking her to call me at home. I also called a former editor whom I had interned with at the *Baltimore Sun* before graduating from college. He told me he would call *Editor and Publisher* to pass on the story. Then I got home and waited for something to happen.

It ended up being a whirlwind several weeks. *Editor and Publisher* ran an article, and, subsequently, more and more news organizations, local and national, called. The *Washington Post* mentioned my situation in Howard Kurtz's "Media Notes," as did the *New York Times* in a piece titled, "In Patriotic Time, Dissent Is Muted" that ran on its front page on September 28. Gersh Kuntzman from *Newsweek* called. My old hometown paper, the *South Bend* (Indiana) *Tribune*, did as well. More newspapers wanted to talk to me than I can remember. At the same time, I knew I wanted to say something more about my situation. Pragmatically, being fired was a difficult thing, but, more importantly, I thought it was a dark day for press freedom and an ethical disaster on the part of Les Daughtry Jr., and the *Texas City Sun*.

I wrote an opinion piece that appeared initially at Salon.com on October 1 and later in several newspapers, including the *Houston Chronicle*, the *San Antonio Express News*, the *Austin American Statesman*, the *Dallas Morning News*, the *South Bend Tribune*, and others. ABC News called and asked me to appear on *Nightline* with Ted Koppel, and I did on October 3. Later, I spoke with Juan Williams on NPR's "Talk of the Nation." My theme throughout those forums was, and remains, unchanged. George Washington once said, "Government is not reason, it is not eloquence, it is a force. Like fire, it is a dangerous servant and a fearful master; never for a moment should it be left to irresponsible action." Irresponsible action is a particular threat when vigilant critics are silenced. It is the obligation of democratic citizens to freely debate the direction their country and leaders are taking. The beauty of republicanism comes from diversity of opinion, not unity of thought. Squashing debate only crushes the sacred duty of the citizenry.

I can admit now, although with sadness, that my views on press freedom and societal debate were naive. As I found out, Americans didn't want debate. We wanted to wave flags and lash out. We wanted sound bites, bumper sticker slogans, and lapel pins. That doesn't mean, however, that I was wrong.

Those who disagreed with me generally have made two criticisms. First, they said my tone was outrageous and inappropriate. I always have admitted the column wasn't perfect. I believe it was necessary to have a strong, clear delivery of what I had to say. But quibbling over issues of tone is semantics and overshadows the larger points brought up in the column. Second, critics dismissed any connection between my firing and First Amendment and free speech issues because it didn't involve the government preventing the column from being published.

My being fired had nothing to do with the government, and it wasn't a censorship issue—the column got published. But that doesn't mean it wasn't a matter of free speech. Relegating freedom of speech to journalists' and others' interaction with the government is a narrow, legalistic approach to the issue that fails to consider the wide-ranging importance it and other rights hold in our society. Foremost among those is the First Amendment responsibilities—not rights—of newspaper publishers.

The notion that freedom of speech is fostered purely through defensive measures, such as negating government interference when it occurs, is misguided. Free speech, the first item articulated in the Bill of Rights, is a cornerstone of our society. In practice, the spirit of freedom of speech must extend beyond government interaction with its citizens. Alexander Hamilton wrote in the opening paragraph of "Federalist No. 1" in *The Federalist Papers*: "It has been frequently remarked that it seems to have been reserved to the people of this country, by their conduct and example, to decide the important question, whether societies of men are really capable or not of establishing good government from reflection and choice, or whether they are forever destined to depend for their political constitutions on accident and force." The only way to make decisions based on reflection and choice is to encourage debate and consider disparate viewpoints.

Many are inclined to say what my former boss, Les Daughtry, said about my column: "I'm a supporter of the First Amendment, and I think reporters and editors have the obligation to be voices of dissent at times, but this was beyond the pale."[14] To maintain a productive, working democracy, it is essential to consider differing viewpoints at all times. There's no asterisk on the First Amendment excluding times of crisis or popular waves of patriotism. We most need dissent when we are so sure of ourselves that we don't want to hear contrary views.

It is often said that we must balance dissent with the needs of security. But, even in a post–September 11 world, constraints on public debate are not a necessary trade-off between freedom and security. Searching airline passengers cannot be equated with silencing columnists. Except in the most extreme cases, such as revealing important government secrets or explicitly inciting armed rebellion, there is no gain to our security from restraining speech. The residents of Texas City would not have been more secure if my column had not been printed on September 22, 2001. In fact, those outraged by what I wrote were better off for reading it. If my criticisms of Bush were right, they heard a truth they needed to hear. But even if I were wrong, the fact that I spoke out makes the truths I contested stronger. As John Stuart Mill wrote in chapter 2 of *On Liberty*, "Complete liberty of contradicting our opinion is the very condition which justifies us in assuming its truth." To be convinced of our beliefs, we have to hold them up against the strongest arguments of those who disagree with us. If, after putting our views to the test, we still believe them, our principles will be all the more founded and strong.

After September 11, even the *New York Times* trod as if on eggshells when it touched on the issue of dissent. On September 28, 2001, Felicity Barringer and Bill Carter wrote, "The surge of national pride that has swept the country after the terrorist attacks on Sept. 11 has sparked the beginnings of a new, more difficult debate over the balance among national security, free speech and patriotism."[15] The debate, Barringer and Carter reported, was "over whether it is proper to speak in ways that seem to contradict the popular theme of national unity." It was shameful to see the newspaper of record suggesting that the right and duty of dissent might need to be rethought in the face of an avalanche of patriotic fervor.

In contrast to such hesitation and equivocation, it is no surprise that the Bush administration became more aggressive. According to Barringer and Carter, newspaper and television reporters "said administration officials stopped returning their phone calls for a time after they expressed skepticism about the

White House assertion that Air Force One had been threatened by terrorists."[16] From the highest levels of government to the people in Texas City who chastised me as a traitor, the message rang loud and clear: don't rock the boat. The sternest admonition came from Ari Fleischer, the president's official spokesman. Referring to *Politically Incorrect* host Bill Maher's unflattering statements in the aftermath of September 11, Fleischer said, "it's a terrible thing to say, and it's unfortunate. . . . They're reminders to all Americans that they need to watch what they say, watch what they do. This is not a time for remarks like that; there never is."[17]

The result was not far from a de facto Sedition Act. The idea that dissent was unpatriotic had taken root. I, along with Dan Guthrie, fired from an Oregon newspaper for writing a column that criticized Bush; Bill Maher; Susan Sontag; and others, served as an example that freedom of the press was not compatible with "United We Stand."

The immediate and widespread result of this swift, crushing campaign against the media was self-censorship. News outlets began to take their material straight from government sources, largely ignoring independent verification and betraying the basic principles of good journalism. There was transparent timidity in many stories and a failure to ask obvious follow-up questions. It wasn't merely "Just the facts" but "Just the facts you want to tell us." To top off the lack of reporting, television networks quickly moved to superimpose images of the US flag over their logos.

The self-censorship climaxed in the disgraceful coverage provided by US news outlets during the run-up to the war in Iraq. Our finest journalists bought the Bush administration case for war hook, line, and sinker without so much as batting a skeptical eye. Now removed from all the hype, we know the discrepancies, deceptions, and outright falsehoods that existed in the narrative about Saddam Hussein's weapons of mass destruction stockpiles. In an unprecedented move, the *New York Times* and *Washington Post* conducted massive internal reviews of their coverage. The results were deeply disturbing. But our two major national dailies had a hard time facing their own facts.

In an editors' note on May 26, 2004, the *Times* acknowledged that, on the issue of Iraq's weapons and possible Iraqi connections to international terrorists, their reporting had been lax and that, when they reported dissenting opinions on the case for war, these often came far into articles buried deep inside the paper—occasionally in stories whose headlines gave no indication that the paper might be reconsidering earlier stories that had been trumpeted on the front page. The *Times* relied largely on anonymous sources and acknowledged not following up on the reliability or accuracy of information on several occasions. Nonetheless, the *Times'* self-assessment was merely that it had found "a number of instances of coverage that was not as rigorous as it should have been."[18] In fact, the paper did a job so poorly that it would warrant an F in introductory journalism classes.

The *Washington Post* performed no better. In the published account of its own internal review, Howard Kurtz came close to admitting failure but repeatedly hedged the point:

> An examination of the paper's coverage, and interviews with more than a dozen of the editors and reporters involved, shows that *The Post* published a number of pieces challenging the White House, but rarely on the front page. Some reporters who were lobbying for greater prominence for stories that questioned the administration's evidence complained to senior editors who, in the view of those reporters, were unenthusiastic about such pieces. The rest was coverage that, despite flashes of groundbreaking reporting, in hindsight looks strikingly one-sided at times.[19]

Even Bob Woodward said it was a gamble for reporters to write about possibilities other than the official Bush administration line. As Kurtz said, citing Woodward, it "might look silly if weapons were ultimately found in Iraq."[20] But an adolescent fear of embarrassment shouldn't stop journalists from following a story wherever it leads. Suppose Bob Woodward and Carl Bernstein had thought that way in reporting Watergate.

Walter Pincus, the *Post*'s defense and nuclear weapons guru, went to his most trusted sources to root out stories on weapons of mass destruction. His findings didn't play well with the party line, and he found nothing but frustration from the *Post*'s editors, who, Kurtz reported, complained "that [Pincus's] hard-to-follow stories had to be heavily rewritten." Liz Spayd, the *Post*'s assistant managing editor for national news, said, "Stories on intelligence are always difficult to edit and parse and to ensure their accuracy and get into the paper."[21] This sounds like special pleading to evade the fact that Pincus dug up ideas that didn't go along with what people wanted to hear.

Some media were more honest. The *New Republic*, instead of going into complex and self-serving explanations, simply apologized to its readers. Christiane Amanpour, CNN's chief war correspondent, admitted that the press had failed to be vigilant leading up to and during the Iraq war. "I think the press was muzzled, and I think the press self-muzzled," she said. "I'm sorry to say, but certainly television and, perhaps, to a certain extent, my station was intimidated by the administration and its foot soldiers at Fox News. And it did, in fact, put a climate of fear and self-censorship, in my view, in terms of the kind of broadcast work we did."[22] After the war started, the situation was exacerbated by the administration's idea of embedded ("in bed with," as the obvious joke went) reporters.

But we shouldn't think that self-censorship arose only from misguided patriotism in a crisis. It has a much deeper source in the corporate conglomeration of media.

The creation of "big media" has brought enormous emphasis on the profitability of news. That, in turn, has led to emphasis on news as entertainment, which is particularly detrimental to newspapers as they compete with television and the Internet. The result of this blend of news with entertainment is a serious resistance to in-depth, serious stories that might touch on unpleasant realities or, even worse, bore readers and viewers. Weapons inspections aren't nearly as dramatic on TV as night-vision shots of anti-aircraft fire over the skies of Baghdad. To the occasional pressures of popular patriotism we must add the continuing lure of profit.

A final and particularly poisonous addition to the mix is the government's abuse of its regulatory power over new media. Paul Krugman at the *New York Times* laid out this compelling and disturbing case in a May 13, 2003, column. Krugman parsed through the ways in which the US government can reward private media companies for doing what it wants. The Federal Communications Commission, chaired by Michael Powell (the son of former Secretary of State Colin Powell), relaxed rules on media ownership, allowing large companies to carve out larger shares of the national market and lifting limits on cross-ownership. To rally support for the plan, Powell resorted to mutual back scratching. "One media group wrote to Mr. Powell, dropping its opposition to part of his plan 'in return for favorable commission action' on another matter," Krugman reported. "That was indiscreet, but you'd have to be very naïve not to imagine that there are a lot of implicit quid pro quos out there."[23]

In an environment such as this, it doesn't take a logical quantum leap to see the potential impact on news coverage. Networks and newspapers, even at the most basic local level (like the *Texas City Sun*, whose parent company owns more than a dozen newspapers across the South), are increasingly becoming part of large national stables. Not only does it restrict the number of available outlets for information, but also executives clearly are aware that raising embarrassing questions about the government could bring unfavorable results for the conglomerate. The censorship isn't overt. It takes place at the individual level, which is what makes it such a dangerous threat to the ethical codes that would prevent partisanship. As Krugman put it, "[W]e do have a system in which the major media companies have strong incentives to present the news in a way that pleases the party in power, and no incentive not to."[24]

Couple the lack of incentives to promote the best possible news coverage with the emphasis that conglomerates place on profitability, and it's easy to see how questionable the information we get is. In addition, this business perspective seems to have seeped into reporting models. Reporters focus on stories for their immediacy and human interest, becoming "up close and personal" and ignoring the wider picture. Twenty-four-hour news channels, with their constant search for new titillation, are the worst offenders. But even our elite newspapers get caught up in the inanities of the daily news cycle.

It was because of the corporate takeover of American media that, by writing my column on September 22, I effectively ended my journalism career. Every other small newspaper in the Houston area was owned by Southern Newspapers, Inc. These papers wouldn't dare give me a job, and moving elsewhere wasn't an option for me. The only other choice—and the only choice practically possible for many—is self-censorship.

I don't know where this story will end. Big media are expanding faster than ever before. News stories are not only edited and fact-checked but also measured for their impact on the bottom line. This system short-changes journalists, readers, and viewers. Worse, it undermines an essential part of our democracy. The only people who benefit are fat cats looking to squeeze every penny out of a newspaper or TV station in order to gather the money for their next acquisition.

The corporatization of the media provides the final, ironic twist to the story of my own career as a journalist. On November 6, 2004, the *Texas City Sun* published its final edition. Citing declining circulation and advertising, Les Daughtry announced that the *Sun* would merge with its main rival, the *Galveston County*

Daily News (also owned by Southern Newspapers, Inc.). For the first time in nearly a hundred years, Texas City no longer has a local newspaper.

NOTES

1. Headlines taken from *Texas City Sun* editions published between September 11 and September 15, 2001.

2. Dan Balz and Bob Woodward, "America's Chaotic Road to War," *Washington Post*, January 27, 2002.

3. Tucker Carlson, "A Conservative's Dilemma," *Esquire*, September 2004.

4. Ibid.

5. George W. Bush, Address to the joint session of Congress, September 20, 2004. Official transcript from the White House Office of the Press Secretary.

6. Tom Gutting, "Bush has failed to lead U.S.," *Texas City Sun*, September 22, 2001.

7. Ibid.

8. Ibid.

9. Ibid.

10. Ibid.

11. Les Daughtry Jr., "Apology," *Texas City Sun*, September 23, 2001.

12. Les Daughtry Jr., "Bush's Leadership Has Been Superb," *Texas City Sun*, September 23, 2001.

13. Ibid.

14. Gale, Daryl, Frank Lewis, and Gwen Shaffer, "Speak No Evil," *City Paper* (Philadelphia), October 4–11, 2001.

15. Felicity Barringer and Bill Carter, "In Patriotic Time, Dissent Is Muted," *New York Times*, September 28, 2001.

16. Ibid.

17. Ari Fleischer, White House press briefing, September 26, 2001. Official transcript from the White House Office of the Press Secretary.

18. From the editors of the *New York Times*, "The Times and Iraq," May 26, 2004.

19. Howard Kurtz, "*The Post* on WMDs: An Inside Story," *Washington Post*, August 12, 2004.

20. Ibid.

21. Ibid.

22. As quoted in Peter Johnson's "Media Mix" column in *USA Today*, September 14, 2003.

23. Paul Krugman, "The China Syndrome," *New York Times*, May 13, 2003.

24. Ibid.

Chapter 9

WHEN THE CANARY STARTED SINGING ...

JASPER BECKER

British citizen Jasper Becker started his career in Brussels and worked for the Associated Press in Geneva and Frankfurt. He later joined the *Guardian* newspaper and reported from Beijing from 1985 to 1989. After the 1989 Tiananmen demonstrations, for which the paper nominated him Foreign Correspondent of the Year, he returned to London. He subsequently left the *Guardian* to join the BBC World Service. He moved to the *South China Morning Post* in 1995. Becker is currently accredited with the *Independent*. Aside from journalism, Becker is an accomplished author. His first book, *The Lost Country* (1992), is a travelogue/political commentary on Mongolia. His second book, *Hungry Ghosts* (1996), is an award-winning account of the famine kept secret by Mao from 1958 to 1962. *The Chinese* (2000) is hailed as the best single volume that introduces China and its people. *Rogue Regime* (2004) is his latest title, which focuses on North Korea. He is currently writing a book on Beijing. Becker is frequently interviewed on television and radio on matters relating to China, North Korea, Hong Kong, Tibet, and Mongolia.

Ａfter the handover of Hong Kong to China in 1997, one of the toughest challenges facing the Chinese Communist Party was to gain control of the freewheeling media there. For more than a century, Hong Kong had been a refuge for dissenting voices in the Chinese world: the prime marketplace for trading hard information, rumors, and political insights.

Hong Kong's Chinese-language press was the first target, and the process of subduing its boisterous voices began well before 1997. Critical voices were targeted, often in creative ways. Some were flattered and won over, others bribed or threatened. Some journalists were fed stories to bring them into a collaborative and dependent relationship. Others were helped with favors; in one case, Chinese officials paid the debts of a reporter's mistress.

With the *South China Morning Post* (*SCMP*), the problem was more difficult. It is in English and therefore widely read in the rest of the world, so it serves as a barometer of Hong Kong's freedoms—the canary in the coal mine. Under the "one country, two systems" mantra, its way of life is supposed to be preserved for fifty years. Thus the process of turning it around, so that its media take a pro-Beijing "patriotic" stance, has had to be carried out gradually to avoid creating undue alarm, especially in the United States.

The *SCMP* was born a century ago when Hong Kong was a British colony, one of China's famous Treaty Ports, but very much in the shadow of Shanghai and Tianjin. It became internationally significant only after 1949 with the communists' victory on the mainland. With both Taiwan and the mainland under tight censorship, the territory took over the role vacated by Shanghai as both the last surviving Treaty Port and the last bastion of free expression for the Chinese—at least on Chinese territory. At some point, it has played a unique role as the last refuge for almost every persecuted writer or politician.

After 1949, it also rapidly became an international media

center, a base for foreign journalists covering wars in the region, especially those in Korea and Vietnam, but also the lesser conflicts.

During and after the Cultural Revolution when China was closed, Hong Kong provided the world's prime listening post for those trying to understand what was going on inside China. Here refugees were interviewed and competing factions in the Communist Party provided their version of what was going on. This was especially important when Mao's regime collapsed and Deng Xiaoping took over. It was in this period that the *SCMP*, along with other newspapers, became a key conduit for information about China.

As the flagship for the English-language media, Beijing also treated the *SCMP* as the mouthpiece for the Hong Kong administration and the tycoons who controlled the economy. As China opened up in the 1980s and Hong Kong investment flowed across the border, Hong Kong boomed and so did the *SCMP*. It was acquired by Rupert Murdoch, and for a while it was the most profitable newspaper of its size. (Daily sales peaked at 110,000.) At one critical point in the early 1990s when Murdoch was struggling to hold his empire together, the *SCMP*'s profits were large enough to forestall a collapse until he renegotiated his debts.

Murdoch sold the newspaper in 1994 to a Malaysian Chinese tycoon, Robert Kuok, who had previously traded in rice, rubber, vegetable oil, and other commodities before expanding into property. Like many others, he moved to Hong Kong and positioned himself as a supporter of both the British and the Chinese. He developed major investments on the mainland, including the chain of Shangri-la hotels, a popular brand of corn oil, and a very prominent real-estate project in Beijing, the World Trade Centre (Guo Mao building), which opened just before 1989. Troops sent to impose martial law in Beijing and suppress the pro-democracy protests shot up the windows of the multistory Guo Mao.

The events around the Tiananmen protests caused a huge rift between Hong Kong and Beijing. A million people turned out to

protest the Tiananmen massacre, condemn the Chinese Communist Party, and voice their support for democracy. The British government had to appease public opinion by confronting Beijing
and insisting on a planned transition to democracy in the colony.
Beijing, however, regarded Hong Kong as a threat—a platform for
subverting the mainland.

The conflict became increasingly acrimonious when new governor Chris Patten arrived and won great popularity for pushing
the cause of direct elections in Hong Kong in defiance of the Chinese. Hong Kong tycoons who had at first supported the students
had, by then, begun to change track. In 1992, Deng Xiaoping
threw the mainland open to radical economic reforms and fresh
investment flooded in. A China fever gripped Hong Kong and
increasingly won the tycoons over as they became confident that
whole new sectors, including real estate, were open to investment, especially in sweetheart deals with Hong Kong's elite.

When I joined the *SCMP* in 1995 to become the new Beijing
bureau chief, Hong Kong was booming and the stock market was
reaching record heights. By then I was an old hand having lived
in Beijing from 1985 to 1989 when I worked for the *Guardian*
newspaper, covering the battle for political reform, which culminated in the Tiananmen protest movement. Six months later, I
left China deeply disappointed by what had happened.

In 1995, China was a quite different place—invigorated by a
great optimism that change could not be held back. The *SCMP*
still had a great reputation for lively and extensive reporting on
China and was often regarded as the bible for those based in the
capital trying to follow events unfolding across the country.
When I joined, the paper had realistic ambitions of becoming a
global newspaper. It wanted to open bureaus across not just
China but also the world, and the paper had the money to do it
now that Murdoch was no longer squeezing it dry.

The *SCMP* was run by experienced professional managers and
editors, including an Australian editor, David Armstrong, who

was quickly followed by a Brit, Jonathan Fenby, who had worked as deputy editor on the *Guardian* and the *Independent*. Even so, the Beijing bureau when I arrived lacked a working computer or a chair that was not broken. I worked in this post over the next seven years, and the paper began to expand its presence in China, opening bureaus in Shanghai and Guangzhou and recruiting a total of six reporters. The years before and after the handover marked the high point of the paper in terms of its influence and profitability. Under Jonathan Fenby's leadership, the paper also recruited an international staff, with correspondents in Bangkok, Saigon, Jakarta, Singapore, London, Washington, Seattle, Tokyo, and other cities. The paper was frequently quoted as the leading authority on events in China; in particular, this was thanks to its long-time China watcher Willy Wo-Lap Lam, who had an inside track on all the maneuvering inside the politburo.

Even so, the Kuoks tried to ingratiate themselves with the new team running Hong Kong after 1997 by first sacking the popular cartoonist Larry Feign and his strip about Lily Wong and later firing the brilliant satirist Nury Vittachi. The new chief executive of Hong Kong, Tung Cheehwa, soon became concerned that he was not being taken seriously enough. Despite the ruckus caused by these sackings, the Beijing bureau seemed safe from direct interference. As an English-language newspaper, we were well treated by the Chinese Foreign Ministry and retained the status of a foreign, that is, a British newspaper. As such the Chinese authorities insisted that all the accredited journalists had to be foreigners rather than Hong Kong Chinese. Reporters representing other Hong Kong papers or Taiwanese newspapers were treated differently.

Being a "big nose" had certain advantages in reporting sensitive events in China because ethnic Chinese could be more easily mistaken for mainlanders and beaten by police or held in detention. It was often the case that those with mainland connections would find their families threatened by the secret police, detained, or penalized in some way. All journalists are kept under constant surveillance by secret police, their comings and goings noted, their phones and apartments bugged, and their staff required to file weekly intelligence reports. In the 1990s, the surveillance became more sophisticated as the intelligence services updated their equipment. Chinese friends would be hauled in, and tapes of private conservations held in restaurants or rooms would be replayed to frighten them. In some cases, people would be detained while on trips and shown video footage of meetings held in private homes that had been secretly taped.

Reporting in China is often extremely dangerous, although mostly for the Chinese. To be sure, some foreign journalists have been seriously injured, including ABC-TV reporter Todd Carrel, who was left permanently crippled by a beating at the hands of government thugs while reporting on Tiananmen Square. As a rule though, it is the people who are interviewed who take the risk. Western journalists are occasionally expelled, sometimes detained and threatened, but it is their sources who end up spending years in prison. Some Chinese are not even aware of the risks they take, while others don't care.

In a country without a free press of its own, the role of the foreign journalist becomes unique. In a large and powerful country like China, this can flatter the foreign correspondent, giving him an exceptional role: He is free to report on things or views that would otherwise be hidden. Yet it can also cause agonizing moral quandaries. Sometimes the reports that journalists write are used as evidence to condemn the very people they tried to help. One case that springs to mind concerned two elderly villagers from an area about to be inundated by the Three Gorges Dam reservoir. The villagers went to Beijing with a petition to complain about the dam. On their return, they were arrested and given three-year prison sentences, and my articles about them were used as evidence that they were "betraying state secrets." On the other hand, I published a book titled *Hungry Ghosts—Mao's Secret Famine*, which describes how over thirty million starved to death under Communist rule. I was neither attacked nor expelled by the authorities.

The knowledge of what the state does to individuals who crossed the often-shifting danger line has induced self-censorship in the minds of many correspondents. This became even stronger in the late 1990s as China began to benefit from a wave of foreign investments. Among those wanting to make a play for China were the heads of major media conglomerates, including AOL/Time Warner, whose chairman, Gerald Levine, made a big play to get into the China market. In my view, he directly or indirectly exerted pressure on his executives to soften reporting on China. Other media tycoons like Rupert Murdoch, who poured money into China hoping to find a way into the world's last great market, used the same tactics. At stake were not just business ventures but also the delicate negotiations between China and the United States over the former's entry into the World Trade Organization. In order to sway public opinion in America, much of which was hostile to China, it was essential to create an image of China as a country on the road to democracy.

Hong Kong media companies came under similar pressures. The Hong Kong tycoons, led by chief executive Tung, who was himself a major tycoon, scrambled to stake out claims in China, especially as it was throwing open its major cities for redevelopment. Those with controlling stakes in Hong Kong's media also hoped to carve out their own markets in the mainland. With the state-controlled media offering such poor fare, mainlanders were (and still are) keen to watch Hong Kong television and all manner of foreign films.

The SCMP had long nurtured hopes of printing paper in China or starting other business ventures. A few small projects were started with Michael Heseltine, the former conservative deputy prime minister, whose publishing house, Haymarket, started several magazine projects. It was thanks to Heseltine's intervention that the foreign ministry agreed to postpone the transfer of the *SCMP* into the ranks of the Hong Kong newspapers and, therefore, under the control of another bureaucracy, the Hong Kong and Macao Affairs Office (HKMAO). This is a small body, but it is led by hardliners whose top priority is to bring Hong Kong under the tight political control of Beijing.

The growing pressure on Hong Kong resulted in the Kuoks deciding not to renew editor Jonathan Fenby's contract after he wrote a column on the anniversary of the Tiananmen protests, a date always marked by candlelit vigil. Fenby had struggled during his four years at the paper to resist Robert Kuok's interference and desire for Fenby to fire journalists Kuok disliked, to ban the use of the word *massacre* to describe Tiananmen, to stop calling Hong Kong figures "pro-Beijing," and to drop the outspoken pro-democracy columnist Emily Lau.

After Fenby left, Robert Kuok had a free hand to begin root-and-branch changes at the paper. He brought in one of his sons, Ean Kuok, to run the paper and replaced Fenby with an American, Robert Keatley from the *Wall Street Journal*, who was on the verge of retirement. One of their first steps was to remove Willy Wo-Lap Lam from his job as China editor, which was followed by his departure from the paper in November 2000. The reason is that the elder Kuok had written a letter to his own paper criticizing Willy Lam for "absolute exaggeration and fabrication" in his description of a delegation from Hong Kong that met with senior Chinese leaders in Beijing.

Also soon to leave was the paper's managing director, Owen Jonathan. Ean Kuok had no experience in publishing and instead began appointing staff from the hotel and real-estate sectors where he had previously worked. Few of them had the same understanding as journalists, and they set about cutting overheads in the same way that may have brought success in other businesses but discouraged any reporting. At the same time, the paper's management proved that it was hopelessly incompetent at launching new business. Huge sums were wasted in the dot-com boom on projects that failed. A cousin of the Kuok family was appointed to run operations in China and squandered tens of millions of US dollars in various ill-conceived ventures that led nowhere.

All those changes ensured that the atmosphere changed radically. People began to be afraid of writing stories about anything controversial and preferred to leave negative stories to the wires. There was a growing inclination to duck stories on Falun Gong and other topics. I ran into difficulties with the Chinese authorities over a series of articles exposing corruption in the Three Gorges Dam resettlement fund, and I soon realized the paper would not support me if things went wrong. Lam's departure was the key event, however, because it led to a protest petition signed by 115 staff members and, therefore, heightened tension. The transitional editor, Robert Keatley, gave the impression he was principally interested in avoiding trouble in his short time there and in collecting a bonus for his retirement.

One of the organizers of the petition was the editorial page editor, Danny Gittings, who was, therefore, the next to be marked to go. This took another year. In the meantime, the paper made the extraordinary decision of hiring a new editor, Thomas Abraham, an Indian living in London. He had never been to Hong Kong or China and had no editorial or management credentials whatsoever. His father, a former ambassador in Singapore, had been a friend of the Kuoks. The Kuoks must have reasoned that it was preferable to hire an Asian rather than another Western "big nose." The obvious thing to do was to appoint a Hong Kong–born editor, but this never seemed to be a possibility, perhaps out of fear that such a person might have strong loyalties to Hong Kong and one of its political parties and would therefore be harder to control. The same line of thinking led to the appointment of China editor Wang Xiangwei, a mainlander who had been trained at the *China Daily* and then sent to England for further training. As the mood in Hong Kong soured and

Tung Cheehwa's performance disappointed even his supporters, there was growing support for direct elections. The last thing the newspaper's owners wanted to do was appoint talented Hong Kong staff members for fear that they might support opposition to Beijing's growing interference in Hong Kong's affairs.

The new editor Thomas Abraham told Danny Gittings he should take a "realistic view" of editorial independence. Abraham instructed him not to serialize extracts from a book on Chinese leadership discussions in 1989, the *Tiananmen Papers*, because the younger Kuok objected and "he signs the checks." The decision was reversed after strong protests from journalists, but in a reshuffle in the autumn of 2001 Gittings was made redundant.

As the last prominent writer left on the team covering political issues, I suppose it was inevitable that I would become the next target. The Chinese foreign ministry had kindly issued a private warning to the Beijing staff that life would become more difficult once the Hong Kong and Macao Affairs Office took over the administration of the *SCMP*. The move followed an angry and very public outburst by Chinese leader Jiang Zemin, who let loose a finger-wagging tirade against the irresponsibility of the Hong Kong press after a junior reporter questioned him about the reappointment of Tung Cheehwa as chief executive of Hong Kong, describing it in terms of an imperial appointment. This was soon followed by the Hong Kong government's determination to push through a vaguely worded "national security law," which many feared could lead to the sort of censorship seen on the mainland. The law allowed for broad interpretations of what constitutes acts endangering state security, and it could include news reporting that supports Tibetan or Taiwan independence or criticizes Beijing's handling of the Falun Gong movement.

The first move was for the HKMAO to draw up provisional regulations. In the first draft, it ruled that only ethnic Chinese journalists could qualify for registration. At first the paper was told that the existing six correspondents could not be accredited at all. Then the authorities said we could be accredited only provisionally for at least six months. I went to Hong Kong to acquire some kind of Hong Kong status as a registered employee in Beijing with a work permit. Amid rumors that the paper had cut some deal behind our backs, life became more and more difficult for me. From January 2000, it became more difficult to get the monthly operating expenses necessary for the continuing operation of the Beijing bureau. The rent was not paid, the salaries of the local staff members were withheld, and our Internet connection was suspended. The situation became so bad that I had to send a warning that we would have to close the bureau unless swift action was taken to resolve these problems.

After the HKMAO took charge, it appointed a full-time official to supervise the paper's coverage. This official began calling China editor Wang Xiangwei nearly every day, issuing direct instructions on what and what not to put in the paper. On one occasion, Wang called me and said that HKMAO had warned us it would be inadvisable to attend an illegal protest in Beijing that was being organized by rural AIDS victims. In fact, I hadn't even heard about it and probably would not have gone anyway. Later, Wang realized he had blundered by telling me that he was receiving direct instructions, and he became more circumspect about how he controlled the coverage. He suggested we spend more time covering routine press conferences and stick to official statements. More and more of our stories became rewrites of stories in the Chinese press or articles from the state-run Xinhua news agency. The interesting stories were left to the Western news agencies, and we were asked to highlight official Chinese reactions.

Increasingly, the paper seemed to want to bury revelations that were embarrassing to China. China stories that ran on the front page of the *International Herald Tribune*, like the Falun Gong's remarkable success in briefly broadcasting its messages across a cable television network in Changchun in March, were stuck at the bottom of the China pages.

For me, the turning point came when I managed to wangle a trip to Tibet thanks to the intervention of the Foreign Ministry's information department. I asked to visit a charity school run by a blind German woman for poor Tibetan children who were blind or deaf. To my surprise, the Lhasa government agreed. However, editor Thomas Abraham did not. He refused point blank to allow me to go. "We have to fill the paper with real news," he said.

I explained that I had been arrested and expelled from Lhasa in 1989 when martial law was declared and had never been allowed back. Tibet remains one of the most sensitive issues for China, and access to Tibet is tightly controlled. Foreign journalists are allowed to go there only once a year on group tours when they are kept to a closely supervised schedule. I had a good record of breaking stories on Tibet from Beijing and felt sure that if I could get in and roam around, it would be easy to find a lot of stories in addition to the feature about school.

Having failed to go to Tibet, I then waited to see what the paper did think was important. When the biggest worker protests in a decade erupted in China's northeast in March 2002, no one in our bureau was asked to cover or analyze it. Every day I spoke to Wang Xiangwei, but he failed to mention the huge story at all and instead wanted me to cover routine foreign ministry briefings. Finally, after a ten-day delay, during which the protests received front-page coverage in every other newspaper, the *SCMP* sent a junior reporter from Hong Kong to the northeast to cover the crisis.

By this time, it was clear to our readers in Beijing what was going on. The omissions were so glaring that everyone remarked upon it, and the paper was losing its credibility as a major source of news on China. I then called Abraham in Hong Kong and asked for a meeting to air my concerns. I brought with me a list of stories that had been downplayed or ignored. It was quite a long one and included stories about Jiang Zemin and Chinese Premier Zhu Rongji that were edited down to make them as bland as possible. Even when we were ahead of rivals with a story about how copies of *Securities Weekly*, a leading Chinese financial journal, had been seized for running a story about the assets of the family of Li Peng, this was cut down and buried. For a while I had managed to get my views published on the editorial pages, but now Wang Xiangwei had insisted that no story about China could be published in the paper without his permission. What is more, I discovered that he was personally responsible for holding back payments for our office expenses in Beijing.

At first, Abraham listened sympathetically but then caught himself as he realized the implications of agreeing with me. He then declared he had total faith in Mr. Wang and the quality of the China coverage. He said if I could not work under Wang, I could no longer continue as the Beijing bureau chief, and he initially proposed a vague designation as a commentator. After seeing Abraham, I then went to see the paper's publisher, a former investment banker named Tad Beczac, who admitted that morale was very low among the staff and that readers were deserting the paper. He knew Abraham was doing a poor job. I warned him that sooner or later the paper itself would become the focus of stories and the pressure would increase. If we lost readers, we would lose revenue, especially since people could easily turn to other papers for their China news. Hong Kong readers could just as easily buy the *Financial Times*, the *Asian Wall Street Journal*, or the *International Herald Tribune* on the streets of Hong Kong, not to mention city rivals like the *Standard*.

Sure enough, shortly after I returned to Beijing, the *Australian* newspaper ran the first story about the *SCMP*, describing the paper's refusal to allow me to go to Tibet. Naturally I was blamed for this, but in fact the reporter heard about it after bumping into our Australian photographer and had diligently called Hong Kong to confirm this and get a response. A week later the axe fell.

After attending a lunchtime briefing, I arrived back in my office to find someone from the Hong Kong office waiting for me. He handed me a letter saying I was being sacked for "insubordination." He insisted I clear my desk immediately, and he set about changing the lock to the office. My computer was confiscated. As it happened, I had to leave the next day to fly to Washington to take part in congressional hearings about North Korea's famine, but my story still managed to attract a great deal of international attention. For instance, the *Asian Wall Street Journal* ran a supportive editorial on May 2, 2002, that praised me and said my dismissal came as a shock to colleagues and readers: "Mr. Becker is prolific and hard-working, but more importantly he is highly regarded for digging deeply into the guts of a story and not shying away from telling an unpleasant truth—even when it might cost him a tongue-lashing from China's media minders or jeopardize his visa. . . . In short, when a journalist of this caliber makes a stand on principle at considerable cost to himself and his family, it's worth sitting up and paying attention," said the paper.

It was gratifying to get so much public support from colleagues around the world. It was clearly and rightly recognized that my sacking was part of a wider trend in Hong Kong. The consequences for the paper were, as I predicted, disastrous. Within the next two months, the *SCMP* unceremoniously sacked Abraham and his deputy editor. Instead of professional staff, publisher Tad Beczac decided that he could run the paper on his own without any editors. The paper went from bad to worse, losing 30 percent of its readers.

Although the paper continued to claim in public that nothing had changed, sales dropped to sixty thousand, which included free copies distributed in hotels and elsewhere. By the end of 2002, the paper, which in its heyday had made more money than the *Financial Times* or the *Daily Telegraph*, was losing money. All the foreign bureaus were closed. By 2003, the newspaper was in an irreversible decline, and almost all the senior staff members had been sacked or fled, including Tad Beczac. The owners who had repeatedly tried to sell the paper without success now saw the value of the shares falling to less than half what they had bought it for.

As I write, the paper has stabilized after the owners rehired a professional newspaper editor, David Armstrong, from the *Australian*. However, its main competition, the *Standard*, now claims to have higher sales and to make more money.

The Hong Kong government's efforts to ram home its "antisubversion law" in the face of widespread opposition collapsed when half a million Hong Kong people took to the streets in June 2003. Tung Cheehwa was forced to withdraw the law. By this time, a great deal of damage had been done to Hong Kong's media industry.

Reuters had moved its East Asia headquarters to Singapore. The BBC had likewise closed its regional offices and moved to Bangkok. One of Hong Kong's English-language weeklies, *Asiaweek*, closed, with the loss of all its jobs. In 2004, it was followed by the closure of the *Far Eastern Economic Review*, with the loss of a further eighty jobs. The hollowing out of the media in Hong Kong is the opposite of what was expected to happen. None of these media groups has managed to make any inroads into the Chinese market or capitalize on China's economic boom. The Chinese-language media have not fared any better where Jimmy Lai, the owner of the most dynamic newspaper, *Apple Daily*, has moved to Taiwan.

There is little comfort for me in having been proved right. Being fired is a horrible experience. It also struck me as completely unnecessary. The Kuoks could easily have resisted the pressure by quoting Deng Xiaoping's mantra of "one country, two systems." This meant that the central government considers Hong Kong to be an international city open to the world where different rules apply. As major investors in China, they had considerable clout and should have been able to find enough allies in the different ministries in Beijing to defend their case. Many people in Beijing thought the HKMAO was being unnecessarily clumsy and were damaging the broad effort to improve China's international image.

The mentality of Hong Kong's elite was that it felt it should anticipate what Beijing wanted, seeming desperate to be seen as more Catholic than the pope. A string of visits to Beijing by executives seeking the views of top officials on the *SCMP*'s work led to hints being interpreted as orders. As no one actually wants to be caught issuing such orders, the paper plunged deeper into a surreal world of totalitarian "doublethink." Everyone had to pretend not to see what was really going on. If you stopped participating in the game, you lost your job, and your colleagues became indignant because you were endangering everyone else's.

Horrible though this is, it must be remembered, however, my situation and those of any journalists in Hong Kong is far better than those on the mainland. China has a record of imprisoning more journalists than any other state in the world. Its record of censoring not only the press but also any media, including the Internet, is unrivaled. Its uncanny ability to keep pace with information technology and to force major companies like Google to bend to its will remains unprecedented. Even so, I am sure that one day China will have a freer press and a commercial media industry, but I now doubt whether Hong Kong will play much of a part.

Chapter 10

THE BURROWERS

GARY HUGHES and GERARD RYLE

Gary Hughes has worked on the *Age* for the past ten years as an investigative reporter and in a number of editorial management roles. In thirty years of journalism, he has held a wide range of positions with newspapers in Australia, including stints as a correspondent in Europe and as Victoria editor of the *Australian* newspaper.

Gerard Ryle is investigations editor of the *Sydney Morning Herald*. He joined the paper in 1998, serving on the news desk as features editor, special correspondent to the United States, and investigative reporter. Prior to that, he worked at the *Age*, which he joined in 1988 from his native Ireland.

As a team, Hughes and Ryle won a number of national and international awards for their investigative journalism, including three Walkley Awards (Australian Pulitzers), two Commonwealth journalism awards, the George Munster Award for Independent Journalism, a United Nations Human Rights Award, and two Melbourne Press Club awards. Individually, they have won a number of other major Australian prizes for science, workplace, and medical writing.

Ryle was recently honored in the prestigious Investigative Reporters and Editors awards in the United States, getting a special citation for an international entry for a story on how public land in Australia was being leased out to major corporations and political donors at rates far below market value.

The hunt eventually led to a conference room lined with legal tomes high above a busy city street. It was here that we were finally faced with two options: reveal our sources or face indefinite jail on contempt-of-court charges.

For more than three years, police and government officials in the Australian state of Victoria had been attempting to shut down our investigation into police corruption, cover-ups, and abuse of power. Police had launched an internal investigation, led by an inspector and a sergeant, to try to catch those within the ten-thousand-strong force who were leaking information to us. We were warned our telephones were being monitored. And both the chief of police and the state's most senior elected official had launched stinging attacks on our credibility and that of our respected broadsheet newspaper, the *Age*, accusing us of "rolling around in the gutter to dig up whatever dirt [we could]." To make matters worse, pressure was also being applied behind the scenes on those running the media company that owned the paper, which sold about two hundred thousand copies a day in Melbourne, the capital of Victoria.

But, so far, everything had failed.

Now, the supposedly independent watchdog on the police, Victoria's ombudsman, had intervened. Under Victoria's statutes, the ombudsman was an independent officer of the state's parliament with the sweeping legal powers of a Supreme Court judge. His task was to scrutinize government departments and investigate police corruption and abuse of power. Now he had subpoenaed us as part of a complex inquiry into our revelations that an undercover police unit, reporting directly to police command, had been secretly spying on political groups and civil liberty campaigners. Members of the covert unit had been so successful in infiltrating a publicly funded community radio station that they hosted its breakfast show. They had so duped peace protesters that undercover officers were acting in key treasury positions within the groups and deliberately embarking on paths designed to make them insolvent. They were bugging meetings of civil liberty organizations, conducting illegal searches, and operating as foot soldiers for a spy network that reached right around the world.

Under Australian law, we knew that the ombudsman had the power to demand that we reveal our sources. Failure to do so could lead us to Victoria's highest court, the Supreme Court, where continued refusal to answer questions would put us in contempt of court and result in jail until we agreed to cooperate. But we also knew that jail would cause a public sensation because of the blaze of national media attention our revelations were receiving. As we were led into the book-lined conference room, placed on oath, and formally warned about the risks of perjury, we were faced with a choice that we had always known would eventually come.

Our journey had begun almost three years earlier when we first decided to have a closer look at a police force that had enjoyed an almost impeccable reputation in Australia. Many other major police departments in Australia had been torn apart by commissions of inquiry. But so respected was the Victoria police that the rebuilding processes employed by other state police forces often involved poaching new team leaders from Victoria.

We had first met in 1993 when we joined an expanded version of the *Age*'s famous Insight investigative team, which for almost twenty years had established the Melbourne-based newspaper as a leader in the field of investigative journalism. When the larger team had been disbanded a couple of years later after internal management quarrels and editorial upheavals within the paper, we decided to go it alone as a two-man investigative team.

Such partnerships were almost unknown within Australian journalism, where investigative journalism had been carried out either by lone reporters or large and often unwieldy teams. Historically, the onerous demands and hothouse pressures of investigative journalism had seen attempts at forming tight working partnerships end both quickly and acrimoniously.

We would eventually develop a template for such investigative partnerships that is still being used. It would include a carefully evolved set of journalistic protocols that covered everything from establishing and running sources and respecting confidentiality, to personal security and ethical decisions on what to publish and when.

Eventually, we were able to work as one. Sources would be run either by one of the team individually or by both, depending on what arrangement the source found most comfortable. If a contact opted to be handled by just one of the team, that member would later brief the other in depth following each meeting or telephone conversation. This included not just what was said but the smallest details on the type of language used, the nuances of the conversation, the mood swings of the source, and the handler's assessment on the credibility of the information. We knew that, professionally, we lived or died by each other's judgments.

Criteria were also put in place regarding the level of confirmation needed before going into print. Documents were considered primary sources only when we were sure of their provenance. Right from the beginning, we were always wary of attempts to discredit us by using faked documents, and elaborate steps were taken to prove the authenticity of such information. Likewise, "new" sources offering unsolicited information were always treated with deep suspicion, and their backgrounds were thoroughly checked to prevent attempts to undermine credibility.

Sources were kept strictly quarantined to prevent cross-contamination of information and to protect their identities. No individual source was aware of the existence of other sources or the nature of the information they were providing. Security surrounding sources extended to them were given code names, so their real names would not need to be used during even private conversations. Because of the nature of our work, the integrity of telephones or even confined office spaces were a very real risk.

The decision to publish was based on a complicated formula

of multiple confirmations from sources, unless the information came from a leaked document we had verified. Such documents would eventually include top secret intelligence files that a previous Victorian government had ordered police to destroy more than a decade earlier but had been illegally kept.

We had a rule that a minimum of two independent sources had to confirm a fact before we would consider using it. Even then, official comment was always sought before publication. The flow and detail of the information reaching us was such that the Victoria police would eventually negotiate an arrangement with the *Age* for a "warning period" before an article was to appear to allow sufficient time for the police to respond in detail.

Initially we targeted police corruption, revealing how officers had been implicated in drug dealing and setting up on false charges those informers who tried to expose their activities. Our first series of articles had exposed how a corrupt senior police officer in a Victorian town had terrorized the local community, dealing drugs and taking bribes. When a former mayor in the town tried to stop him, he and other corrupt police officers set her up on false charges and had her hauled into court in handcuffs. Another citizen who turned informer and wore a "wire" to help catch the corrupt officer in an undercover sting operation was also later set up and jailed on false charges after drugs were planted in his house. Our revelations led to lengthy debates within Victoria's parliament and calls for independent judicial inquiries. Police command, realizing the revelations would continue, at first adopted a friendly approach. We were invited in by one of the force's most senior officers for a "chat." He made us an offer: If we backed off and dropped what we were doing, he strongly implied that we would be rewarded with a succession of exclusive crime stories that would keep our editors happy.

Such cozy inside deals are unfortunately commonplace in the Australian media, where a reporter working a beat relies on staying friendly with sources to maintain the flow of information.

The Victoria police, which was the first police force in Australia to have a professional media relations department, had raised such deals to an unprecedented level. Not only did crime reporters have to rely on police for their stories, but also the force knew it could—and often did—embarrass uncooperative reporters by leaking "exclusives" to their competitors. The result was a team of crime reporters in Melbourne who worked hand-in-hand with police officers and dare not upset them. That, in turn, had resulted in a force that considered itself above public scrutiny and beyond the grasp of accountability.

We scoffed at the deal, preferring instead to gamble our professional credibility on our ability to find genuine stories rather than rely on "sanctioned" leaks. The senior policeman who made the deal would later resign, after being effectively sacked for failing to stem the flow of embarrassing leaks to us over internal cover-ups.

Soon we began publishing a succession of articles revealing that police were failing to notify the ombudsman of internal allegations of corruption and misconduct, as was legally required. In one crucial case, police command had kept secret the discovery of a marijuana crop worth AUS$1.2 million found growing on a remote outback property owned by a senior Victorian police officer. The officer was never charged over the crop, claiming a tenant had grown it. In another case, we were able to show how police had failed to properly investigate initial allegations that some officers had been taking bribes to tip off glass replacement companies about broken store windows. When these allegations were eventually probed by the ombudsman, it was found that hundreds of officers had been caught up in the bribery scandal.

Following these further embarrassments, police command changed tactics and launched public attacks on us and our newspaper in an unsuccessful bid to destroy our credibility. Other media outlets cooperated with police, carrying the attacks by the chief commissioner and later the most senior elected politician, Victoria's Premier Jeffrey Kennett. Police Chief Neil Comrie described us as "vultures" with reputations for digging up gutter dirt and said we were distorting the facts in an attempt to trigger a royal commission, the most powerful type of independent inquiry possible under the Australian legal system. "Then they can just go and park themselves in the royal commission for an hour or so each day and retire to the pub," he said on Melbourne's most popular radio station. Jeffrey Kennett unleashed similar vitriol, telling people that the *Age* was only fit for wrapping up "dead cats" and other rubbish. "You cannot trust the *Age*; it is an appalling affront," he said. "If you want to feel good . . . do as I do, don't read the *Age*, or if you're still buying it, rip it up."

At the same time, police attempted to isolate the *Age* and its ability to cover the crime beat. It not only stopped supplying information to the newspaper but also took the unprecedented step of placing a public ban on anyone within the force talking to Gerard Ryle, including its media liaison officers. It was a blatant attempt to destroy Ryle's ability to work as a reporter. The ban made good copy for the *Age* and did nothing to stop the flow of information out of the force. Even the details of a secret "crisis" briefing held by police command to assess the scope of corruption problems within the force and take action to ward off an independent inquiry were promptly leaked and published.

A secret internal investigation was also launched into our sources with the police force, including monitoring the telephones of both us and those belonging to police officers under suspicion. They also attempted to reconstruct our movements through such measures as checking airline passenger lists. But those same sources were so well placed that we were quickly not only warned of the investigation but provided with the name of the inspector within the internal affairs division who was leading it.

The pressure also increased behind the scenes. Chief Neil Comrie called the *Age*'s editor, Bruce Guthrie, to a meeting, where Comrie tried to persuade him it was in the newspaper's best interests to stop our investigation.

Pressure was applied on Bruce Guthrie by one of the media company's directors, whose commercial interests included another corporation with lucrative police contracts for information technology. Guthrie, who was subjected to savage public attacks by the police commissioner and the Victorian premier, refused to give ground, saying that as long as he remained editor, the *Age* would continue to publish without fear or favor.

The state government eventually threatened to withdraw lucrative government advertising from the *Age* and place it with the rival Rupert Murdoch–owned daily, in a bid to blackmail the paper into ending its investigation into police corruption as well as dropping a separate probe into casino licensing. Again the editor resisted, although the threat brought even more pressure on the firewall of independence that had traditionally separated the *Age*'s editorial stance and its commercial operations.

Our work contributed to the biggest corruption inquiry in the history of the state of Victoria and led to the removal of an assistant commissioner and the disbanding of the police force's internal affairs division. Over the next three years, more than 10 percent of the force (over one thousand police officers) was implicated in corruption inquiries.

The waves we started would later overwhelm the police drug squad, which was also disbanded amid allegations that some police officers were, in fact, running parts of Victoria's drug trade instead of policing it.

In the meantime, we kept burrowing.

Early in our investigation, we had heard whispers about the activities of a secret, undercover intelligence unit working within the Victoria police. But some of our most trusted sources warned us against investigating the unit, saying it could end our careers. There was no public record of the unit's existence, and even within the force its covert activities were known only by a handful of senior commanders. There was good reason for such secrecy.

In 1983, a newly elected state government had ordered that

the Victoria police disband its Special Branch, a unit within the force that had breached civil liberties by spying on the political opponents of the former conservative governments and others considered security risks. Tens of thousands of dossiers had been compiled on individuals and organizations such as trade unions, peace groups, and civil liberty campaigners. A hangover from the darkest days of the cold war, the Special Branch had used covert surveillance and infiltration in its relentless hunt for "Reds under the bed."

We were told that the Victoria police command had defied the orders of its political masters. While going through the charade of publicly disbanding its Special Branch, it had secretly transferred its activities to the Operations Intelligence Unit (OIU). Hundreds of dossiers that police claimed were incinerated had also been illegally kept and transferred to a secret headquarters in a nondescript building in Melbourne's inner suburbs. While details were sketchy, some of the OIU's activities appeared an extraordinary abuse of power, including infiltrating a public broadcasting radio station, bugging meetings of civil liberty groups that campaigned against excessive police violence, conducting covert surveillance on left-wing politicians, and carrying out searches without the necessary warrants.

We knew, however, that the evidence for any public exposure of OIU's activities would have to be irrefutable, given that police had always angrily denied previous claims about the illegal retention of Special Branch dossiers. Indeed, the state ombudsman had failed during an earlier full-blown inquiry to find any evidence that the dossiers had been improperly kept, despite the considerable statutory powers at his disposal.

Gaining irrefutable evidence would mean not just breaking through the tight security surrounding the Victoria police but penetrating Australia's covert intelligence community, as the OIU was closely linked to the national Australian Security and Intelligence Organisation (the equivalent of the CIA), Australian military intelligence, and similar special units within other state police forces (all of which were also secret). Indeed, the OIU was the gatherer of raw, on-the-ground intelligence, which, feasibly, found its way around the world given the close links between Australia's intelligence community and both the British and United States intelligence communities.

What followed was a two-year quest. While working on a range of other investigations, we began the painstaking task of piecing together the secrets of the OIU. Reluctant sources were cultivated and their trust slowly won. Many feared that the promised confidentiality would not be kept and that the Victoria police and the state government would exert its influence over the media to stop the story ever going to print. Clandestine meetings were held with sources that knew enough about the capabilities and reach of the OIU to avoid using telephones. At one stage, we were given a fast course in countersurveillance techniques by sources frightened of exposure.

Finally, in late 1997, the breakthrough came. The two years of meetings and delicate negotiations with contacts culminated in a high-risk rendezvous at a secret location. For a limited time, we were given access to the OIU's own top secret records, including a computer database containing personal details of twelve hundred individuals. Details of how the breakthrough was achieved, of identities of sources, and even of the nature of the material accessed remained confidential. But the form of the material and the source's refusal to allow computer files to be electronically copied meant that the records had to be laboriously copied by hand into notebooks under tight time constraints.

While this breakthrough was crucial, it was not the end of the investigation. The sources were impeccable, and we were confident the material was genuine, but we made the decision to obtain further confirmation. This meant weeks of meticulous cross-referencing dozens of incidents and scores of names and facts with public records and newspaper archives.

For instance, if we had details about a particular—usually public—event, we searched the old newspaper archives on microfilm to confirm dates, times, and events described in the documents we had transcribed. Those who had been targeted for surveillance by undercover officers were traced and interviewed. Confirmation was even obtained confidentially that the two false names used by the undercover officers infiltrating the public radio station were still on the station's employment records. (The station apparently was a particular favorite of one senior police officer who liked to tune into the radio show hosted by his operatives on his way to work. For those wondering about the value of such an operation, just think: If you were a fringe group organizing a protest or meeting, where would you go for publicity? Information like time, place, and likely turnout was the bread and butter of the OIU).

In October 1997, the *Age* published the first of more than twenty articles that composed the first part of the investigation, proving beyond doubt that the Victoria police had not only defied government orders by effectively continuing to covertly operate a special branch but also gone well beyond the role of an enforcement agency in a democratic society. The indisputable details of the daily activities of the OIU over a five-year period were laid bare, including the times, dates, and targets of covert missions; how the missions were conducted; and the results that were obtained. The articles also provided a rare insight into the exotic world of the covert operative, describing in detail how undercover officers led a James Bond–style existence, riding powerful motorcycles equipped with fake registration plates and secret radios and using bank accounts set up in false names.

We took an ethical decision not to publish information on ongoing operations or the personal details of unit members and the false identities they used to avoid placing serving or former officers at risk.

The articles caused a furor, prompting a series of public meetings and demonstrations that focused public attention on the activities of police intelligence units throughout Australia. A vigorous national debate ensued on the legitimacy or otherwise of such activities. After Victoria police commanders initially attempted to deny knowledge of the OIU's activities or the existence of an electronic database, we used the *Age*'s Web site to publish a full list of the twelve hundred names and organizations listed, along with their secret file numbers. It was one of the first examples in Australian journalism of such coordinated use of print and the Internet.

The revelations also forced the ombudsman into launching what would prove to be one of the longest and most complex inquiries in Victoria's history, resulting in three volumes of findings being tabled in state parliament.

In January 1998, the story took a new turn. We obtained from our sources some original Special Branch dossiers—the same documents ordered destroyed in 1983. The dossiers, containing personal information on a variety of targets, including an anti-Vietnam War protester and the wife of a high-profile trade union leader, showed how records had been carefully compiled on where people went, whom they met, and what they said. They appeared to be irrefutable proof that police had defied government orders and illegally retained dossiers.

Although confident of the authenticity of the files, we again set about the elaborate process of confirming the material. The subjects of the files were traced and interviewed and the events to which the subjects referred were cross-checked with independent sources. A series of articles exposing the existence of the files became the second installment of the *Age*'s expose of the OIU. The dossiers were then handed to the ombudsman, who confirmed them as genuine, ending more than fifteen years of police denials that such material existed.

But it was this same ombudsman inquiry that led to us facing jail for refusing to identify our sources. The questioning of the ombudsman's investigators was heated. We refused to divulge the identities of sources or anything that might lead to them being found, including the exact nature of the OIU records we had seen. At one point, Ryle was directly threatened with jail if he continued to refuse to answer questions.

But we stood by our earlier agreement to take the biggest professional gamble of our careers. We believed that the public benefit of what we had revealed and the attention it had attracted would lead to a public uproar if we were jailed. Any attempt to force us to reveal our sources would be seen publicly as yet a further attempt at covering up police wrongdoing. And the subsequent embarrassment to the police and government from such a row would outweigh the desire within the police force to catch our sources. The gamble worked. We were allowed to walk free, our sources still protected.

The three volumes of the ombudsman's report confirmed what had been written about the OIU's improper activities. The result was a fundamental change in the way covert intelligence was allowed to be gathered by the police, including the introduction of external monitoring of the selection of targets and a culling of thousands of files.

The nature of the battles investigative journalists face worldwide to report the truth differs, as does the professional and personal price they pay.

In Australia investigative journalism has to be conducted in a media industry where ownership is highly concentrated. Only two main daily newspaper publishers operate in the market, and one of these, owned by Rupert Murdoch, controls an overwhelming majority of the market. Commercial television networks rest in the hands of just three owners. Publicly owned media outlets are restricted to one mainstream national television and one radio network.

It may surprise many Americans to learn that there is no guarantee of freedom of speech in a country like Australia. We operate in a climate where the libel laws are among the most restrictive in the world.

It is not enough for the story to simply be right. Journalists will most likely still be sued even if they can prove that the story is right, which means there is an ongoing debate about whether the "public good" of publishing some of the information in the series of articles outweighs the risk of defaming some government officials and local businessmen, resulting in legal action.

In addition, access to government information is routinely blocked in Australia, with minimal access allowed to government officials to discuss the merits of decisions made.

The Freedom of Information laws are often jokingly referred to as the "Freedom from Information laws." The rules as defined in the legislation are often applied haphazardly and routine appeals can often mean a wait of up to six or twelve months for the most basic information. By then it is of course often too out-of-date to use.

The lack of media diversity and the relatively small Australian market make publishers and broadcasters particularly susceptible to commercial pressures from governments, government authorities, and large corporations. Falling sales and television ratings have seen companies slash editorial budgets, especially in the resource-hungry area of investigative journalism. This cutback in quality journalism has, in turn, seen media outlets increasingly— and unquestioningly—rely on a flow of news from governments, government agencies, and a booming public relations industry.

In such a small market, it is also not unusual to find yourself ruffling the feathers of powerful interest groups.

At the same time we were under attack from the Victoria police, we were battling on another front following an investigation into breaches of medical ethics by some of Australia's most powerful and influential scientific and research institutes.

In between investigating the police, we had produced a series of reports that made international headlines. We revealed that for twenty years medical researchers had used orphanages and baby homes for tests of experimental vaccines. Many of the babies and young children in those homes were wards of the state, under the guardianship of the government. Detailed case studies published in the *Age* showed that researchers had repeatedly used these nameless children in trials, monitoring the effectiveness of vaccines and recording the adverse side effects.

The key ethical issue raised in the reports was the question of consent. No one involved in conducting the experiments, which included renowned scientists and doctors, could provide an answer to the question of who gave consent for orphans and state wards to be used as medical guinea pigs. Nor could that answer be found by government inquiries launched in response to the investigative articles and a recently completed Senate hearing into mistreatment of children in institutions, which, in August 2004, also concluded that the long-term health impacts of the experiments also remained unknown.

But the ethical issues raised did not deter the research and medical communities from attacking us, describing our reporting as sensational and irresponsible. Again, rival media outlets, which enjoyed cozy relationships with the research community and unquestioningly reported "exclusive" medical breakthroughs by those same research institutes, provided a platform for the attacks. The *Age* stood by the reports, which were followed up by such respected publications as the *Lancet* in Britain and prompted a debate over medical ethics and the acknowledgment of the need for stricter guidelines covering consent for children used in medical trials.

The scientific and research communities harangued us again after we revealed that Australia's postwar advances had been aided by dozens of Nazi scientists secretly brought to the country after the collapse of Germany in 1945. The articles detailed how a famous researcher at one of Australia's most prestigious universities had been a key figure in the scheme, helping to choose which Nazi scientists to recruit, including former members of Hitler's Stormtroopers and chemists from I. G. Farben, where poison gases used in extermination camps were developed.

More recently, Hughes incurred the wrath of the international pharmaceutical industry and some of Australia's peak professional medical organizations when he exposed how drug companies were spending millions to secretly fund such groups as part of their marketing strategies. The investigation showed how some supposedly independent expert medical organizations had been set up and run by public relations companies working for pharmaceutical corporations as part of disease-mongering campaigns. In October 2004, Hughes was under attack again, this time from federal health authorities after he revealed in detail how the Australian government knowingly released batches of Salk polio vaccine in 1961 that were contaminated with the SV40 monkey virus, which has since been linked to a range of cancers. Hughes used documents buried in the Australian government's own national archives to disprove repeated claims by health authorities that there was no evidence that Australian polio vaccines had been contaminated, as had occurred in the United States.

The reality of investigative reporting in Australia is that journalists sometimes find themselves battling a public relations company as much as the issue they are investigating.

For instance, when Ryle (who by then had moved to the *Age*'s sister publication in Sydney, the *Sydney Morning Herald*, whose investigative unit he heads) revealed that the Australian Red Cross, an arm of the respected International Red Cross, had failed to distribute millions of dollars collected for victims of a horrific bombing incident in the Indonesian island of Bali, he found himself up against a combination of slick public relations and government indifference. The story was one of the biggest in 2003 because so many Australians had been killed or injured in the bombing the previous October.

Many were so haunted by the sickening images of the dead

and wounded that almost US$11.1 million was raised, with the Red Cross promising that ninety cents in every dollar collected would go "directly to the victims." The truth, however, was that seven months after the event, only a small portion of the money had reached those most affected.

Only US$3 million had been spent, and some money was going to projects unrelated to the tragedy. The banks were taking a large slice, and thousands of dollars were being spent staging public relations events that were later exposed as a lie.

The revelations had a massive public impact, dominating the national media for almost two months and resulting in government inquiries in the states of New South Wales and Victoria. By the end of the first week, the Red Cross had made an unprecedented public apology and began handing out checks to victims for claims that had earlier been refused.

To restore public confidence in its organization, the Red Cross hired outside public relations experts and began an aggressive national advertising campaign. The Red Cross also preempted the government inquiries by announcing an inquiry of its own to be conducted by the respected accountancy firm PricewaterhouseCoopers. This so-called independent inquiry was commissioned and paid for by the Red Cross, which set its own terms of reference. The inquiry's final report carried many disclaimers and noted that those preparing it did "not seek comments from the victims of the Bali tragedy or other affected persons." Indeed, of the twelve people interviewed, eleven were Red Cross personnel and one was the Red Cross's external auditor. As the report further disclosed, the Red Cross blood service (an arm of the Red Cross) was a client of PricewaterhouseCoopers. Furthermore, the person who headed the review was the external auditor of the Red Cross for five years until 1999.

Not surprisingly, the Australian Red Cross embraced the results when the report declared that there was no evidence of fraud or misuse of the funds collected for the victims of the Bali bombings.

"We didn't diddle anyone, we didn't double-cross anyone," the national chairman, Rob O'Regan, said when the report was released. Such an allegation had never been made.

But arguably the real betrayal of public interest came after it emerged that both government inquiries later relied almost entirely on the findings of the PricewaterhouseCoopers report. Rather than do any investigating of its own, the government simply relied on the validity of the report and cleared the Red Cross of any wrongdoing. None of the victims of the tragedy were ever interviewed.

The influence of public relations companies is growing and is probably best reflected in the fact that the number of public relations graduates emerging from Australia's colleges and universities now outnumbers new journalists. The Fairfax newspaper group, where we work, is one of the last bastions of investigative journalism in Australia, although it is not immune from commercial pressures. The future of genuine investigative journalism in Australia remains under threat. While media outlets increasingly turn to using the investigative journalism tag as a marketing ploy and providing the public a facade of quality, real commitment wanes.

Chapter 11

PUTIN, THE MAFIA, AND THE MASS MEDIA

A TRUE CRIME STORY

ALEXANDER PUMPYANSKY

Alexander Pumpyansky is editor-in-chief of the weekly magazine *Novoye Vremya* and its English sister paper, the *New Times* (Moscow). A professional journalist, he worked for fifteen years in the newspaper *Komsomol-skaya Pravda*, where he became managing editor and worked as a correspondent in New York. For eight years, he worked as deputy editor-in-chief of the weekly newspaper *Mosckovskiye Novosti* (*Moscow News*). Pumpyansky has worked at the *Novoye Vremya* (*New Times*) since 1985. Pumpyansky also served on the board of the International Press Institute (IPI) from 1992 to 2000 and is an IPI fellow. He is the author of numerous books and scripts for documentary films, including participation in the Soviet-American serial *The Unknown War*. His most recent books are *Humpty Dumpty Sat on the Wall* (literary essays) and *Two Leaders: History as an Earthquake* (political essays). In 1976 the communists banned him from practicing journalism (the unofficial term for his crime was "bourgeois objectivism"). The ban was only lifted during the *glasnost* period. He won the Vorovsky Prize in 1986 for the best publications on international affairs, and in 1989 he received the Journalist of the Year Prize from the Interpress Service Agency, which was presented at the UN Headquarters in New York. In 1997 Pumpyansky received a Johns Hopkins University diploma for excellence in international journalism.

The *Novoye Vremya* magazine (its English-language version is known as *New Times*) is unlikely to move back to the building it has occupied for half a century. Almost overnight the magazine that had weathered the convulsions of recent years and was one of the nation's few independent publications, found itself literally on the street. Its offices were vandalized: All the partitions were torn down and the parquet flooring ripped up. The raiders also searched the journalists' desks looking for anything juicy, and, as editor, I know that a lot could be discovered there.

THE UNINVITED GUESTS

The *Novoye Vremya*'s time in Pushkin Square came to an end on the afternoon of an ordinary working day on February 19, 2004. The day team had approved the final design of the magazine cover and dispersed to their rooms, some to write, some to do the magazine makeup. No one had an inkling of what was about to happen when the guards reported uninvited guests.

Afterward a team quite different from the day staff made its appearance: The locked door to the reception room could stop for only a moment the dozen or so aggressive musclemen. On the other side of the thin glazed door came the order "Break it down!"

This act took place on a normal working day in the heart of Moscow.

Actually, it was not quite an ordinary working day. The *Novoye Vremya* staff had not known an ordinary working day for almost six months from the night in September 2003 when one of the magazine executives got the call that "Some strange men have forced out our guards and seized the building!"

The "strange men" introduced themselves as employees of the OOO (known under Russian law as a society of limited liability)

Primex company and showed the document asserting their ownership rights over the building that had been the *Novoye Vremya*'s property for almost half a century. Where had the OOO obtained those rights? The men displayed a contract of purchase. Bought from whom?—See for yourself, they said. It came from the OOO Koncept company. What Koncept company?

"Sorry, we don't know. Not our business. Our concern is to buy."

APRIL FOOL'S DAY: WHEN THE "JOKE" WAS PLAYED

Since that day, enough time has passed to allow us to trace the events like a detective on a case.

April 1, 2003. Let us keep in mind this date, which seems to have been chosen with a purpose. On that day, the *Novoye Vremya* financial manager Dmitri Nikolayevich Minakov signed, clandestinely, what was nothing less than a contract for the sale of the building. Later, in justification, he would say that the document was "just a valueless piece of paper," that the contract was "a formality," "had no legal effect," and was "invalid from the very beginning." Much later he would stop the excuses and refuse to offer any explanations "without his lawyer's [being present]." His position did little for interoffice relations but was well suited for the later court hearings.

To this day the editors have not seen the deed. Was it actually signed? There can be no doubt about this because it set off a chain reaction of serious consequences. But where can the document be found? Minakov will have to answer this and many other questions in a court of law: Criminal proceedings have already been instituted against him.

Did the financial manager have the right to sign a deed to sell the editorial office building? Of course not. However, a solution can be found to almost every problem if one sets one's mind to it. It came to light that four months before April Fool's Day, the financial manager had registered, also clandestinely, new Articles of Association of the OOO *Novoye Vremya* Editorial Office. The new articles differed from the previous ones on a single decisive point: the financial managers' authority was extended fantastically, and he was given, in fact, the authority of a general director.

The founders of the OOO *Novoye Vremya* were the *Novoye Vremya*'s journalist staff when the magazine was registered as an independent publication and an OOO in 1991. A majority of the founding journalists no longer work for the newspaper. All the names, however, are well known to the public. It turns out that on November 15, 2002, a founders' conference took place and resolved to amend the articles of association in favor of Minakov. The conference proceedings record that fourteen founders attended, among them the editor-in-chief in his capacity as the general director.

As a matter of fact, under the law on limited liability societies, a financial manager's authority can in no way equal that of a general director. So even if the founders had the idea of passing such a strange decision, it would have been illegal. The curious thing is, however, that nothing of the sort was decided. Not one of the founders had attended the fateful conference of November 15, 2002. The editor-in-chief at that time was in Guatemala, ten thousand kilometers (6,214 miles) away from Moscow, as evidenced by his published reports, visa stamps in his passport, and airline tickets!

No such conference of the founders took place. The record of the proceedings is a fake. The editor-in-chief/general director's signature on the new articles of association was forged. All this was undertaken so that four months later the financial manager's signature under the deed of sale could be taken as valid. As a matter of fact, one more founders' conference had to be faked. It took place, allegedly, on the same historic day of April 1, 2003. The founders, supposedly, "approved the big deal" of the building's sale.

April 1 is a day for fooling. To repeat for the sake of clarity: There was no second founders' conference, just as there had not been a first one. There was nothing but the proceedings.

A PARADE OF PHANTOMS

Be that as it may, April 1, 2003, was the day that the purchaser company OOO Koncept made its appearance. As is befitting, OOO Koncept has (or had on that date) a "founder"—a college student who supplemented his income by renting out his passport. There is also (or was at that moment) a general director employed as a messenger by a certain lawyer named Dmitri Gennadyevich Akimenko with whom Minakov did business. As time passed, the masks would be changing mysteriously and disappearing.

Koncept has neither assets nor operations to its name—that is, it has nothing except its symbolic name. All it ever did was purchase the building in Pushkin Square. Actually, I am wrong. It has done one more thing—the company sold the building. To whom? The Primex company.

Primex is the twin sister of Koncept. Their institution followed one and the same schemes by one legal entity and one physical person. What is most significant in this case is not the remarkable coincidence of both legal entities originating from the Tver region but that the registration forms of the Koncept and Primex bear one and the same contact phone number.

THE BONA FIDE PURCHASER GAME

The so-called resale of the Pushkin Square building by Koncept to Primex had a special significance. It was a game known as "hunting for the bona fide purchaser."

The bona fide acquisition is a legal notion specifically explained and finally legalized by the Constitutional Court's decision of the summer following some very dramatic developments.

A wave of housing swindles had hit the nation. Racketeers of various kinds would sell to their accomplices flats that did not belong to them. The latter would resell the flats to unsuspecting people and then vanish with the money. After some time the tricked owners would claim their property. Courts would satisfy their appeals and rule that the people—who had sometimes paid all their savings for the flats—would be evicted. The victims were left to locate on their own the sellers and resellers who had disappeared without a trace. The substance of the Constitutional Court's ruling was that the bona fide purchaser must not be victimized and was to be allowed to keep the title to the property.

Of course, the Constitutional Court acted with the best of intentions. But in real practice its ruling immediately produced a scheme for criminal appropriation. For a fraud to succeed, it was enough to show a chain of resales to imitate bona fide purchases. That was done in the case of the *Novoye Vremya*.

Actually, each Koncept and Primex twin had a part in the ploy. Koncept's deal was vulnerable, made with falsified documents, and its fraudulence could be proved in a court of law. But this poses no problem. When this happens, the Koncept company will vanish into thin air because it is actually a nonentity, a phantom company. The crucial factor by that time would be the listing of the building as the property of the Primex company, which would subsequently declare that it has never even heard of any malpractice and pretend to be a bona fide purchaser.

Actually, like the Koncept company, the phantom Primex company was also to disappear. Having bought the building, Primex sold it right away to another sister company known as Effekt. (All those transactions were on paper only.) The scenario was that the latter company (or some other concern after it) would be a "one hundred percent bona fide purchaser: the more links in the sale chain, the harder to expose is the fraudulence. However, there was a glitch in the plan; the case got extensive press coverage, and the third 'deed'" was not registered officially and was rendered invalid. The Primex owners will have to go on playing the role of the "new" owner. But the main target had been reached: The company has obtained a real document, the certificate of ownership, made on official paper and properly signed and sealed. Now the contract could be shown to be binding.

It was the culmination of the process and the key link of the criminal master plan. Several faked signatures, a fraudulent contract, and a series of virtual quasi-sales, with the help of a couple of dummy companies and the building in Pushkin Square, in downtown Moscow, has been seized from its proprietor—quite literally seized in a perfectly "legal" manner. As a result, a fraudulent performance has given birth to a new reality and a new crooked law.

THE RAIDERS SHALL NOT BE TRIED

Now comes the next phase: the materialization of a crooked law.

A certificate of ownership is not enough to take possession of a building—it must be supported by a separate document. There is a court ruling to this effect. Those behind Primex preferred mob law and the use of a loophole in the law, which says, "A [raider] shall not be tried."

It would be next to impossible not to see that the seizure of the building by sullen musclemen was a glaring and rude violation of the law. But the law finds itself at a loss about how to deal with such people. Later, a document certifying their property right is proudly produced and can be contested only in a court of law. But trials may take years, including those regarding the illegal seizure of a building. Without a court order, no bailiff would drive out a raider, so a misdeed can be righted only in the same way, that is, by use of force. However, the use of force would be, first of all, against the law and, second, usually beyond the ability of the lawful owner to carry out.

That was exactly the type of seizure that happened with the *Novoye Vremya* building. It even happened twice. The first seizure took place on September 17, 2003, when the sullen men produced a certificate of ownership to the magazine's guards and drove them from the building. This happened on a Thursday night; four days later, on Sunday, at about 8:00 a.m., the raiders attempted to clear the building of the magazine's editors. However, two of the magazine staff members succeeded in locking themselves in the lobby and managed to call other mass media. The information was immediately put on air by the Echo of Moscow on the radio and the TV channel Rossiya. On hearing the news, deputies of the state Duma Vladimir Lukin and Nikolai Gonchar alerted the authorities, and the Interior Ministry issued appropriate instructions. The raiders were frustrated in their attempts to take over the building.

Five months later, on February 19, 2004, the locked doors of the lobby failed to stop the raiders. Physically restraining the journalists and turning out their pockets, the raiders forced all the magazine's staff out into the street. The magazine's property (computers with files, lockers with archives, desks with materials and personal belongings, a library collected for sixty years) was thrown into a heap on the floor. After that, they methodically set about destroying the interior, partitions, and structures.

The destruction of the building was intended as a signal to the journalists that said, "You shall never come back. The editorial staff is not to work here." The ruination also signaled the beginning of the presale preparations. The raider was readying the building for the "commercial client"—meaning the one who had placed an order for the building to be seized.

THE SPECIFICS OF THE SEIZURE BUSINESS

One feature of the new Russian seizure business is that the raiders have no fear of the law. They play cat-and-mouse games with the law and turn it upside-down. In fact, they usurp the law. This is exactly how they managed to acquire the certificates of ownership. Even less do they fear the specific officers of the law. The necessary documents (counterfeit articles of association of the *Novoye Vremya* magazine, the illegal deed of the sale to the Koncept company, a fake resale deed with Primex, and the like) received official registration at breakneck speed on a par with the president's decrees and without verification. Local police treat them tenderly and address them by their first names. Court sessions, however urgent a case might be, are postponed mysteriously or resolved in their favor. Invisible bonds exist between them and an army of government officials and bureaucrats of different levels in endless offices, law enforcement bodies, and political headquarters. That is why the captors are immune from prosecution, even though their actions may be criminal. Crime is putting on quasi-legal robes.

KNOWN AND UNKNOWN "HEROES"

Let's have a closer look at the principal actors of this story.

We mentioned earlier the nameless "heroes": a class of officials, lawyers, bailiffs, and so forth and those government servants who serve other masters and use their official positions to promote the interests of crime. Without them the legitimization of the criminal seizures would have been impossible. The individuals' names are supplied in the order that they appeared in this story.

Dmitri Nikolayevich Minakov has been the commercial director of the *Novoye Vremya* for the last five years. He is the man who spearheaded the scheme that started with a few fake documents and a search for a person inside the company who could arrange the forgery—someone prepared to set up the company and step aside. At the beginning, the man would be unaware that swindlers were using him, and he probably believed that he was merely acting under the influence of petty and pardonable temptations. But he will find he cannot go back, and soon he turns into a direct accomplice of the crime.

The way it happened with Minakov may be of psychological interest. Sadly, it can have no effect on the final outcome. Be that as it may, a few days after the initial seizure, and without any explanation that might have helped the investigation, he perplexed the editors with a wire, "Please accept my voluntary resignation." He sent the message in duplicate and was gone.

Dmitri Gennadyevich Akimenko is an untraceable person and a self-styled lawyer. He has two grounds for saying so—first, an identity card that he offers when necessary and, second, a workplace where he rents a desk in an office adjacent to the Court of Arbitration at 23 Novy Arbat Avenue. The signboard of the court serves to sanctify his presence there. Actually, he is not employed by the Court of Arbitration or any other court. Nor can his name be found in the legal profession registries of the city of Moscow or Moscow region. In effect, he is not a lawyer.

Then what is he? An exhaustive answer to this question may only be supplied by a court of law. But the type is already known.

In Russia our lives have a huge black hole—our constant need to deal with petty bureaucrats. Getting any certificate, permission, licence, and so forth is a headache for anyone. But, in these situations, as if by magic, a savior would appear, an intermediary, a middleman, a go-between—language has lots of names for this species. He knows the layout of the corridors of power and the right doors to open. He knows what wheels should be "oiled," the size of the "remuneration," and where it should be "dropped" to settle a matter. He knows intimately every loophole in the law.

For some time, the self-styled lawyer Akimenko was Minakov's principal adviser, and it was he who introduced the Koncept company—the first link in the swindle.

THE INSTITUTE ON THE FRUNZENSKAYA EMBANKMENT

Nikolai Vladimirovich Nesterenko, the deputy to the general manager of Primex, was actually the field commander of the storm troopers' team. He is twenty-nine, a native born Russian from the northern Caucasus and a former sportsman with expertise in hand-to-hand combat and experience as a bodyguard. Nesterenko owns a cherry-colored Mercedes and collects tributes from street vendors. He was given the job of seizing and holding the building. He enjoys his hard-hitting position: "I'm pretty high in our structure, and it's a very large one."

Nesterenko's professional activities are not limited to *Novoye Vremya* alone. Here is one more daring exploit of his.

The following is an excerpt from the orders of Khamovniki district prosecutor on starting an investigation following the appeal of Sergei Reznichenko, general director of the Research Institute of Elastomer Plastic Materials (OAO NIIEM): "On 04.02.07 unidentified persons numbering about thirty burst into the building housing the property of the OAO at the address 10 Yefimova Street, Moscow, claiming to be its new proprietors."

The research institute is not the editorial office of a liberal weekly but a defense enterprise with classified laboratories. Nor is it a four-story building but ten stories, eleven thousand square meters (36,091 square feet), close to the Frunzenskaya embankment.

Who were those thirty men?

To quote the NIIEM general director's appeal to the prosecutor in central Moscow, "The attackers were led by Mr. N. V. Nesterenko who introduced himself as Director of OOO Bizneskontrakt [and] as the new owner of this building."

Nesterenko is making progress in his career: At Primex, he is a deputy to the general director.

The technique is identical. For starters, fake documents and powers of attorney were used to alter the founding documents of the NIIEM. Then, the District Court of Shatsk in Ryazan region ordered Moscow's Office 4 of the Taxes and Revenue Ministry to register the changes in the National Registry. These changes recorded the appointment of a certain Marat Neshanovich Yusupov, the general director of the NIIEM. The presiding judge of Shatsk left for extensive leave to the United Arab Emirates—for obvious reasons. His ruling legalized everything. Subsequent steps followed the same scheme, the only difference being the names of the companies. On January 21, 2004, the registration of the sale of the building was entered by Viyur-grad to the same Biznes-kontrakt, with Nikolai Nesterenko as its boss. The latter's statement to the Khamovniki Office of the Ministry of the Interior follows:

> In December of 2003 I made the acquaintance of the director of Viyur-grad by the name of Pavel, his surname I do not recall. He said he was the proprietor of the building. We met in an office near Tishinka Square, its full address I do not remember. As he had been recommended to me by people whom I know well; I would not like to name them; I had had no doubts of his legitimacy. He showed his Certificate of Ownership; I verified it through my channels. The certificate had been registered. Indeed, on these grounds I made the decision to formalize the purchase.

It is an illuminative self-portrait by a bona fide purchaser painted by a former bodyguard and master of hand-to-hand combat. Anything to add to it? If you please!

On New Year's Eve 2002, in the formal language of the police, "unknown persons burst into the building known as OAO Giprokhim's property styling themselves as its new proprietors." Giprokhim, yet another institute of scientific renown, is a large building on Shcherbakovskaya Street close to the metro station Semyonovskaya. The "unknown persons" were under the command of the omnipresent Nikolai Nesterenko. By what right? By the right of being a "large stockholder" and, of course, a deputy to the general director of the OAO Giprokhim. The young man's scientific interests are extensive.

THE FIVE PROJECTS

The parade of so-called heroes would have been incomplete without one more person, Dmitri Valeryevich Port.

In the case of the plastic materials institute, Port had been armed with a paper called "OAO NIIEM . . . Authorizes Legal Council D. V. Port to Represent the Company's Interests." We in the *Novoye Vremya* knew Mr. D. V. Port well enough from that September night of the first seizure when the councillor presented an identical power of attorney but issued by Primex.

He is inseparable from Nesterenko's goons. "How are things at the Frunzenskaya embankment?" we asked him. We got a bright smile and, "Wonderful! But don't you know we have five projects of this kind?"

We do. They include, by the way, the famous department store Moskva in Leninsky Prospekt. At this property, a Primex offshoot is fighting off the department store. It is important to realize that we live in the epoch of absolute interchangeability—raiders and defenders of property can exchange places. In any case, they operate with the same means and for the same reason: There is no law to fight lawlessness.

Primex, Koncept, Biznes-kontrakt, Viuyr-grad. Each of these pretends to be ordinary independent companies and bona fide purchasers. Actually, they are part of a pattern of operation, and even their operatives are the same. Their men are not chance employees—their various elements and lines are remarkably well developed. An operation employs a spotter, a traitor, a storm trooper, a consiglierie (to use the description in *The Godfather*, the person who provides legal advice). It is a network of individuals. But who holds the net in his hands?

THE MAN BEHIND THE SCREEN

Perhaps we should introduce Mr. Antimoni at this juncture. It is his proper name.

He is the man behind the screen.

Yevgeny Grigoryevich Antimoni was born in 1969. Among the solid men of shady business he enjoys a bad reputation. On hearing his name almost everyone is capable of recalling some special story involving Antimoni. Particularly popular is the alleged story from his early years in business when he attempted to swindle a Chechen group in a large petrol deal. The operation could have ended sadly for the man. It was only thanks to his connections that he was merely thrown out of a speeding car and left in one piece.

Currently, Antimoni's calling card, and probably his screen, is his position as a proprietor of a chain of beer restaurants, Kruzhka (Tankard). He was introduced to the *Novoye Vremya* editors by Minakov, who enthusiastically described him as an important investor who could tap large resources of Russian emigres in the United States and an unlimited potential "to settle matters" in Moscow. Antimoni liked the building and brought with him a batch of handsome plans: "We'll turn the place into a hotel named Pushkin, 30 percent for you and 70 percent for us."

After the editors explained, showing all possible respect, that Antimoni had wasted his money on the plans, he bluntly asked to buy the building. The editors' response was equally blunt and worried Minakov: The editors' board should have been more cautious because the man was dangerous. It would have been better to find a consensus with him. The editors thought the discussion was at an end, but they were mistaken. Antimoni found his own response.

Of course, a raid is not the end of the chain. Usually there is a customer lurking behind him who has concrete plans for the property in question. One day he may decide that there are too many editorial offices in Pushkin Square while entertainment establishments, hotels, and casinos are too scarce. So the raider moves into business.

ROBBERY AS A BUSINESS VENTURE

Yet it can be said that Antimoni is not just a name. He is the embodiment of the open quasi-legitimate seizure of property—robbery as a business venture.

This kind of activity has many names, such as a hostile takeover or "greenmail." Those in this business are sometimes called raiders. It is quite an industry. These days almost every large business group in Russia has a specialized unit, from professional jurists and economists up to storm troopers, that looks very much like organized criminal gangs.

All the time we hear reports of more and more seizures: a department store, a museum, an editorial office, an institute, or factories ranging from alcohol distilleries to ore beneficiation plants or paper mills. Ever more ownership certificates and sale contracts are turned out right and left, and, in every case, they follow a nearly identical scheme: one or two faked signatures, a decree from some faraway court, an immediate resale, and the involvement of a Nikolai Nesterenko as host.

This kind of business is fantastically profitable. The costs of seizing and keeping a unit ranges from about a million dollars to as much as two million in particularly difficult cases. The real price of the loot can be five, ten, fifteen, or perhaps even more millions. Experts evaluate the cost efficiency of this business at 700 percent a year. The figure is an average; in case of a complete success, it is incalculable. But a complete victory for a raider does not always happen.

Sometimes negotiations are called for. But, of course, not with the proprietor whose prospects are too gloomy. The proprietor will have to part with at least one-half of what he holds in his first encounter with the raider. A half can be saved if he finds a powerful protector capable of a long, protracted war. The outcome will depend on a correlation of different forces. As the process progresses, the sides enter negotiations and look for a compromise. Even in the worst cases, the raider's costs are compensated, and he receives a bonus of some 300 to 400 percent.

The market continues to expand and is already assessed at billions of dollars. The law has washed its hands of the matter.

This process has an important objective background. It has been accurately described by Nikita Kirichenko, a remarkable journalist and economist who met such an untimely death, "No legitimate property has yet emerged in Russia." Since no legitimate property has emerged, any property rights can be challenged, and any seizure of property can be legitimized. It all depends on manipulation.

In real life, the law (the authority at all levels, including law enforcement agencies and the courts) does not protect property owners and lawful proprietors. Like a Wild West cowboy, a proprietor is totally alone, as he has to fend off an invisible enemy springing up at him from nowhere. And he has to face a lot of unfortunate discoveries. He has to learn all too soon that "the dispute of rights" turns into "a war of budgets and influences." With endless discussion of the "dictatorship of law," that very law has turned into a pure (and very dirty) ritual.

Law as a cover for lawlessness is a perfect breeding ground for the foulest robbery passed off as a redivision of property. The right to violence is being privatized. The country is being turned into a province ruled by stick-up men and field commanders. Everyday business is impossible and any normal activity is threatened. This is the worst kind of government default and a formula for disaster.

IN PLACE OF AN EPILOGUE

When the *Novoye Vremya* was thrown out of its building, its publication was suspended from April to June. In mid-2004 the magazine published an editorial in the first issue printed after the disaster. Using the editorial, we pursued two goals—first, to provide the reader with as many facts about what had happened and, second, to focus the authorities' attention on the core of the problem. We thought the story was so self-evident that a triumph of justice was merely a procedural matter. After all, we had done all the work expected of the law enforcement bodies. We carried out an investigation, traced the different phases of the crime and its cover-up, named names, and described the specific part each person had played. More than that, we showed that ours was not an exceptional case, that the criminal story was in actual fact a social model. We acted on the assumption that the state would intervene to right a wrong. After all, is it not the duty of law enforcement to see that no crime goes unpunished? Moreover, regarding the political elite, it must realize that such cancers cannot be tolerated in society. Procrastination is deadly.

There has been no reaction from the state.

We won half a dozen suits in the arbitration courts and got a ruling that annulled the initial deal (the sale of the building to Kontsept) as invalid. But so what? We felt as if we were entangled in a cobweb. Piecemeal litigations with phantom companies can drag on until the end of time, while the actual criminals thrive and pull the strings off-stage. By the way, this too is a component of the criminal process: to use this endless cycle to wear down the opponent. The consequence is a waste of time and money. Naturally, the resources available to the editors of a none-too-rich magazine when compared with, say, the persons who contracted the crime are somewhat different.

Little progress has been made in the criminal case that could have solved the crime. The investigators, who allegedly toiled for many months, managed not to ask "the other side" a single "uncomfortable" question, not even one concerning the initial facts regarding founders' conferences that had never happened, and the investigators failed even to mention the subsequent acts of banditry that were witnessed by many. Unbelievable as this may seem, it is a hard fact. The editors appealed to the top officers of the Ministry of the Interior and the Prosecutor General and the President's administration and brought accusations of sabotage and corruption against specific and very highly placed officials, backing the accusations with facts. The response was exactly nothing. Why? To this question, at least, we did get an answer—even two.

Editors of a liberal magazine do not come under the protection of the state. They are outside the law. The official stand is "The political bodies wash their hands of disputes between economic agents." Unofficially, the position is "You are in opposition, so it is silly to count on the authorities' protection. Nobody in the Kremlin would shed a tear if there is one fewer liberal magazine. You are not that stupid not to realize this."

We were perfectly aware of this, that in Putin's Russia the state is not the people but the authority, that the state machinery serves the ruling regime and not the society. But we were indeed naive to think that the notions of law and order had a certain independent value of their own. Nothing of the sort. The authority is free to ignore us. The authority is selective and cynical. Its only concern is its own self-perpetuation. Such was our first discovery.

But our second discovery was even worse. The Russian state is worse than bad—it just does not exist. It may seem a strange statement about Russia, where it is in one's best interest to profess loyalty to the state; nevertheless, it is a fact.

There is a joke in the legal community. A young judge asks advice of his elder colleague—how should he act in a particular case? The plaintiff has offered $100,000 for a ruling in his favor, while the defendant has offered $120,000. The judge's elder colleague replies, "Suggest that the plaintiff add twenty thousand more and rule on the facts of the case." The advice was worthy of King Solomon.

Courts do not dispense justice; their rulings are bought, good and right ones just like the bad and unfair ones. It is common knowledge. The law enforcement bodies are not geared to protect law and rights. The bureaucracy does not serve the cause it is called upon to serve. It serves itself, both as a class and as one entity, and individually, with each member toiling to line his pockets.

Everything and everybody is corrupt. The corruption is more than plain bribing or the occasional dishonesty of an official. It is a complete system that permeates everything from top to bottom.

The FSB Mafia that has come to power in Russia under Putin styles itself as "state builders" and also "enforcers." The Mafia pretends to be building up "the vertical lines of authority" without which the state would disintegrate. No assertion can be as far removed from reality.

"The vertical lines of authority" is a rickety affair by definition. It is not a method of keeping the society in a state of balance. Such balance calls for a more complex structure: the separation of three powers. This is a principle willingly forgotten in Putin's Russia. Added to them must be the "fourth estate," the independent mass media, the watchdog of democracy that they keep chained up.

An unmanageable democracy is dangerous for the "enforcers." The idea of the vertical lines of authority is intended precisely to instill manageability so that instructions can be passed down from the top. That is, everyone and everything must work when ordered to do so. The vertical lines of authority are called upon to support the power of one person; anything else is of little concern. It is absolutely unsuitable as an instrument for solving the problems of a society.

The motto of such a society is well known: "The cobbler should stick to his last." The good side of the cobbler-bureaucrat is his awareness that one must work only on orders from above. But he is not a simpleton; he is sly. He is aware that the remainder of the time can be spent working for his own benefit. In reality the last in question is divided among grabby hands, each millimeter privatized. The marriage of the all-powerful and all-controlling bureaucracy to the wild market has given birth to a fantastic, unbridled, and irreversible corruption.

Of all the people at the top, only one man attempted to allow justice to prevail in the *Novoye Vremya* case. Ombudsman Vladimir Lukin, we thank you for your effort! I have a suspicion, however, that even a person with real power could not change the situation. There is no worse tool with which to fight bandit capitalism than the vertical lines of authority, rotten to the core as they are.

Chapter 12

INFORMATION WORTH FIGHTING FOR

MICHAEL McKINNON

Michael McKinnon is the freedom of information editor on the *Australian* newspaper. He has worked at a number of Australian newspapers, including the *Townsville Bulletin*, the *Sunday Mail*, the *Herald Sun* and the *Courier Mail*. Before becoming a journalist, among other jobs, he worked on a cattle ranch in North Queensland. He holds a BA in history and politics and a Master's of Public Policy. When not battling governments for the truth, McKinnon annoys his family, enjoys fine wine, and playing jazz and blues guitar. He is an obsessive and hopeless golfer.

Canberra July has always been bitterly cold. Often accused of lacking a heart, the nation's capital was a birthplace I had happily left in my late teens in the late 1970s, and its bracing air still elicits memories of early morning fogs, pallid sunshine, and a cleanliness typified by streets without litter and a long-standing ban on billboard advertising. The city has changed. Bustling cafes and restaurants and a growing private sector have transformed a city designed as a home to the politicians and the bureaucracy of the Commonwealth of Australia, yet it still remains the heart of the nation's government.

It was a battle against government secrecy and censorship that had brought me back to Canberra to the Administrative Appeals Tribunal (AAT) in 2004. A battle for truth about how much income tax cuts are really worth to ten million citizens and whether a suspected Australian terrorist David Hicks was legally held by our closest ally—the United States. The potential news value of the stories was obvious. But underpinning the cases was the strategic decision to dramatically improve the effectiveness of Australia's tired and often abused Freedom of Information (FOI) Act by overturning the long-standing precedent from a case called *Re Howard and Treasurer* widely used as a rubber stamp for censorship for almost twenty years.

My journey to the Administrative Appeals Tribunal (AAT) had started about fifteen years earlier with my introduction to the vexed Freedom of Information Act as a young journalist on a regional daily newspaper, the *Townsville Bulletin*. Like a problem gambler, I won a jackpot with the first ever bet and have never left the casino of FOI—despite the appalling odds and unabashed and consistent cheating by the government.

The beautiful small city, blessed by endless sunlight and its closeness to the Great Barrier Reef in North Queensland, provided a superb grounding for any journalist forced to cover issues ranging from massive mining projects, racism, and politics to the local agricultural show and cane toad races.

I had left Canberra unhappy with a job in the public service and, given my love of the written word, a failed and deluded attempt at an electrical engineering degree. Bewildered by immaturity and unsure whether I possessed any potential at all, I had only one plan: to travel north to North Queensland, where my younger brother John had already gone. Almost as far from the then-cloying confines of Canberra as you could go.

My father, Bill McKinnon, was the widely respected and well-liked secretary of the Department of Immigration and former head of the Industry Assistance Commission who died too young of a heart attack on the golf course in December 1988.

I had grown up steeped in a public service where bureaucrats still provided full, fearless, and frank advice in the best interests of the nation. Public servants did not have political views, and I still remember as a child my father declining to tell me whom he voted for. So I traveled north and ended up out bush first on a sheep station for a few months and then chasing half-wild cattle on half-wild horses on two hundred square miles of cattle property. In a year when I learned horse breaking and shoeing, rum-fueled brawling in bush pubs, and fixing an old four-wheel drive motor fencing wire when stranded thirty kilometers (seventeen miles) from home, my thoughts were never far from what I would do. Somehow in the hours in the saddle or the stockyards, inspiration found its way to me.

I would get a degree, become a journalist. It meant leaving the bush, although the bush never left me, nor did the memories of the bemusing and sometimes bizarre array of characters that live in the vast interior of the continent. Mustering a mob of 150 horses at flat gallop, the sound of the stock whip cracking through the ghost gums at dawn, and the incredible harsh beauty of the Australian outback once enjoyed and endured can't be forgotten. I then worked a variety of jobs to support my studies: a builder's laborer, street sweeper, night club bouncer, and musician, although my parents remained a loyal and regular last resort for money. I also managed to gain a degree in politics and history, edit the university student publication, and become Student Union president while at Townsville's James Cook University.

With studies complete, an optimistic raft of letters applying for journalism jobs across Australia were dispatched to sad and universal rejection. Word of mouth led me to a cadetship on the local free weekly where my choice of profession was confirmed in the interview when told drinking beer was a useful skill for any journalist.

A couple of years later, after transferring to the local daily newspaper, the love-hate relationship with FOI started. I was sent out to cover a politician announcing that a disused power station would be torn down. As an election promise, the story was forgettable, but as I wandered around outside the dilapidated and massive brick structure, I noticed blank 7.62-millimeter ammunition liberally strewn around the ground—a sight well remembered from two years in the Reserve Army training with the old SLR rifle. Peering through the plastic stretched between ancient window frames, free-floating asbestos looked like a snow storm within the interior—a storm that could deliver a bitter harvest of cancer to the infantry soldiers trained at the makeshift urban warfare training facility. Exposure to asbestos causes grave and inescapable risks of incurable cancer. A series of stories followed, but it was my letter to the Department of Defence asking more questions that finally led to the cancellation of further training. The army also promised and carried out an internal investigation into the issue but refused to release the findings.

Enter the FOI Act, legislation allowing citizens to lodge a request for government information and within thirty days receive a decision on access and minimal costs. At least that is what the law says and what politicians ostentatiously claimed would occur when the act passed through both houses of Parliament more than twenty years ago. In practice, FOI requests for nonpersonal information are extensively delayed, incredibly complex, costly, and thwarted by wrongly applied exemptions, leaving the process generally spurned by journalists as too hard, too slow, and too costly. So I lodged my first FOI request, which was processed quickly and cheaply, and gained a complete copy of the 3rd Brigade report into training exercises between 1984 and 1989 at the disused power station. Few if any FOI requests have ever been so easy, and the documents yielded a truth that demanded to be told.

More than a thousand soldiers had been exposed to asbestos, and they had continued training despite warnings from a senior army medical officer. Soldiers were issued with masks if they asked, but the masks were known to be totally inadequate. The report also admitted airborne asbestos levels would have been increased by the presence of a large number of troops running, searching, and firing blank rounds and grenade simulators, with some soldiers "showered with asbestos dust." The investigation also brought home to me the importance of journalism to individuals. Such a reality can sometimes be lost by journalists amid the competition, cynicism, emotional fatigue, and alcohol abuse. Sure, each soldier who trained at the facility had his or her medical record annotated—leaving a permanent record if medical help and compensation were needed, but the real importance of the story to individuals was hammered home while out at a club one night. A group of young soldiers—or "diggers," as they are also known—asked me whether I were "the journalist who wrote the asbestos stuff,'" which I freely conceded. I recall being told, "Your money is no good in this bar, mate," and about a dozen soldiers then proceeded with boundless and frightening enthusiasm to show their appreciation.

All had trained at the facility. All held some fears about the long-term impact of the asbestos nestled in their bodies, despite a soldier's typical bravado. All argued that the truth would never have come out without the newspaper's investigation.

And each of them owned my story far more than I did. Unlike the soldiers, I would never be forced to recall training amid deadly white clouds and fear whether a cell had started the first unstoppable mutation of cancer decades after exposure.

My career then took me to the *Sunday Mail* in Brisbane, also owned by News Ltd., but I failed to adapt and understand the needs of a newspaper catering to management's perceptions of what interested a Sunday readership market. I still had some success with FOI, but my knowledge of politics and governments was still insufficient and hampered any systematic approach to FOI.

I needed a better education.

For private reasons, I moved to Melbourne—a city of four seasons in a day with incredible ethnic diversity and history. The city lives consumed by its devotion to Australian Rules Football—a uniquely Australian game best watched live to be understood. (If in doubt, support the undisputed best team—the Saint Kilda Football Club!) I found casual, part-time work at the News Ltd.–owned *Sunday Herald Sun*, but my real interest was the master's degree in public policy (M.P.P.) program at the prestigious Melbourne University.

One tutor, the erudite economics professor Neville Norman, fondly recalled my father from the Industries Assistance Commission and seemed determined to ensure that the son grasped at least the rudiments of the science of economics mastered by his father. Juggling study and work, I managed to complete the degree and honed my knowledge of government. I still used FOI for investigations but had to pay the costs because I was a casual worker. And once again, a perception that Sunday readers could not or would not be interested in reading breaking hard news seemed to dominate the paper.

Unfortunately, with my degree finished and a heavily pregnant wife, I was fired. A senior manager yelled at me like I was a dog. I sharply corrected him. I was sacked. My shiny new master's degree—paid for from savings—seemed pointless. In my desperation, I contemplated sinking to undreamed-of lows—public relations, spin doctoring. Call it what you will, repellant as it was, it seemed the only odious option.

As I left the newsroom, I noted a notice board advertisement calling for a new deputy editor for the business section of the daily paper, the *Herald Sun*—again owned by News Ltd. With absolutely nothing to lose, I applied and received an interview with the paper's business editor, Stephen Mayne, who subsequently set up and is still running Australia's leading political Web site, Crikey.com. Cadaverous in appearance, Mayne remains a very clever man, although, on occasion, he is seemingly untroubled by mundane issues like accuracy and balanced reporting.

He was certainly not fooled by my application, noting correctly within minutes that I had never actually written a business story or shown even a passing interest in the area. However, impressed by the newly conferred degree, Mayne gave me some casual work and eventually permanent employment covering the small business sector. A long way from politics and government, but a welcome regular paycheck. My bleak outlook had improved, and I was about to be the welcome beneficiary of one of the lasting and great joys of journalism—break a big enough yarn and the world will be your oyster.

One of the continued stories in the round was a report commissioned by the federal small business minister Geoff Prosser on fair-trading and the small-business sector. The key recommendation of the May 1997 report was beefed-up protection for small retail businesses being bullied by large shopping centers over leases.

Yet the minister remained lukewarm about the recommendations despite the political importance of a small-business lobby measured in the millions of voters. He would not even pay lip service to the issue by fobbing it off to a committee for investigation and obscurity. Puzzled, I organized someone to check the parliamentary pecuniary interests register in Canberra, where elected members are obliged to record their financial details. Prosser modestly stated that he owned "Bunbury—various lots."

Even more puzzling, I thought.

Bunbury is a city south of Perth in west Australia where

Prosser was the local member of Parliament. I went to work on Saturday on my own time and phoned the first real-estate agent I could find in Bunbury, asking whether the minister owned any retail tenancies in Bunbury. The answer will remain with me for life: "What doesn't he own," the helpful man advised. After nailing the details, including an interview with Prosser where he was only really concerned about whether his tenants liked him (which they did), I wrote the story but could not convince the news desk of its value. It appeared on page 64 on June 9, 1997.

Prosser's businesses included some eighty retail tenants. As minister he had refused to endorse some key recommendations of an inquiry, which argued for commonwealth action to protect shopping center tenants. He rejected accusations of a conflict of interest; however, further details of his business interests and conflicts with the ministerial role emerged, and on July 11 the minister was sacked.

Around the same time, I also met News Ltd.'s founder for the first and only time, Rupert Murdoch. Quietly spoken, he seemed friendly and unassuming despite the unquestioned talent and energy that has transformed ownership of a small afternoon newspaper in South Australia into one of the world's largest media companies.

Another newspaper headhunted me and with a major offer in hand—the *Herald Sun*. I met with the *Herald Sun*'s likeable, well-regarded and rough-hewn editor Peter Blunden. He promised to match the money and, more importantly, offered me a posting to the News Ltd. National Bureau.

Finally, I was reporting from the Canberra press gallery—the pinnacle of political and government reporting in Australia. I was going back to Canberra to grasp a long-cherished dream on the second floor on the Senate side of Parliament House, where the gallery was seen as the most competitive arena in Australian journalism.

The quick and obvious first lesson was, more often than not, the government, with its spin doctors, controlled the news agenda. The leaders of the pack—senior political reporters—receive leaks or background briefings but are largely expected to follow the government line or "spin" on the issue. Lesser lights are fed lesser scraps, with a newly arrived journalist left to rummage in the remaining rubbish.

Sure, the pack would hunt the government ferociously and without fear or favor on any given issue, but the daunting challenge of meeting the demands of day-to-day coverage precluded much investigative journalism even by the leading talent assembled in the gallery.

As News Ltd.'s group economics and immigration reporter writing for leading newspapers in each state, time constraints made FOI investigations very difficult. Inflation, balance of payments, growth, and interest rates required a daily, determined slog. Nevertheless, research and talking to bureaucrats helped the development of new approaches and showed just a glimmer of the real possibility of FOI.

For example, I had developed—with some welcome free assistance—a database of government records. One story arose after I managed to track down a consultant employed to improve the prime minister's publicly funded wine cellar. On September 8, 2000, the published story received enormous interest, even though I regarded it as insignificant in public policy terms compared with other work. The yarn started simply: "Prime Minister John Howard has spent $8,000 of taxpayers' money for a consultant to tell him what wines to drink."

What was the government's response? The PM's senior press secretary found me and roundly abused me, pointing out I would never receive another leaked yarn. I replied that given that I had never received a leaked yarn from the PM, this was a somewhat hollow threat. More importantly, the yarn opened my eyes to another important value of FOI—it breaks the cycle of dependency of journalists where stories are farmed out to a favored few who will ensure the "right spin" is adopted.

Despite the endless attraction of working the gallery for three and half years, I decided to move. Canberra's cold, dry climate was creating havoc with my asthma-affected son, Tom. Frequently hospitalized for days at a time, Tom was advised to move to Brisbane, the capital of the state of Queensland, with its hot and humid climate. A small child in a hospital bed desperately gasping for air makes any decision easy.

Typically, with my son's health at stake, Peter Blunden took an immediate and keen interest in helping my transfer, although News Ltd. had already resolved the problem. I was assured a job working for the *Courier Mail* with its editor-in-chief Chris Mitchell, who was committed to improving FOI in Australia. A widely read and intelligent man, Mitchell relished chasing and breaking stories like few others, and he understood that the future of newspapers depends on providing fresh, accurate, and interesting news.

I recall at our first meeting in Brisbane when Mitchell asked me what I wanted to do. My reply, "I want to really get on top of FOI—make it work," was greeted enthusiastically. I argued that FOI—despite its flaws—could be made to work, and I was soon appointed FOI coordinator as well as an editorial writer. One FOI application lodged with the Australian Taxation Office (ATO) was already pushing the boundaries of government censorship.

I had lodged an FOI request with the ATO when, while in the Canberra gallery, I discovered a $200,000 report called "Simplifying Personal Income Tax" that had been prepared by consultants. The request was refused. I then applied for an internal review of the decision, and the ATO again refused access. Under Australia's FOI Act, the next step was an appeal to the Administrative Appeals Tribunal. But legal advice is expensive, with an AAT appeal possibly costing hundreds of thousands of dollars in legal bills. Naive and optimistic, I decided to represent myself, arguing against the formidable legal team assembled by the ATO and paid for by taxpayers.

The result was stunning and gave me the insight that would eventually lead to my legal challenge in Canberra in 2004.

On October 25, 2001, the *Courier Mail* published the front-page story from the case. Up to 5.5 million Australians would not have to file income tax returns under radical plans under consideration by the ATO. Despite the ATO's claims that the report's release would cause confusion and "ill-informed" public debate—arguments from *Re Howard and Treasurer*—the AAT had found that the document was of "overwhelming public interest," as it discussed possible changes to the tax system and public reaction to those changes. "It is, in simple terms, the public's document," the tribunal said.

It was a defeat for the public interest arguments from *Re Howard and Treasurer* and showed the issue of income tax might prove a key weapon in the war against secrecy and censorship.

Under the FOI Act, documents can be exempted from release for various reasons, although the object of the act is to extend as far as possible the rights of all Australians to access government documents. Almost all exemptions contain a test where documents can be released if in the public interest.

Sadly, the present Australian prime minister, John Howard, as a young opposition minister, had lost an FOI battle in 1985 when the then AAT president, Justice Davies, defined public interest in the case. According to the judgment, there were five factors contrary to disclosure of information. These factors suggest a profoundly stupid electorate best left untroubled by any inconvenient information about the government.

First, the higher the office of the persons involved in communications and the more sensitive the issues, the more likely the communication should not be disclosed. Second, disclosure of communications made during the development of policy tends not to be in the public interest. Third, disclosure that will inhibit frankness and candor in future communications is likely to be contrary to the public interest. Fourth, disclosure leading to confusion and unnecessary debate resulting from disclosure of possibilities considered tends not to be in the public interest. Finally, disclosure of documents not fairly disclosing the reasons for decisions subsequently taken may be unfair to a decision maker and may prejudice the integrity of the decision-making process.

These factors all ignore the real intent of the FOI Act—to improve transparency so the public is better informed and the government more accountable. Secret government is bad government. But the case of *Re Howard and Treasurer* has been used repeatedly to keep secrets from the electorate as an argument that the public has no right to know about policy under consideration because the electorate's knowledge will hamper government!

For two years, I worked as the *Courier Mail*'s FOI coordinator, further improving the processes used to get stories and developing new approaches in the relatively benign environment offered by the state government. The investigations yielded ample front-page stories on state-based issues and proved FOI could be made to work.

About that time, Chris Mitchell was appointed editor-in-chief of the country's only national broadsheet—the *Australian*—also published by News Ltd. Without his support and news judgment, my stories would have been buried. In late 2003, after an offer from Mitchell, I was appointed Australia's first ever FOI editor on the leading newspaper in the country. Reporting directly to Mitchell and given a free-ranging brief to "break news" and push back the boundaries on FOI, I had landed my dream job.

While it took some months to lodge and battle new requests, by early February the next year, I was starting to produce significant national stories. In Australia, there is a system of free medical care in which the government subsidizes visits to a doctor. This is called bulk billing, and access to free medical care had remained a key issue for many political parties.

In early February 2004, I used FOI to obtain documents that revealed that bulk billing was in free fall, with rates dropping by as much as 1 percent a month and bureaucrats unable to predict how far the decline would go. This contradicted the prime minister's statement to parliament two months earlier: "Any suggestion that bulk billing has disappeared or is disappearing, given the rates of bulk billing in Australia at the present time, is factually incorrect."

Within days, then federal health minister Kay Patterson announced reform plans, and bulk billing remained a key issue throughout the 2004 election campaign. Typically, the health department has since learned the error of such openness and opted for censorship using taxpayer-funded lawyers in the AAT. In 2005, the department fought my subsequent request for more-up-to-date documents right up to the AAT, where I lost the case representing myself. It was an appalling judgment. Apparently, it was not in the public interest for Australians to know about reform options considered by their government of a taxpayer-funded free health system!

Another success was in September 2004, when I used FOI to reveal that almost one million Australian families effectively lose sixty cents of every extra dollar they earn, despite five years of the Howard government's welfare changes and tax cuts. Over two years, FOI produced many stories, including fraud and corruption in indigenous organizations, a major government agency making 1.3 million mistakes in a four-month period, more than 250,000 children living in homes afflicted by domestic violence in an "expensive epidemic" costing AUS$8.1 billion a year, Australian soldiers sent to Afghanistan to fight the Taliban suffering severe side effects from an anthrax vaccine, and more than AUS$35 million owed to workers under a government scheme set up to protect employee rights after companies go broke. But the majority of FOI requests were still denied, delayed, or answered only in part because of public interest exemptions arising from *Re Howard and Treasurer*.

The existence of those dreaded public interest arguments were a primary motivation when I lodged two FOI requests with the treasury relating to income tax and the First Home Buyers Scheme (FHBS) just weeks after starting on the *Australian*. At the same time, I lodged a request with the Department of Foreign Affairs seeking information on whether suspected terrorist David Hicks was being legally held by the United States government in Cuba. The information I sought from treasury on income tax related to so-called bracket creep. In Australia, when workers are pushed into higher income-tax brackets by rising wages, the government collects more revenue, which it claims credit for when it is handed back as tax cuts. I had sought information on whether the FHBS had been responsible for fueling a residential housing boom that had ruined the dream of home ownership for many Australians.

All three requests were refused—again on internal appeal, leaving me no option but to challenge the AAT as an unrepresented client. The tribunal would judge the public interest arguments for and against release, and I was quietly confident, having won some eight appeals out of ten representing myself. But on the doorsteps of the court, the government struck a massive blow in favor of censorship. Under a little-known area of the FOI Act, ministers can issue so-called conclusive certificates stating document release cannot and should not occur. The key difference is the issue judged by the tribunal is not the public interest in favor or against release but whether it is reasonable for the certificate to be issued. And typically, the certificates, particularly those from the treasurer, relied on the appalling arguments from *Re Howard and Treasurer* to justify their issue.

The editor-in-chief was immediately supportive and understood what was at stake. The certificates had to be challenged, or, in the future, the government would use them at every turn to hide embarrassing secrets. While attempts were made to directly negotiate with the government, a paltry offer of a handful of documents was easily judged to be meaningless. Government lawyers released hundreds of largely boring pages a few weeks later because these papers could not be lawfully exempted from release. The government had simply offered us documents we were going to receive in any case. I decided to pursue the David Hicks documents myself because that certificate was based on security and protection of international relations with the United States—a much more difficult challenge. Hicks was probably a terrorist. He had trained with the Taliban and supported its loathsome philosophies. But he remained innocent until proven guilty and deserving of protection from arrest by a foreign power—even one as close and warmly regarded as the United States is in Australia.

While the costs were formidable, we decided to proceed. A superb legal team was assembled. An array of excellent witnesses and solid arguments were developed to be presented to the acting head of the AAT and Federal Court Judge Justice Downes, with both the bracket creep and FHBS appeals now joined together as one appeal.

My plan was to run the Hicks appeal straight after the treasury case—so I could learn from one how to attack the other, given that I would be able to watch closely the strategy and tactics of my legal team. Even so, both cases were complicated by secret hearings in which the government gave its evidence to the judge behind closed doors.

Our witnesses challenged the very basis of *Re Howard and Treasurer*. Lawyer Alan Rose was president of the Australian Law Reform Commission when it undertook a review of the 1982 FOI Act. He was also a former secretary of the commonwealth attorney-general's department and the Department of Community Services and a deputy secretary of the Department of Prime Minister and Cabinet.

Rose argued that the release of the subject matter in the *Australian*'s FOI requests would be "of interest to many citizens in Australia" and help voters make an informed choice at the ballot box. Critically, he testified that the government's public interest arguments—that, for example, bureaucrats would not give free and frank advice if they knew it could be publicly released—simply did not reflect the reality of the public service at work.

Peter Dixon was a professor at Melbourne's Monash University and director of its Centre of Policy Studies, specializing in economic modeling. One of Australia's foremost experts, Dixon argued all taxpayers were affected by, and potentially interested in, bracket creep. He told the tribunal that "with access to the Treasury documents, it is likely that applied economists in Australia, including myself, would improve their analyses of the extent to which the Government's tax cuts in the 2004–2005 budget and earlier budgets are genuine, that is, in excess of compensation for bracket creep. Such analyses are important in assessing the extent to which tax cuts represent a dividend from good economic management." The cases lasted about three weeks, with some of my other appeals to the AAT now being held over because of the importance of the decision to future cases.

Effectively, we argued that the public had a right to know and that *Re Howard and Treasurer* represented an outdated and patronizing view of the public and what it could understand.

After three weeks of costly and lengthy legal arguments, the cases concluded. And just before Christmas 2004, the decisions were e-mailed to my computer terminal. It took only minutes to work out that I had failed. Not only had I failed to push back *Re Howard and Treasury*; a new case would be used to justify secrecy and censorship—with my name on it. I could accept the Hicks decision—even if I had proved he was denied consular support and treated as special case—because of the security issues. But the treasury decision came like sledgehammer to the stomach. The AAT had found a new concept: Release of the treasury documents would be against the public interest because it would interfere with the "smooth" running of government. AAT acting president Justice Downes found both certificates were issued reasonably.

"The primary role of government is to govern. Interference

with the smooth carrying out of that role will be against the public interest," the judgment said. "There remains a legitimate potential public interest in letting government get on with its role without unnecessary intrusion and distraction." Justice Downes saw the Australian public, media, and analysts as easily confused and unable to distinguish provisional and tentative findings from final conclusions and to have complex data accurately explained. At a number of times in his decisions, Justice Downes could have chosen to improve or damage the role played by secrecy and confidentiality in the Australian government, but at the most critical points in the decisions, Justice Downes made findings or used reasoning which will be exploited by Australian governments, state and federal, to justify claims for secrecy.

Sadly, despite the talented legal team and buckets of money and time, I lost. The editor-in-chief was thankfully supportive, but I knew the concept of freedom of information legislation as a means of attacking secrecy had received a terrible wound, possibly fatal, as any minister could now use a conclusive certificate to impose censorship without fear of challenge.

Compelled by failure but without real hope, I sought approval for funding for an appeal against the judgment to the full bench of the Federal Court. Last week, the response came. The appeal would be funded.

McKinnon v. Treasury may still end up being the death knell of FOI in Australia if it stands. It may still dramatically improve the government's ability to censor potentially damaging information and thwart informed choices at the ballot box. But not yet; instead, the learned judges of the Federal Court may decide democracy and its citizens not only deserve but demand open and accountable government.

Chapter 13

CLUELESS IN COUP COUP LAND

MICHAEL FIELD

Michael Field has been covering the Pacific since 1975, with the last fifteen years spent as the correspondent for Agence France-Presse (AFP). A New Zealander, he has worked for the main domestic news agency and newspapers before working as a volunteer in Botswana and in Samoa, where he became editor of a government newspaper and the prime minister's press secretary. As a result of that experience, Field wrote the book *Mau* on the independence struggle in the Pacific nation. New York's Commonwealth Fund awarded Field a Harkness Fellowship to attend the John F. Kennedy School of Government at Harvard. Based in Auckland, Field has covered the major dramas and issues of the Pacific for AFP, has written papers and articles for specialist regional publications, and occasionally lectures on Pacific politics at universities in New Zealand and Fiji.

At a kava ceremony in Tau, I was welcomed by a talking chief in the stilted phrases of his office.

In my reply, I alluded to the common origin of the Polynesian somewhere in Asia and the wonderful voyages our ancestors had made in peopling Polynesia.

The talking chief replied: "We thank you for your interesting speech. The Polynesians may have come from Asia, but the Samoans, no. We originated in Samoa."

He looked around with an air of infallibility, and his fellow scholars grunted their approval.

In self-defence, I became a fundamentalist. I said; "The good book that I have seen you carrying to church three times on Sundays says that the first parents of mankind were Adam and Eve, who were created in the Garden of Eden."

In no way disturbed, the oracle replied; "That may be but the Samoans were created here in Manu'a."

A trifle exasperated, I said; "Ah, I must be in the Garden of Eden."

I took the silence that followed to be a sign of affirmation.

—*Vikings of the Sunrise* by Peter Buck (1938)

Traditional culture is everything in the South Pacific. For a journalist to offend, change, or challenge it or offer anything other than unswerving admiration is to take a risky road. This is why the little preceding tale from celebrated New Zealand Maori anthropologist Sir Peter Buck (1880–1951) is my favored opening talisman. Coming from the youngest branch of the Polynesian family, Buck perhaps felt he should have easily understood his older cousins, but at times, he found himself struggling with the profound arrogance that sustains many who live on small isolated islands scattered across the South Pacific. Extensive contact with the outside world makes little difference, and Buck's words produce a wry recognition among the small band of correspondents who get to cover the islands of Melanesia, Micronesia, and Polynesia. Everything is different; no means yes, and "off the record" ensures it will be tomorrow's headline. Simple things make all the difference; a double-negative question in Polynesia can be guaranteed to result in reporting mistakes, while hospitality and politeness obligations mean contacts often give reporters the answer they think they want rather than the real answer. Culture, while providing the color, warmth, and sense of purpose for its people, also carries the dead hand of censorship; many local reporters will not go into areas normally the provenance of chiefs, while outside reporters often face the high-level criticism of being cultural imperialists at worst or insensitive clods at best.

For all that, and for the problems and dramas further on in this chapter, one of the secrets of South Seas reporting is its sheer richness and often-startling originality. While the Western media can lightly dismiss the Pacific Islands with the tag "paradise," the region offers up marvelous stories of drama, intrigue, confusion, lust, and love in a form that many of our big city compatriots would never come across. As it happens, many of the major characters of big news stories in the Pacific are approachable and accessible in a way outsider journalists would find both bewildering and touching. I feel a fondness for the Pacific people and a strong belief that the fisherman struggling on the Tarawa lagoon each day to feed his family has as much right as any Wall Street broker to his point of view. What has always struck me though is that there are so few reporters in the Pacific seeking out the stories; the bright lights of a different kind of fame seduce many more.

Growing up in New Zealand did not set me up for a career covering the Pacific. Although much of the rest of the world views New Zealand as a couple of South Pacific islands, in my youth that nation simply did not see itself that way. Rather, it was a somewhat misplaced extension of Britain. Perhaps this is why so many good New Zealand journalists ended up in Fleet Street, the emotional headquarters of the Kiwi reporter's soul. I went the other way and found myself one day sailing into the harbor of Fiji's capital, Suva. Wisps of rain swept through the surrounding high mountains of Viti Levu Island, and an appropriately named peak called Joske's Thumb seemed to give assent to the arrival. It was intensely green with many shades of blue. The Suva market was full of things I had never seen—taro, breadfruit, mango, papaws—while the sellers were astonishing-looking people, big Polynesians from eastern Fiji; the strong-looking Bau Islanders, with proud stocks of black, crinkly hair; and Indians, descendants of contract labor brought in by the British to grow sugar cane. This South Seas world had captivated others earlier—Robert Louis Stevenson, Paul Gauguin, and Herman Melville, among many others—and lured with its intimacy and culturally rich characters. The world of spin and control, so evident in much of the West, has yet to plague the Pacific Islands, and access to presidents and prime ministers is blessedly easy—so long as they know the reporter will take them seriously. However, in the last decade, as economic decline and corruption have begun to beset the islands, reporting has taken on an edge and a unique kind of danger associated with civil unrest and coups.

Living in the United States, I had missed Fiji's first coup in 1987. The army's number three, Lt. Col. Sitiveni Rabuka, marched into the old Legislative Assembly chamber (a room I later spent a big part of my reporting time in—two coups and a change of occupant) and overthrew a government led by an indigenous Fijian but dominated by Indians. Ironically, Rabuka had studied military coups at the Indian Army Staff College. If the Pacific had been paradise found before that, it certainly was paradise lost after it. He promptly imposed censorship, and several reporters found themselves detained and roughed up. Fiji won more international media attention than its eight hundred thousand people might have normally warranted because Rabuka, dark, witty, and handsome, had the kind of media persona for which any politician would sell a soul or two. Moreover, Fiji, as a major tourist destination, was attractive to cover because it had good hotels, nightclubs, and telecommunications. Situations in other Pacific countries were not so easily covered, and the mainstream media mostly ignored them.

One such was the island of Bougainville in the eastern part of the sprawling nation of Papua New Guinea (PNG). An Australian mining company, CRA, created one of the world's largest open-caste mines in the center of the island. The local people, resentful of the environmental damage and the way in which they received few benefits, tried to break away from PNG. From around 1989, the island plunged into a vicious war that went mostly unreported. Several colleagues—including Sean Dorney of the Australian Broadcasting Commission and Mary-Louise O'Callaghan of the *Australian*—were notable for their coverage, often at high personal risk, but, for the most part, the war was conducted in a journalistic no-go-zone and claimed around 5 percent of the 180,000 people. The main guerrilla force, the Bougainville Revolutionary Army (BRA), was sometimes denied credibility simply because, as one international editor put it to me, "How can we take an organization called 'bra' seriously?" I covered the conflict at some distance for a while, but by 1996 it had begun spilling out of the island and across the narrow Bougainville Strait into the Shortland Islands, part of the separate nation of the Solomon Islands.

For most Americans, the Solomon Islands meant one story—Guadalcanal, Red Beach, PT109, a young John F. Kennedy, and a line on the Marine Corps monument. For the four hundred thousand people of the Solomons, it is an astonishingly beautiful and until recently peaceful nation trying to live by its tourist moniker, "The Happy Isles." Bougainvilleans and Solomon Islanders are ethnically related, so it was not altogether surprising that the war would spread across the border and go almost unreported. In 1996, I went up to the Shortlands to find out what was happening.

One of the curiosities of Pacific journalism is that you now and again come across interesting, dramatic stories that are completely unreported, with no sign of competitors on the wind. Such was the case in the Shortlands, which was living in terror as warring factions from Bougainville brutalized the Solomon Islanders. The Papua New Guinea Defence Force (PNGDF) mounted regular helicopter and fast-boat raids across the border. In these parts of the world, the locals often think reporters can do more than we can, and some welcomed my presence. Others took shots at me, all fortunately missing. A Solomon Islands immigration officer—who called himself "Billy the Kid"—gleefully arrested me and said he would have to escort me back to the capital. Several days of dangerous traveling revealed his real motive; I was his ticket out of hell. My stories on Agence France-Presse's wire—as well as photo spreads in the *New Zealand Herald* and the now sadly defunct *Pacific Island Monthly* (published in Fiji, it was Rupert Murdoch's smallest publication and closed during the 2000 coup there)—gave much-needed attention to this conflict.

A year later, in March 1997, O'Callaghan broke the news that PNG had hired foreign mercenaries to fight the war and reopen the copper mine. The PNGDF revolted, and the country's capital, Port Moresby, saw what amounted to a coup. I covered the revolt around the dramatic Parliament buildings, much of the time concerned for my own safety, given Moresby's infamous mix of criminal gangs and political opportunists. What was more worrying, and continues to afflict Pacific reportage, is that the drama brought in scores of reporters unfamiliar with the territory or culture and motivated mainly by ratings. What was known as the "Sandline crisis," after the name of the British mercenary firm, was somehow transformed into an Australian story in which rumors of Australian takeover moved from a long shot to the main agenda item—at least in the traveling media's eyes. Almost in spite of the media's headlines during that crisis, there were behind-the-scenes efforts to end the conflict, and, in one of those treasured moments that make Pacific journalism special, in April 1998 a small group of journalists were present in Arawa, Bougainville, for a truce ceremony. Most of BRA's guerrillas came out of the hills and, in the presence of unarmed Australian and New Zealand soldiers, literally broke their spears. That day, which saw headlines and coverage around the world, was a special but fleeting moment.

Around 1997–98, the Solomons was hosting film crews shooting the Oscar-nominated movie *The Thin Red Line*, which told of the wartime experiences on Guadalcanal. (Its stars Sean Penn, George Clooney, Woody Harrison, et al. did not have to risk Guadalcanal's malaria—their scenes were filmed at an Australian tourist resort.) Odd things were happening behind the scenes—several boats were stolen, a couple of people assaulted, a number of rapes. Only slowly did it dawn locally that this was the beginning of an ethnic conflict. The combatants used a patchwork of old World War II weapons as the indigenous people of Guadalcanal fought for control of the island from migrants from neighboring Malaita Island. The capital Honiara, a former US wartime base on Guadalcanal, became a Malaitan enclave, and for local reporters this meant that covering a story beyond the end of Henderson Field International Airport and out in the countryside was risky to the point of being impossible. The small group of foreign journalists who did go beyond key bridges often hoped that skin color alone would be enough to prevent harm.

In 1999, Dorney and I went out to a distant village where Rabuka—the former coup leader who had just lost a democratic election in Fiji—was a commonwealth-appointed peace negotiator. The day before, another reporter and I had been in the same area when rebels emerged from the palm oil plantation to surround us. My colleague panicked as the men raised their weapons at us, but I had found the experience rather different and somewhat dangerously found myself believing, if not in my own invulnerability, that doing harm to me would have no point and so would not happen. We survived that day, and, on the next day, we attended Rabuka's talks, where rebel leader George Grey held court. A bank clerk in regular life, he had donned combat fatigues and wore an unusual headgear made up of curtain rings.

"We are fighting a holy war," he announced. "The trees are fighting, the stones are fighting, and women and the children are fighting."

I talked to Grey, trying to figure out this hatred of Malaita people, which had been going on for something like thirty thousand years.

"Do you know what we call them," he asked me. "Dog sperm."

Of course, it was a vile comment, but some of the people at the peace talks under the huge spreading tree had that week been involved in murder and pillage at a nearby village. Cultural sensitivity had not saved them. I used the quote in my piece for AFP, and then it bounced back into the Solomons, where it was picked up by the small Honiara newspaper the *Solomons Star* and the state-run Solomon Islands Broadcasting Corporation (SIBC). What was surprising was the way in which SIBC and the *Star* used the comment and then accompanied it with suitable outrage on the nature of culturally insensitive foreigners. In the University of the South Pacific's newspaper *Wanasolwara*, SIBC general manager Johnson Honimae said, "Overseas journalists don't care what happens as a result of their stories. If that reporter was in Honiara, he would have been killed." In fact, I was in Honiara and somebody managed to leave a World War II–era .50-caliber bullet on my hotel pillow as the quote got around town.

As we left the peace talks in the village, another group of rebels surrounded our car and decided they wanted to take us prisoner. There were several hundred rebels, and, as if drawn from some boy's own adventure novel, they were mostly naked other than a loincloth that hid little. They carried axes, bows and arrows, and a frightening array of homemade weapons that amounted to little more than a wartime bullet strapped onto bamboo. Friend and foe alike would have been in trouble had they ever been fired. I ended up outside the car and was roughed up; my watch was stolen, and I was becoming seriously concerned for my future. By chance, Rabuka and a commonwealth diplomat, Ade Adefuye, happened along the road. For the rebels, it was a startling moment; they had heard of fellow Melanesian Rabuka but had never seen him. Rabuka caused me a moment or so of concern when he pointed to me and told the rebels, "They are not with us." A soldier with long experience in Lebanon, Rabuka knew what he was doing, and I was impressed with his cool command of the scene, casting his eyes around to work out who was where and who had what. We were freed, and much later Adefuye, who is from Nigeria, told me, "Man, you were shaking." No question. Unusually, while we had roadside discussions on freedom and liberation, international media outlets that did not have people on the ground began reporting that Rabuka and the journalists had been kidnapped. I still do not know how that story evolved. What was also intriguing was that the South Seas beat of mine is very intimate, too; within a year, in another country and another coup, the same cast of characters were names in a new notebook.

Four years later, the ethnic conflict ended when Australian forces, acting under the mandate of sixteen Pacific nations, landed and restored order. D-day was in marked contrast to the start of the conflict; dozens of journalists were on the scene, and the Australian Department of Foreign Affairs flew in its best spin doctors to control things. On "Red Beach"—the same Red Beach that in 1942 the US Marines had come ashore on—the media managers had reporters placed in the best spots, with the sun and reflecting sea accounted for, so that the landings would get the best coverage. One photographer had come with small Australian flags, and he gave one to a hapless Solomon Island woman who was doing her gardening. He encouraged her to wave it at the landing soldiers, and after he took this spontaneous shot, he collected the flag and wandered off to find another subject. The force consisted of soldiers from several Pacific countries; the Fijians, with years of peacekeeping experience, quickly settled in and had no problem with the media. If, through some extraordinary accident unforeseen by the spin doctors, a reporter managed to speak to an Australian soldier, then the grunt was prepared for this eventuality. He or she would whip out a laminated card that carried all the approved responses they could give to a reporter.

Journalism in the South Pacific is young. The *Fiji Times*, now owned by Rupert Murdoch's News Corp., was founded in 1869 and claims in its masthead to be the first newspaper published in the world each day—a benefit of proximity to the international dateline. With no written language until English missionaries arrived, the Pacific was and largely remains a predominantly oral culture. The first newspapers and then radio tended to be run by white settlers and were supportive of the colonial governments. News from outside world came in with sailing ships and banana boats. Until late in the twentieth century, Pacific Islands received spasmodic news. Niuafo'ou in Tonga is also known as "Tin Can Island" for the way mail and newspapers were stuffed into big biscuit tins and tossed overboard. Island swimmers would recover the news. While shortwave radio had an important role for the island elite, it is the Internet and global satellite television that has had a seismic effect, even on the remotest of islands. The Solomon Islands offered a dramatic example of this. In the midst of the ethnic conflict, scattered villagers kept contact with the outside world through e-mail. Each tiny village had a laptop computer, solar power, and a trained woman who could take dictation from illiterates who wanted to send messages or obtain goods. A small, community-based Internet provider kept the whole thing operating on shortwave, outwitting the bad guys who were tearing the nation apart.

The shortwave radio broadcasters in the region—Radio Australia and Radio New Zealand International—continue, although these days mostly in a rebroadcast form on local island radio services. BBC Television and CNN now reach into and affect Pacific nations. Several American religious broadcasters and the Chinese government also pump in satellite services. Only a few nations—Kiribati, Solomons, and Tuvalu—have no television services, and the effect of that for visiting reporters is often to find a population affectingly naive about cameras. The crushing isolation that colored life in the South Pacific has been lifted, and it cuts both ways: The outside world can now get to hear more of the Pacific than it used to, and reality has replaced the romantic vision that has cursed the place ever since the first sex-starved white sailors stumbled across Polynesians. This exposure to the outside world on a hitherto unknown scale has impacted strongly on local media. Often the global media swamp them; newspapers in the region are bulked up with wire service copy that some pay for, and vast amounts of news, features, and photos are looted off the Internet.

However, this new information flow threatens the political status quo, particularly in Polynesia, where aging male chiefs have always held power. Journalism does not sit comfortably with them, particularly when they find that those who write and tell stories are young, untitled, and often female and are usually better educated. Admittedly, the South Pacific has been spared the excesses of the worst journalist oppression. Reporters have at most been roughed up, and there have been odd incidents of arson and abuse, but death and injury have yet to be a consequence of a story. Still, the dreaded word *culture* sometimes feels like a hand grenade in a newsroom and creates tensions among journalists themselves.

Culture itself is news and often the key motive behind the headlines. In 1987 Rabuka had staged his coup because he believed indigenous Fijians had a God-given right, literally, to rule in a country where, at that time, Indians and Fijians made up around a fifty-fifty split. By 1999 Rabuka had seen the light and backed off a racially based constitution, and in general elections that year, he was ejected from office, replaced by Indian Mahendra Chaudhry. Fiji newsrooms reflected the national tension; the year Chaudhry was in office was afflicted with a racist hostility among reporters. On May 19, 2000, a year to the day after Chaudhry's election win, bankrupt businessman George Speight led a group of special forces soldiers into Fiji's new Parliament and took Chaudhry and his government hostage. Speight, who could not speak Fijian, proclaimed he was doing it for "the vanua," the people of the land, the indigenous, the extended family, the clan. Speight took it to mean even more than that, a kind of master-race concept. Speight's coup was devastating for Fiji, but also inept. He failed to take control beyond the Parliamentary Complex, and Fiji's fiercely competitive media found themselves with unexpected freedom to report. Making matters even more confusing was that, while a hostage situation existed with politicians held captive by terrorists, the police and the military did nothing to block access for much of what was to become a fifty-six-day-long standoff. Speight seized Parliament just before lunchtime; by the afternoon, he had held a press conference and a swearing-in ceremony. Reporters were able to come and go, almost at will, along with hundreds of coup supporters. Armed rebel guards usually demanded only some form of identification to get in: I used a press card issued to cover a New Zealand tour by a British royal some years before.

For many reporters involved, it was an extraordinary novelty, covering the Pacific and being on the inside of a hostage drama. Speight held daily press conferences. As his media manipulation grew, timed for the mainly Australian television news shows, some reporters began showing signs of the Stockholm Syndrome and referred to Speight by his first name. One even took pleasure at taking bullets out of the rebel cartridges. His horrified photographer got him to pose for a picture with a bullet between his teeth. That was then sent to his employer, and the guy was on the next plane out.

For those of us who had a long experience with Fiji, the scene was a nightmare. The town outside had been ransacked; schools were closed; there was a nightly curfew. Moreover, the government was bundled up in a room nearby and occasionally beaten, while nearby Speight backslapped his way through press conferences. Many of us found the thought of laughter being heard by the prisoners nearby hard to take. Lives were at risk. Yet at one press conference a row broke out among reporters when a BBC microphone stand offended television rivals. They protested so much that Speight's thugs physically manhandled the BBC's Phil Mercer in order to please them—who said dog doesn't eat dog?

Throughout the crisis, the fact that the media were daily entering Parliament and giving a wider voice to Speight and his gang was a matter of fierce controversy. Diplomats, while often pumping us for information on what was happening, condemned us for going in. The occasional foreign minister would also weigh in from a high moral platform.

Veteran Radio Australia correspondent Graeme Dobell, who was present in Suva part of the time, described the free access to the Parliament as an "extraordinary experience. . . . Partly, the access was possible because this was not just a terrorist crime. It was also part of a political process. . . . Usually the only areas reporters could not visit were the chamber and executive offices where the hostages were held."

Certainly, there were issues to debate, and early in the crisis reporters were more the story than observers. One such moment occurred when the military decided it had had enough of the open access and erected barricades around Parliament. Speight, accompanied by his usual media crowd at the time, then marched out to confront the barricades. The military appeared determined to defend its barricades, but Speight marched toward them, surrounded by the media, who formed a tight protective scrum around him. I was standing with the soldiers at the first barricade; any attempt to halt Speight and his men would have involved hitting reporters who were around him. Speight got to the barrier and with his followers, closely followed by the media, tore the barricade down. Speight then headed to another barricade. This time his men kept his media behind him; pictures showed the coup leader boldly walking toward barricades he knew were not going to be a barrier to him. Journalists were not just covering the story; they were the story, the tools of Speight's tactical skills.

Media management is tricky at the best of times, and, a couple of days later, it went wrong. Just outside Parliament, gunfire broke out, wounding two soldiers and an Associated Press Television cameraman, Jerry Harmer. Speight later accused the media of "stampeding" and play acting to achieve a bigger pay raise. On the night of May 28, 2000, things worsened when Speight's people left Parliament and went across town to attack the Fiji TV studios following a current-affairs program they took exception to. They trashed the place. Nobody was hurt, but Fiji TV was intimidated by the event, and a large number of foreign reporters loaded up a fleet of taxis and left town. Part of the fear was racially based. The hundreds of supporters who crowded into Parliament to be with Speight were mostly hill tribesmen, and media mythology had it that they were not too far removed from cannibalism.

The real risk came later in the siege. Speight used to send word of planned press conferences down to the main business hotel. Unusually, he set one up for just after dark, and, in the tropics, it gets dark very quickly. Only a small group of local and foreign reporters bothered to go, and Speight did not show. Those of us on the inside did not know that outside the rebels had locked the gates and were not letting anybody else in. After an hour of waiting, we voted to leave and were on the way out when an Australian reporter changed her mind and said she would stay. It was a case of all in or all out, so we stayed. Speight showed up and announced we could not leave while allowing us to keep equipment and mobile phones. For very little effort, Speight, in the space of half an hour or so, was able to escalate the tension and press home to the increasingly impotent military that he had not played his whole hand yet. He could watch it all play out on BBC and the Internet. Again, the individual reactions were something of a revelation. Some reporters telephoned homes and partners; others phoned their newsrooms. Some found it terrifying; others were indifferent to it on a personal level, just seeing a good story. As one who was not worried, I had not a case of bravado but rather a kind of situational rationalization. Of course, the rationale could have been completely wrong, and in such ways are reporters killed elsewhere.

The intimacy of the Pacific that makes it so attractive to work in came out in the coup. At one point, the commonwealth secretary general, Don McKinnon, arrived to try to negotiate an end to the crisis. With him was the Nigerian diplomat Ade Adefuye, whom I knew from the Solomon Islands. After a couple of behind-closed-doors negotiations, he wanted to dictate his notes at two in the morning. In the Solomons, I had helped him draft a peace treaty; in Fiji I typed up the notes of what had happened—in the full knowledge that I could also have them exclusively for an AFP story. Rabuka, who had no role in the 2000 coup, also tried to negotiate an end to the siege. At his press conferences, he seemed to draw comfort from having reporters he knew around him. When that comfort was not rewarded with soft questions, he would seem hurt by what he perceived as aggressive questioning. The intimacy showed in numerous other ways, tip-offs from people who you might not normally expect to be important and access to key documents through the inevitable extended family leaks. Secrets cannot be kept for long in the Pacific. Many of the Pacific's presidents and prime ministers are refreshingly accessible to the media—sometimes they even answer their own phones.

The one question not really tackled by the reporters but that vexed authorities around the Pacific was, why did reporters keep going into Parliament? My view was simple: One had to because that was where the story was. The presence of so many reporters so close to the action prevented a worse tragedy, and subsequent court actions revealed the plotters did intend at various points to kill their hostages, particularly the prime minister. For most Western reporters, the issue of crossing police lines in hostage or terrorist situations simply does not arise; police will not allow it. The physical risks were plain enough, as Jerry Harmer illustrated, but Fiji, like much of the Pacific, swims in a sea of rumor and half-truth, and actually being on the ground is essential. After it was all over and the hostages were freed (but never allowed to return to government), Speight and company were arrested. I spent a large part of two years sitting in the Fiji High Court watching various trials; the court sat in the room that had been the debating chamber that Rabuka had stormed in the 1987 coup. In the court hearings, much of the crucial evidence came from media accounts of events as well as testimony from reporters who attended those press conferences. Speight's vanity ultimately got him, and he was convicted of treason and jailed for life.

One last word on the Fiji coup and why I gave this "Coup Coup" title to the chapter. The 2000 coup was Fiji's third and easily the most protracted, with reporters and photographers staying for weeks at a time in a Suva hotel. Suva is a small town. The international media were a subject of fascination, awe, and contempt for the locals, so finally the *Fiji Times* asked me to write an inside story on international media life.

"This is a story of hardship, of long hours of tedium, terrible food, wet and cold clothes, per diems and lying, tragedy and yes, worst of all, mixed up laundry orders," I began the piece.

Recounting some of the worst parts of media life, I wrote, "Much of what we write and broadcast would shock people in Fiji, possibly because it seems mostly superficial and often inaccurate (most stories mention sugar production figures and the ratio of Indians to Fijian; like it really matters?). . . . Places like Fiji are expected to provide to readers [around the world] a good-guy-bad-guy story; victims-and-oppressors. Nothing complicated, okay?"

As it turned out, the story really irritated most of my colleagues, and I had a difficult couple of days. Perhaps it was the way I ended it.

So, if you really want to bug the international media get a camera and notebook and run like hell through the lobby of the Centra.

Dozens of reporters and cameramen will run after you—because you will look as if you know what the next story is. We of the international media don't have a clue.

An anonymous but brilliant subeditor gave the feature a headline that came quickly to be the catchphrase used by everybody, politicians, reporters, and academics: "Clueless in Coup Coup Land."

Rebellions and coups are undoubtedly dangerous to cover, but the simple reality for foreign reporters in the Pacific, and perhaps anywhere else, is that driving is easily the most dangerous activity they are likely to take part in. Malaria is a very real risk in some places, and I have been afflicted with both dengue and ciguatera fish poisoning—both endemic—and know they can easily be fatal in some circumstances. Covering general elections in Fiji one year, several of us hired a small boat to go upriver to a troubled village when, seemingly out of nowhere, a church choir group climbed into the boat, and drowning seemed a very real prospect.

Another occasionally significant part of the Pacific beat are disasters, mostly hurricanes, sometimes drought, earthquakes, and, blessedly rare, tsunami. Experience does not necessarily help in the face of disaster, as Sean Dorney, twenty years working in

Port Moresby, found when a tsunami hit PNG's northern coastline at Aitape in 1998. The disaster in which over two thousand people died had no equal in his experience, particularly because of the tensions between those involved in the rescue work and those trying to report it. He recalled a helicopter pilot who worked tirelessly to save lives and his outrage that film crews were interested only in pictures.

In a world where journalists are often killed, the trials and tribulations of Pacific reporters can seem almost romantic by comparison. *Time* magazine's Australia edition in 2002 put out a special Pacific issue and noted how one of its reporters had heroically drunk kava in her pursuit of stories. Kava, a mildly narcotic ceremonial drink, is widely quaffed, but so many Western media practice a form of "Paradise Journalism" that reduces Pacific people to the status of noble savages and make reporters seem akin to explorers. Non-Pacific reporters, often on airline freebies, declare how beautiful the beaches are and how happy the natives. Cultures and societies are reduced to one dimension—dancing and kava. Another popular line in Western stories is to refer to the beauty of the singing in the dozens of Christian church services across the Pacific. No doubt, the singing is beautiful, but seldom does anybody bother to explore the tyranny of the churches behind the singing. Newspapers that do, mostly in Fiji and Samoa, often find themselves slammed over their coverage. Christianity is a strong part of culture in the Pacific and is thus embraced by its politicians. If one applies the Western model of the first three estates of power—the clergy, the nobility, and the bourgeoisie—one sees in the Pacific a remarkable concentration in the hands of just one man. (It is never a woman.) The Marshall Islands, Samoa, and Tonga have had heads of state and government who are also the senior figure in church and in traditional nobility. In places where this occurs, high rates of youth suicide are also features of the local culture; some think this is more than a coincidence.

An attack on the church can often be portrayed as an attack on culture. In 2003, for example, a Nigerian-based German faith healer, Reinhard Bonnke, was in Fiji and attracted enormous audiences. President Josefa Iloilo and Prime Minister Laisenia Qarase gave him audiences. The police stopped the traffic (police spokesman Mesake Koroi defended this, saying Bonnke was "a diplomat of the biggest nation—heaven"), and one hundred thousand people went to his traveling miracle shows. But when the *Fiji Times* questioned his miracles, government information minister Simione Kaitani issued a statement that the paper "anti-Christ." Several religious groups organized a boycott of the newspaper.

Fiji has often seen arrogance from leaders toward the media. When newspapers revealed that the state-owned National Bank of Fiji was lending F$220 million in sweetheart deals to political friends and allies who were not paying it back, finance minister Berenado Vunibobo said press freedom was an imported idea. Journalists should face up to their responsibilities and stop covering the bank's misfortunes "hysterically" he said. The bank went broke, and the money was not repaid.

For Western reporters who try to cover more than just the paradise routines, banning orders follow. Kiribati, in the central Pacific, was an intriguing example of a small nation unable to cope with journalism. Its one big moment in global history was the Battle of Tarawa during World War II, when US Marines seized it from the Japanese. On the 287-acre islet of Betio the battle raged for three days, at a cost of six thousand men killed. Bones and bombs still emerge sixty years on. I had gone there in 1999 to research an intriguing wartime story about executions, but the environmental story was of more immediate news interest. So too were the international intrigue and censorship, all under the watch of President Teburoro Tito. His predecessor, Ieremia Tabai, had been trying to run a radio station in competition with the government station, but, for several years, Tito's government refused it a licence to operate. A nation of low-lying atolls, Kiribati has in recent years been on the international stage, claiming it faced doom through rises in the sea level that resulted from the impact of greenhouse gases from unthinking industrial nations. While the question of its sinking or not has been the subject of fierce controversy, what I found was an environmental disaster entirely of local making.

Tarawa, grossly overpopulated and without appropriate infrastructure, is a fetid rubbish dump dominated by human sewage. Before going there, I had known that the Chinese government had eighteen months earlier built a satellite-monitoring station on Tarawa, one of only two on-shore facilities the government had outside of China. (The other was in Namibia.) Although a civilian facility that was part of China's space program, it was six hundred miles south of Kwajalein. At that atoll in the Marshall Islands, the US Army maintained a vast base for testing ballistic missiles fired from California and the development of the Star Wars missile defense system.

I was staying with a former cabinet minister in Tarawa, and he took me to see the base. When we got there, two local women were engaged in a dispute at the gate with the Chinese boss of the base. It appeared to be over money for services rendered, and the Chinese man was embarrassed to see a former government official there. Without inquiring who I was, he suddenly invited the two women and the two of us into the base and then left us while he went off with the women. I cannot say I picked up any great secrets; the two Chinese technicians we could talk to were complaining that they could not pick up some football game from the satellite, while the computers I could see merely proved that the Chinese space program ran on Windows 3.1. The satellite dishes that were working were aligned toward the Kwajalein track. My stories on the base created a political storm in Kiribati and played a significant part in the eventual fall of the Tito government. But before that could happen, Tito had me declared an "undesirable migrant" for writing "untruths" about the country's development problems. Neighboring Nauru also imposed a ban on me in sympathy for Kiribati; consequently, I was unable to cover a sixteen-nation Pacific summit there. The subsequent Kiribati government kicked the Chinese base out, diplomatically recognized Taiwan, and lifted the ban on me. Tito, out of a job, then announced his intention to go into a new career—journalism.

The Kingdom of Tonga has a population of around one hundred thousand, ruled by King Taufa'ahau Tupou IV, who has absolute powers and has total control over the Legislative Assembly. Labeled "the Friendly Isles" by explorer James Cook, Tonga is an instructive example of the way in which the Western media fall for the Noble Savage–Paradise Island label. Tongans are portrayed as passive, happy, and loyal subjects of a kindly, fat king. Stories were either of the alleged contentment of Tongans or, perhaps worse, the fat king's amusement at the apparent blind loyalty of his followers. Behind the scenes, but entirely accessible to those who went there, was a growing democracy movement. In 1981 schoolteacher 'Akilisi Pohiva started a radio program called *Matalafo Laukai*, or *Voices of Concern*, for broadcasting on the state's Tonga Broadcasting Commission (TBC). Local people discussed events, and, after clearance by TBC executives, they were broadcast, although often with chunks ordered removed.

In 1984, Pohiva did a program on a large salary increase for cabinet ministers. The show was banned and Pohiva fired from government service. He successfully sued them, with Chief Justice Geoffrey Martin noting in his judgment that guidelines used by TBC on Pohiva's program "display a remarkably tender regard for the dignity of government."

Pohiva founded the newspaper *Ko e Kele'a* ("conch shell") and represented commoners in the third of Parliament elected by universal suffrage. *Kele'a*, an unashamed political pamphlet, was the only competition to the government's weekly *Tonga Chronicle*, a worthy but uncontroversial newspaper owned by the government and published weekly in English and Tongan. *Kele'a* hit the streets with claims of corruption in high places. The *Taimi 'o Tonga* (*Times of Tonga*) was more in the newspaper tradition, although plainly leaning toward the democratic cause, followed it in 1989. I was making regular visits to Tonga, particularly because the head of the Catholic Church in the kingdom, Bishop Patelisio Finau, was quietly agitating for democratic change. Through a mutual friend, I arranged a meeting, and he launched a broadside against the royals. I would like to think the resulting story, which got solid regional play, was the result of my insightful interviewing techniques, but the reality was the bishop had something he wanted to say to a wide audience. He confessed that his attitude toward the Tongan system had changed when, as a priest, he had gone to the prison and given the Last Rites to condemned men just before they were hanged.

He accused the kingdom's elite of "enslaving" commoners and creating an atmosphere of oppression and fear. I asked him whether the word *enslaving* was a bit strong; he thought for a moment and replied no, *enslaving* was the word he wanted to use. The rulers were blinded by power and did not hear those with no voice. Tongans were "more Tongan than truthful." This, he said, created a false loyalty built up around kin connections and a concept of obedience.

"We would betray the truth to be Tongan," he said.

It was strong stuff, and the king, in one of his few media interviews, said Pohiva and Finau were Marxists out to destabilize the country.

Each trip I made to Tonga increasingly seemed like my last. The one that proved to be my last was unusual. I had gone to see the bishop just prior to my departure, and he offered to drive me to the airport. I resisted, but he insisted. I never saw him again—he had a heart attack a couple of weeks later and died. In addition, I was banned from the kingdom by police minister Noble 'Akau'ola.

The trigger had been coverage of one of the king's schemes to make money by selling Tongan citizenship and passports to Hong Kong people ahead of the return of the then Crown Colony to China. It was later proven to be unconstitutional, but even before it got to court, I had received the list of all the new Tongan citizens, which featured some major Asian crime figures and the then exiled Filipino dictator Ferdinand Marcos and his wife, Imelda.

For the *Taimi 'o Tonga* life was no easier. Its publisher, Kalafi Moala, was Tongan born, but, as a US citizen, he had effectively lost his Tongan citizenship. Living in Auckland, New Zealand, he was regularly banned from entering his homeland. A later police minister, Clive Edwards, at one point sent a squad of police to the newspaper office to seize letters to the editor that had been published. Editor Filo 'Akau'ola and two letter writers were tossed in jail and were eventually convicted of the crime of making Edwards angry. In the kingdom, it is against the law to make any public servant—except laborers—angry.

Soon after Edwards repeated his predecessor's ban on me, telling reporters that I had been banned for describing the king as a "baboon." Edwards was never able to specify when and where this piece of reportage occurred—simply because it never had.

My troubles were but a shadow of what Moala faced. The absurdity of the royal rule was underlined in 1996 when the kingdom's life-appointed justice minister, David Tupou, went to the Atlanta Olympics without formal permission of the Speaker, Noble Fusitu'a. In the Assembly, 'Akilisi Pohiva submitted a motion to impeach Tupou. *Taimi 'o Tonga* published the motion before it was tabled, so Edwards had Pohiva, Moala, and *Taimi 'o Tonga* editor Filo 'Akau'ola jailed on a trumped-up charge of offending Parliament. They were eventually released after twenty-eight days of imprisonment—during which time Moala managed to sneak out messages to his wife on toilet paper while she ran the newspaper.

Cultural issues make it difficult for foreign reporters to operate in the South Pacific, but it is infinitely harder for the locals. Fiji journalist Jale Moala, who has edited all the country's main publications and now lives in New Zealand, says the basic principles of journalism apply in the Pacific as they do anywhere else. But social and economic environments are smaller and developing, "factors which contribute to the constriction of scope and leverage that make a political reporter's work even more difficult." Covering Pacific politics was a great challenge, Moala says: "This is because politics in the region is so often mixed up with issues like culture loyalties that it can become difficult for reporters to maintain impartiality and direction, especially if they are themselves part of the cultural group involved."

At first blush, some of it strikes one as petty, except that authorities often hold on to the imagined slights and return the favor with interest with detention at border posts and denials of visas. The issue was highlighted on April 19, 2004, when Fiji's founding prime minister and paramount chief, Ratu Sir Kamisese Mara, died in a private hospital in the capital Suva. He had been president during the May 2000 coup, and, typically for the South Pacific, it was never clear—and remains murky to this day—what really was happening, but in the course of events the military sacked Mara by declaring martial law. Mara was a broken man and soon after suffered a stroke. His publicly funded medical treatment around the world was expensive and lengthy, meaning his condition was a matter of genuine public interest. Therefore, when early that Monday morning he died, it hardly seemed an issue as to whether it should be reported. Fiji custom required the nation's other senior chiefs be advised first, and not by telephone. Heralds had to carry the news and deliver it in person via ornate ceremony to the scattered islands and villages. Of course, the news spread quickly on the so-called Coconut Wireless—the gossip networks—and, thanks to the Internet, expatriate Fijians in other countries heard what had happened. Fiji media, however, did nothing. The Fiji TV head of news and current affairs, Netani Rika, admitted later there had been a lot of debate over what to do if the main evening news bulletin came up and the announcement was still not ready to be made. A Radio Australia correspondent in Fiji, Samisoni Pareti, alerted his Australian bosses that Suva was gripped by news of Mara's death—but could not file on it, as he had been his chief and it was against protocol. By mid-morning in New Zealand, I heard the rumor and quickly confirmed it with a family member. To my surprise, the AFP report, five hours after the death, was the first announcement and had other media outlets quickly following. Information minister Simione Kaitani slammed this—"They should have known of the Fijian protocol and should have respected it."

Protocol had not, in this event, worried me at all; so many people knew informally that it had felt like I was breaking old news. Still, my next trip to Fiji was again gripped with the uncertainty over whether or not I would be allowed in.

For all its stresses and complications, South Seas journalism has a compelling uniqueness about it. The stories are big and accessible, and they can be eccentric and amusing, while still touching on issues that are important in people's lives. No other story quite demonstrates this than the 2003 events in the Fiji cannibal village of Nabutautau. The old cartoon strip of the trussed-up missionary in a native cooking pot pretty well came to pass in that village high in the striking interior of Fiji's main island of Viti Levu. There, in 1867, English missionary Thomas Baker and eight Fijian followers were clubbed to death and their bodies cooked and eaten. The natives even tried to eat his shoes and subjected them to days of boiling in an attempt to soften them; the battered soles in the Fiji Museum testify to their pre-Nike durability. Soon afterward, the Nabutautau converted to Christianity but felt cursed for their sin. During the intervening years, they have tried to make peace with Baker's spirit, but rather than make things better, the region became the major production ground for marijuana. In 2003 another group of Christians, of a fundamental and particularly political strain—in favor, for example, of keeping

Fiji for the indigenous and making heathen Hindus convert— arrived and staged an elaborate apology ceremony, inviting in ten Australians who were, three generations on, descendants of the boiled missionary. I had word of it several weeks before, but the inaccessibility of Nabutautau and the uncertainty of the cere- mony itself deterred most other reporters—including CNN, which wanted to carry part of it live. At AFP, we took a punt and, despite some heroic if not downright dangerous mountain driv- ing, got there in time to see Prime Minister Laisenia Qarase arrive by helicopter. Large, barely dressed Fijian warriors guarded the area—who repeatedly and loudly kicked one poor dog out of the presence of guests. Several dignitaries took it upon themselves to tell reporters how they could stand, where they could stand, what they could do—and "take off that hat." Just as culture can tor- ment reporters in the Pacific, there are always practitioners of the culture who arrogantly and at times aggressively beat up on reporters, especially foreign ones. It pays to go into areas with a basic knowledge of protocol to avoid the bullying.

The ten Australians found it all somewhat perplexing—poor ancestor Tom Baker was more by way of an amusing and very dusty old closet skeleton by now. But as one of them, Dennis Rus- sell, put it, they were following the Aussie "mateship" ritual: "They want our help, so we're happy to help."

The ceremony concluded with a reenactment of the ambush of Thomas Baker and to the well informed, it was obvious that the villagers were not really sorry because the missionary had acted in a culturally inappropriate way and had gotten what he deserved, a lesson perhaps for pushy journalists. The story too had some intriguing twists and turns and links to coups and shady characters that needed a lifetime of Pacific experience to work out. The reward was a story well used around the world and a personally rich experience commemorated with a couple of unusual pieces of cannibal cutlery.

NOTES ON SOURCES

Most of the quotes and comments mentioned were from interviews I conducted for AFP, unless credited to other newspapers. These are the sources mentioned in the chapter.

Buck, Sir Peter. *Vikings of the Sunrise.* Christchurch, New Zealand: Whitcombe and Tombs, 1938, pp. 293–94.

Dobell, G. "The Strange Saga of Speight's Siege in Suva." In *Coup: Reflections on the Political Crisis in Fiji,* ed. B. V. Lal with M. Pretes. Canberra, Australia: Pandanus Books, 2001, pp. 126–36.

Dorney, S. "Covering Catastrophe in Papua New Guinea." *Asia Pacific Media Educator* 7 (1999): 137–42.

Moala, J. "Copy versus Custom." *Pacific Journalism Review* 7, no. 1 (2001): 29–34.

Chapter 14
WALKING THE TIGHTROPE

CHARLES ARTHUR

Charles Arthur is a specialist on Caribbean politics and economics, a correspondent for Latin America Press, and a contributor to the Economist Intelligence Unit and *Oxford Analytica*. He is the author of numerous articles for a variety of publications. Following his first trip to Haiti in 1993 when he served as a human rights monitor for the United Nations, he has returned to that country many times. Since

1994, he has been the main consultant for the UK-based Haiti Support Group, a development education and solidarity organization. He is the coeditor, with Michael Dash, of *Libète: A Haiti Anthology* (1999), and his most recent book is *Haiti in Focus: A Guide to the People, Politics and Culture* (2002).

They try everything, to gnaw at us, to bury us, to electro-cute us, to drown us, to drain us. It's been going on for more than 50 years, and why should it stop? They can still try to crush us; to machine-gun us; to ignore, slander, bully and seduce us; to deflate, empty and dis-tort us. It's been going on for more than 50 years. Is there a reason for it to stop? Yes, one. Things must change in Haiti. . . . For freedom of the press, Radio Haiti Inter, at the service of the Haitian people.

—Jean Léopold Dominique

On April 3, 2000, at the usual time—just after 6 a.m.—Jean Dominique arrived for work at the offices of Radio Haiti Inter. *Inter-Actualités*, a daily news show that he hosted along with his wife, Michèle Montas, was due to go live at seven. When Dominique drove to the station entrance on the Route de Delmas, a busy road connecting the upscale suburb of Pétionville and downtown Port-au-Prince, the night watchman, Jean-Claude Louissaint, opened the metal gates. According to station staff, a man had earlier presented himself to Louissaint, saying he needed to speak to Dominique. He had asked Louissaint to point Dominique out to him when he arrived, then waited at the gates. When Dominique pulled into the station courtyard and parked his car, the unsuspecting Louissaint duly identified him. As Dominique walked toward the station entrance, the man approached, pulled a gun, and shot Dominique repeatedly in the head and chest. The gunman then turned, shot Louissaint twice, and fled in a car waiting for him outside. Moments later, Michèle Montas arrived to find the two men dying on the ground. The vic-tims were driven to a nearby hospital, but both were pronounced dead on arrival.

The sixty-nine-year-old Jean Dominique was Haiti's best-known journalist and a veteran democracy activist. His murder deeply shocked Haitians across the social spectrum. On hearing about the attack on his friend and adviser, the then president, René Préval, rushed to the hospital. Former president Jean-Bertrand Aristide and prime minister Jacques Edouard Alexis, along with almost the entire cabinet, the chief of police, and the national human rights ombudsman, all came to pay their respects to the family of the deceased. The government announced three days of national mourning, and political parties and civil society organizations issued statements denouncing the murder.

All through the morning of April 3, crowds of people who had grown familiar with Jean Dominique's distinctive voice and militant approach over decades of radio broadcasting massed in front of the Radio Haiti Inter studios. Women's groups organized a march to demand that the killer be found and charged. Over sixteen thousand people, including thousands of peasant farmers who came by bus from points across the country, attended a funeral service held at the national soccer stadium in the capital on April 8. At the service, President Préval posthumously awarded Dominique the country's highest medal of distinction in recognition of his "inestimable contribution to the construction and reinforcement of democracy."

Outside Haiti too there were strong reactions. In the New York metropolitan region, Dominique's broadcasts that were relayed by the Brooklyn cable radio station Radio Soleil were popular with the three-hundred-thousand-strong Haitian-American community. Speaking the day after the murder on Amy Goodman's *Democracy Now* program, the Haitian-American political activist Ray Laforest said, "Radio stations in Brooklyn are full with calls expressing people's shock and anger, and people are denouncing the murder. . . . People are looking for ways to express not only their outrage, but also to recognize the tremendous work that he has done." Writing in the *Los Angeles Times*, longtime Haiti watcher Amy Wilentz expressed widely held sentiments: "Dominique is dead, unbelievable to those of us who worked in Haiti during the past three decades, when his was the voice . . . of passionate engagement with the ideal of freedom. . . . One cannot begin to say how sorely Haiti will miss him."[1] Human rights organizations and media freedom monitors across the world condemned the murder and demanded justice. Koichiro Matsuura, the director of UNESCO, said the assassination would "distress all those who believe in Haiti's democratic future and all who fight for freedom of speech."

In Haiti, a police and judicial investigation into the murders began but failed to yield immediate results. The clamor for justice remained unabated, and speculation raged about the motive for the attack and the identity of those who had ordered it. Radio Haiti Inter was off the air for a month but reopened at 7 a.m. on May 3. At the time, Guerlande Eloi, a Radio Haiti Inter journalist, explained, "Today is international press freedom day, and we wanted to honor Jean, who died because he wasn't afraid to talk."[2]

Despite being what one government-sponsored lawyer called the "best-financed investigation in Haitian history," the case moved slowly in the face of numerous obstacles.[3] It soon became clear that powerful interests were in some way involved in Dominique's murder—interests who did not want their roles revealed. In response, in September 2000, a group of concerned Haitian citizens formed the Foundation to Echo the Voice of Jean Dominique, an organization that vowed "to keep alive the memory of Jean Dominique and the causes for which he gave his life, and to encourage justice and an end to the impunity which reigns."[4] The foundation found willing supporters among the membership of many of Haiti's civil society organizations, especially those concerned with human rights and freedom of speech. Outside Haiti, human rights organizations, media freedom outfits, development aid agencies, and solidarity groups remained focused on the case, publicizing the twists and turns it took and castigating the Haitian authorities for the lack of progress. The Hollywood film director Jonathan Demme, who had befriended Dominique while filming in Haiti in the 1980s, even helped assemble "The Alliance for Justice for Jean Dominique," an impressive list of actors and celebrities from all over the world who signed up for "a movement dedicated to the identification and incarceration of the parties responsible for the journalist's death."[5]

The murder, and the contentious judicial investigation into it, became a key issue for all those involved in the fight for rights and justice. Jean Dominique was not an ordinary journalist or even just a journalist. His murder represented a high-profile assault on the media, but it was also a direct attack on those engaged in the long struggle for representation for the country's poor majority, in the struggle for a real participatory democracy in Haiti after decades of dictatorship.

Jean Léopold Dominique was born on July 30, 1930, into a starkly divided society. The roots of modern-day Haiti lie in the 1791–1804 revolution, during which half a million black slaves in the French-controlled colony, known then as Saint Domingue, rose up and overthrew their white masters. This revolution brought an end to slavery; however, racial, social, and economic divisions deriving from the colonial regime exerted strong influences on the shaping of postindependence society. Within a few decades, a subsistence economy developed in the interior of the country as, in ever increasing numbers, former slaves squatted idle or abandoned land or carved new plots out of marginal land on the hillsides. Meanwhile, in the coastal towns, a minority elite—composed of mulatto landowners and black officers from the revolutionary army—came together. With opportunities to invest in agricultural production limited by a labor shortage, this elite was obliged to look for new ways to perpetuate its wealth. It focused on the distribution and export of the produce grown by the peasant farmers and the control of state revenue, in particular, the levying of taxes. The basic structure of the independent, but deeply divided, nation of Haiti was, and to all intents remains, a majority rural population of small-holding peasant farmers and an urban-based commercial and political minority. Against this economic backdrop, two essentially separate social realities developed. On the one hand were poor and mostly black peasants (and later shantytown dwellers), communicating in the Creole language, maintaining certain African traditions and lifestyles, and developing rituals and ceremonies to serve the spirits of Vodou. On the other was a mainly mulatto and urban elite, writing and speaking French, seeing itself as European, and professing allegiance to the Catholic Church.

These divisions remained intact into the twentieth century, and the family to which Dominique belonged was firmly located in Port-au-Prince's mulatto elite. However, contrary to the norm whereby members of this class would remain isolated from, and not a little fearful of, the poverty-stricken masses, Jean Dominique did not experience the normal social segregation. He got to know something of the reality of the lives of the majority population at an early age when he accompanied his father, an import-export broker, traveling throughout the Haitian countryside on business. His interest in agriculture stirred, Dominique on leaving school attended the national Agricultural College at Damien, just outside the capital, and in 1952, he went abroad to study agronomy, specializing in plant genetics, at the University of Paris. On his return in 1957, he began a career as an agronomist, working to improve citrus fruit and cacao production.

By this time, the black nationalist François "Papa Doc" Duvalier had come to power, and Dominique soon became embroiled in the political fallout as the first elements of what was to become a notorious dictatorship were set in place. Dominique's brother, Philippe, a lieutenant in the Haitian Army, was arrested and executed on July 29, 1958, on suspicion of plotting a coup against Duvalier. Because of this family connection, Dominique was jailed for six months in the central city of Gonaïves. On his release, he found it impossible to continue as an agronomist because all jobs in that field were provided by the state—a state that was to remain under the control of the father and son Duvalier dictatorships until 1986. Instead, he immersed himself in a passion for cinema that had developed during his years in France. He codirected the first film made in Haiti by Haitians—the sarcastic documentary about a beauty contest, *But I Am Beautiful, Too* (1962), and, in Port-au-Prince, he formed the country's first cinema club. It screened European films provided by foreign embassies but was soon closed on Duvalier's orders after a screening of *Night and Fog*, Alain Resnais's documentary about Nazi concentration camps—the similarities with the dictator's prisons run by the Tontons Macoutes force were evidently too obvious.

Seemingly stymied at every turn, Dominique could easily have joined the thousands of others from his class who emigrated in search of the freedom and opportunities denied at home. He did not, however, join this "brain drain" to North America, Europe, and Africa that was to cost the country dearly in the decades to come, but he stayed and took up freelance journalism, writing about cinema for newspapers, radio, and television. He began his career as a broadcaster with a one-hour time slot on the program *TJ Publicité* on Radio Haiti, the country's oldest radio station. In the late sixties, Dominique and his cousin leased the whole station from the owners, the Widmaier family, later renaming the station Radio Haiti Inter.

Dominique took his first steps on the journey to becoming Haiti's most famous broadcaster and journalist at a time when the gap between the majority have-nots and minority haves was growing still wider. "Papa Doc" Duvalier and—after his death in 1971—his son, Jean-Claude, stole foreign aid and stepped up the already heavy taxation of the peasantry. Instead of investing in the important agricultural sector, the Duvaliers increased the exploitation and, in so doing, compounded structural problems already afflicting the rural economy. Over successive generations, the individual land holdings belonging to peasant farmers had been divided into smaller and smaller plots. Agricultural methods had remained primitive, and the continual need to produce crops to live on meant that farmland was consistently overworked. As yields decreased, peasant farmers could not afford to leave land idle or allow trees to remain where new crops could be planted. Declining production, in turn, was forcing farmers to supplement their income by cutting down trees to make and sell charcoal. Without tree cover, topsoil was being progressively washed away from hillsides and mountain slopes by heavy tropical rainstorms and flash floods. Yields declined still further. With the rural sector increasingly unable to support a rapidly expanding population, an exodus toward the coastal cities, especially the capital, Port-au-Prince, began. Hundreds of thousands arrived in search of a living and found nothing but a daily struggle to survive in squalid shantytowns to the north and south of the city.

One estimate suggests that between 1976 and 1985, the percentage of the population living in extreme poverty rose from 48 to 81 percent. In this context, obstacles to the free flow of information and ideas remained entrenched. Fewer than half the country's children attended school, and those who did received an extremely poor education. As a result, the majority of Haitians could not read or write. Against this backdrop, Jean Dominique's Radio Haiti Inter introduced a number of innovations that transformed radio into an accessible and popular medium for the majority—a move that had potentially far-reaching political consequences.

Perhaps the most significant break with previous radio practice was that newscasters began to use the Creole language, the language spoken and understood by all Haitians, rather than French—a language understood by only an educated minority, estimated at as little as 5 percent of the population. Until Dominique introduced a daily program in Creole—hosted by Joe Tony (Ti Tonton)—the only other Creole broadcast was the government's program, *La Voix de la République d'Haiti*. As

Dominique himself said, the use of Creole on Radio Haiti Inter meant that "the poor people of the country, whether workers or farmers or jobless people, were able to speak through the radio . . . to make people know what was their life, their daily fight. . . . The use of Creole was a new element in the slow process of fighting for freedom, for justice, and for the end of exclusion."[6]

The other groundbreaking departures from radio tradition were Radio Haiti Inter's decisions to broadcast domestic as well as foreign news and to use eyewitness reports. Dominique's reporting of one incident in particular greatly contributed to his growing popularity among listeners. In January 1973, a group demanding the release of political prisoners took the US ambassador in Haiti, Clinton Knox, hostage. Dominique's nonstop eyewitness reporting of the drama of the negotiations, Knox's eventual release, and the flight out of Haiti of twelve prisoners and the three hostage takers brought him to national prominence. This and other reports on political events introduced eager listeners to the concept of a free media reporting without state restrictions. In a 1997 interview, Dominique described his journalism as "a very revolutionary process, making the Creole-speaking audience familiar with what was going on in Nicaragua in terms of the Sandinista revolution; what was going on in Iran in terms of the fight against the Shah; what was going on in Haiti in terms of striking workers at the factories around Port-au-Prince [and] the farmers in the Artibonite Valley fighting against the Tontons Macoutes."[7]

It was not only by the reporting of the hard news of political struggle that Dominique's station came to play an increasingly important role in the developing mobilization to free Haiti from the straight-jacket of dictatorship and inequality. The role of Radio Haiti Inter in promoting a cultural alternative to the elite mainstream is often overlooked. According to Michèle Montas, who joined the station as a journalist in 1973, Dominique used the station to challenge the taboo that existed in the rest of the Haitian media in terms of a participatory and inclusive identity.

In a recent interview, she said, "The stress put on two determining elements of that Haitian identity, a language, Creole, and a religion, Vodou, has helped to free the creativity of quite a few artists, in music, literature and the visual arts."[8] She cited as examples the first break that the station gave to the musicians Manno Charlemagne and Marco Jeanty; how Dominique produced the first Creole adaptation of the quintessential Haitian novel, Jacques Roumain's *Gouverneurs de la Rosée*; and how he encouraged the revered author Franketienne to write the first entirely Creole-language novel, *Dezafi* (published in 1975).

During the late 1970s, when the United States pressed the Duvalier dictatorship to relax its repressive grip and reduce censorship of the media, Dominique took advantage of this space to broadcast editorials that criticized the government. His passionate style of speech and colorful turn of phrase gave these editorials extra appeal for an audience hungry for ideas and desperate for change. Under the umbrella of the Catholic Church, peasants, students, teachers, and community activists were meeting to discuss the country's problems. Human rights, social justice, and democracy became issues for discussion, and Radio Haiti Inter and other media were spreading news of a fledgling pro-change movement. Then, in 1980, the period of relative political liberalization in Haiti was brought to an abrupt end. On the night of November 28, 125 people, many of them journalists, were arrested at gunpoint, and soldiers closed the doors of numerous radio stations, including Radio Haiti Inter, as well as newspapers like *Le Petit Samedi Soir* and *Inter-Jeune*. Recalling these events years later, Dominique made a clear connection to the then election in the United States: "The dictatorship and the Tontons Macoutes had to live with us because of President Carter and his human rights policy. But ten days after Reagan's election victory, the Macoutes said, 'Human rights are dead.' . . . They ransacked the station, arrested all the staff, and destroyed the facilities."[9] Dominique was not at the station at the time of the arrests and, on hearing the news, took refuge in the Venezuelan embassy. From there, he fled to the United States. The rest of the staff members of Radio Haiti Inter were eventually freed from jail and, together with a number of other journalists and human rights activists, were expelled from their homeland. Dominique and Michèle Montas—by this time married—together began a life of exile in New York that was to last over five years.

The crackdown on criticism and dissent won the Duvalier dictatorship a few more years, but, by the mid–1980s, the grassroots movement that Dominique and Radio Haiti Inter had, in many ways, nurtured and encouraged grew more determined. Although the station was closed, its influence on radio communication continued to be felt. Many of the innovations introduced by Dominique were taken up by the one radio station that enjoyed a certain immunity from state repression. Radio Soleil, the Catholic bishop's station, became an outlet for voices from the popular movement for change and the country's main source of uncensored news. Although the protection of the Catholic Church hierarchy was enough to keep Radio Soleil on air until December 1985, it still faced difficulties, as Father Hugo Triest, the station's director at that time, remembered: "As most of the bishops had been appointed by Duvalier, we had a certain space in which to work, but we were not free from harassment. Employees of the station were beaten up, telephone lines cut, and at one point they jammed the signal from the studio to the antenna. We had to go to the antenna, six kilometers away, and broadcast from there."[10]

By late 1985, protests and unrest fueled by food shortages were spreading throughout the country. Fearing a revolution, the US government—which had up until then regarded the Duvaliers as a staunch anti-Communist ally—withdrew its support. On February 7, 1986, Jean-Claude Duvalier and his entourage fled the country, and the United States put its weight behind a military governing council that it hoped would oversee a transition to an electoral democracy without disturbing the status quo. Within a month of the fall of the Duvalier regime, Jean Dominique was back in Haiti. In a staggering outpouring of acclaim, a crowd of around sixty thousand people gathered at the airport to welcome him home from exile. Radio Haiti Inter's equipment had been destroyed, but donations from ordinary people both in Haiti and the diaspora in North America poured in to help rebuild the station. In November 1986, the station was back on air. Film director Jonathan Demme, who began to make a series of documentaries about Haiti at this time, recalled the enthusiasm with which Dominique resumed his work: "With no lurking secret service in evidence to 'play cat and mouse,' Jean ratcheted up the ante, spewing Creole, people power, unbridled criticism of the still deeply-entrenched dynasty that Duvalier left behind, and scathing indictments of the United States' efforts to 'discreetly' continue the American control of Haiti."[11]

Over the next five years, the previously marginalized majority began to mobilize and participate in a range of activities. Peasants, women, workers, and students launched marches and strikes to demand justice and a purge of Duvalierists from positions of power. Grassroots organizations swelled in size and number, setting up self-help schemes such as credit cooperatives and self-defense strategies such as vigilance brigades. Successive military governments responded with repression, and Radio Haiti Inter was attacked numerous times because of its determination to report the unfolding struggle for a participatory democracy. In Dominique's words, "It lasted five glorious years, even though twice the military destroyed the station, including the attack at 2 a.m. on November 29, 1987. The military came and started shooting. We fought back by throwing rocks at them from the roof! I remember CBS phoned me from New York, and I told them I was being shot at, right then!"[12]

The attempt to hold elections in November 1987 resulted in a bloodbath, with the army and resurgent Tontons Macoutes gunning down voters as they queued at polling stations. Free elections were finally held under United Nations supervision in December 1990. Dominique told the *Miami Herald* that he felt that every terrible thing he had been through had been worth it. "You must understand, for Haitians to vote is more than it is in your country," he said. "It is the way for millions of people who live in dirt and poverty to prove to themselves that they are human. It is the difference between eternal darkness and light."[13]

The election victory of the radical priest Jean-Bertrand Aristide, the head of the pro-change movement called Lavalas, appeared to be a major step toward a more inclusive and participatory society. As president, Aristide strongly promoted the use of Creole and, in doing so, fortified a trend toward broadcasts and publications in the language. The post-Duvalier era of increased media freedom had been baptized in Creole: *baboukèt-la tombe!* ("The muzzle is off!"), but the military coup d'état of September 30, 1991, put it firmly back on. President Aristide fled into exile, and the media, the radio stations in particular, were the military's first targets.

For Radio Haiti Inter, the "glorious years" were over. "One week after the coup, they shot us up again," said Dominique. "On October 2, I interviewed the exiled President who was in Washington. One hour later they came, shooting in broad daylight. On October 15, I decided to stop broadcasting after they came to my home during the night."[14] Once again the station was closed, and Dominique was forced into exile, not to return until US troops intervened to restore the constitutional government three years later.

Rebuilding the station for a third time, Dominique and Montas took up where they had been forced to leave off. Their *Inter-Actualités* program again became one of the most popular morning shows. Montas read the national news, while Dominique wrote and read editorials and commentaries that included fiery tirades against corrupt politicians and businessmen. Dominique and his team of journalists also specialized in the sort of investigative reporting that was, and still is, all too rare in Haiti. Whereas other stations focused almost entirely on news about the government and events in the capital, Radio Haiti Inter would investigate and report on stories and issues relevant to ordinary people, particularly to peasants and the inhabitants of small towns. For example, if a peasant organization occupied idle farmland, Radio Haiti Inter would send a reporter. The same would happen with allegations of corruption in the Organization for the Development of the Artibonite Valley or complaints that the flood of imported rice from the United States was forcing down local rice prices. When in 1999 peasants in the Léogane region started falling ill after drinking alcohol laced with ethanol, Dominique spearheaded a high-profile investigation and public information campaign warning of the dangers of mixing indus-trial spirits with homemade rum and warning off the unscrupu-lous businessmen profiting from the distribution of ethanol for this purpose.

Such reports made Dominique extremely popular with ordi-nary people throughout Haiti, especially among peasants in the countryside. He saw such an approach to news gathering and broadcasting as being part of a clear political position: "We are fighting for popular participation. We are against exclusion, because the majority of people in this country are excluded from political life."[15]

Over three decades, Dominique's distinctive voice, probing interviews, and scathing commentaries were broadcast over the airwaves and had become part of daily life. His particularly politi-cized form of campaigning journalism had transformed the medium of radio and made it a vital tool for the sharing of ideas and information. At the same time, his commitment to the idea of social inclusion and participatory democracy had helped ener-gize and mobilize a movement that had brought an end to a twenty-nine-year dictatorship and developed the potential to transform the nation. In the face of repeated violence and threats, and despite two periods of exile, he had refused to be intimidated or silenced. For all these reasons, and more, the murder of Jean Dominique in April 2000 was deeply shocking for the people of Haiti. But perhaps most shocking of all was that, after surviving through dictatorships, military coups, and attacks on the station he had built, Dominique was shot down just as it appeared that the transition to democracy in Haiti had finally been achieved.

In early 1995, the reinstalled President Aristide had disbanded the Haitian Army, and a new police force run by the Ministry of Justice was in the process of being built. Parliamentary and presidential elections were successfully held, and the first peaceful transfer of political power in recent Haitian history took place when René Préval succeeded Aristide as president in February 1996. For all those Haitians who hoped that the country had finally turned a corner and would at last enjoy some stability and a chance to prosper, Dominique's murder was hard to comprehend. Marleine Bastien, president of the advocacy group Haitian Women of Miami, gave an idea of its impact when she told the *Miami Herald*, "Haitians in the United States have always thought about when we could return to Haiti. But the murder of Jean Dominique makes us think only about how to get our families out."[16]

Compounding the sense of unease was the difficulty in identifying the probable culprits for the murder. Dominique's widow, Michèle Montas, articulated these thoughts when she noted that in the past the threat would obviously have come from the Duvaliers and the military leaders who followed. "Then it was much easier to find out who the enemy was. Now, you don't know. It's very difficult to determine who's who." Speaking just weeks after the murder, Montas said, "I cannot say who killed my husband, but there are a number of people who were interested in doing so."[17]

Early suspicions focused on members of the country's economic elite because, as Montas recalled, Dominique did not let vested interests stop him from following a story. "Jean's investigations touched a number of very powerful interest groups. For example, he focused on the scandal in 1997 when 80 kids died from taking toxic medicine. Pharval [a local pharmaceutical company owned by the influential Boulos family] paid a number of journalists to keep their mouths shut, and it worked, except with us."[18]

As a commercial entity, the station's pursuit of the truth caused problems because, despite all the political upheaval in the post-Duvalier decade, Haiti's wealth continued to be concentrated in the hands of the very small elite. Radio Haiti Inter—in common with other commercial media—had to look to this sector for advertising revenue, but this was the very same sector that opposed the movement toward democracy in the 1980s and supported the 1991 coup d'état. In 1995, Dominique admitted his station was feeling the pinch. "We are with the poor people, those 'in the street,' and because of that, advertising, which is our sole source of revenue, is nearly completely absent. There is a practical boycott by the business community and we are suffering."[19] Four years later, the same problem still existed. A consortium of business groups, many of which were owned by the same families that had previously crossed swords with Dominique, canceled their advertising contract with Haiti Inter in protest against unfavorable coverage of their attempts to enter electoral politics. The station suffered a 20 percent drop in revenue and, as a result, had to abandon plans to extend its FM broadcast coverage to more remote parts of the country.

It may be that the murder of Jean Dominique was ordered by members of the elite who saw themselves threatened by his exposés of their corrupt business practices or who were angered by the ridicule that he poured on their attempts to enter the political arena in the hope of derailing the moves toward democracy. However, most observers of the tortured and so far inconclusive murder investigation now believe that the intellectual authors are most likely to be found in the Lavalas Family political party that Dominique had once supported but later distanced himself from.

When, in the later half of the 1990s, the Lavalas movement that had brought Aristide to power at the beginning of the decade split into opposing factions, Dominique criticized the one that controlled the government for implementing the neoliberal policies called for by the international financial institutions. But he remained close to the president, René Préval, who served until February 2001. Both men were former agronomists, and they shared an interest in promoting the political involvement of the peasantry as a means of improving the fortunes of the rural sector. Together they are believed to have been instrumental in the establishment of a new organization of peasants in the central Artibonite region called KOZEPEP. Although Dominique was himself a member of the Lavalas faction that coalesced around Jean-Bertrand Aristide—constituted as a political party called the Lavalas Family in late 1997—there is speculation that powerful elements within that party viewed KOZEPEP as a potential rival.

Suspicions that Dominique was the victim of a power struggle within the Lavalas Family party are enhanced by the open dispute that developed in 1999 between Dominique and Dany Toussaint, a former army officer and Aristide loyalist. Toussaint had been head of the interim police force in 1995 and subsequently built a significant power base among the Port-au-Prince youth who supported the Lavalas Family Party. He made no secret of his political ambitions or of his desire to exert control over the newly established police force. Following the murder of the incoming police chief on October 8, Dominique broadcast a public warning to Aristide about elements that he feared would lead the Lavalas Family Party away from its roots in the mass movement. Toussaint countered by sending his supporters to demonstrate outside Radio Haiti Inter, and in an editorial broadcast on October 19, Dominique made the following comments about Toussaint: "I know he has weapons. I know he has enough money to pay and arm henchmen. Here I have no other weapons than my profession as a journalist, my microphone and my unbreakable faith as a militant for change, real change. . . . If Dany Toussaint tries something against me or the radio station and if I survive, I'll close the station down and go into exile once again with my wife and children."

Toussaint did nothing to dispel suspicions when, following his election to the Senate representing the Lavalas Family Party in May 2000, he claimed parliamentary immunity in order to avoid having to answer the questions of an investigating judge. The Senator justified his lack of cooperation with the investigation by suggesting that he was being "set up" by political enemies. He accused a US Embassy employee of bribing some suspects already detained as part of the investigation to implicate him in the planning of the murder.

Suspects have been interviewed, and, as a result, some have been cleared, while others believed to have been involved in planning and carrying out of the attack have been arrested. Some of those are still in detention, but some have escaped. One key suspect died on the operating table, and, when police asked for the body for an autopsy, they were told it had disappeared from the morgue. Another detained suspect was dragged out of a provincial town police station and killed by a mob. Charges have been made, and charges have been dropped. Investigating judges have been appointed and then dismissed. The one judge who appeared to be making the most progress fled the country in fear for his life, then returned with increased police protection, and finally was not reengaged to continue with the case.

The investigation became part of the long and increasingly violent struggle for political power between President Jean-Bertrand Aristide's Lavalas Family Party government and the opposition movement, a struggle that culminated in the overthrow of that government in February 2004. While opponents charged that President Aristide himself was deeply complicit in obstructing the judicial process to identify the killers, Aristide supporters, in turn, say such accusations are just another part of a long-running smear campaign to tarnish the populist leader's image. In Montas's opinion, Aristide was complicit in at least the cover-up. "It is a betrayal," she said. "I was once sure he couldn't have given the order to kill Jean. Now I don't know."[20]

Neither the killer nor those who hired him have been definitively identified, and the repercussions of Dominique's murder continue to be felt in Haiti. Journalists have become the frequent target of attacks and threats as the country has degenerated once more into violence and a political quagmire. Scores of journalists have sought asylum abroad, while for those who remain the fate of Jean Dominique acts as an effective deterrent against any form of investigative journalism.

In an open letter to her husband read on air on the first anniversary of his murder, Michèle Montas declared, "We know that they assassinated you, Jean, because you had the credibility to say NO to politicians of all stripes, greedy for power and money; NO to violence; NO to corruption; NO to exclusion; NO to impunity."

On Christmas Day 2002, gunmen attempting to enter the residence of Michèle Montas shot dead her security guard, Maxime Seide. In February 2003, she closed Radio Haiti Inter, saying that the staff had received one death threat too many. In mid-2004 she said,

> Radio Haiti Inter is not over. More than any media, we have been harshly struck, faced death, forced to close at least seven times, gone into exile, been shot at or sabotaged. But every time we have bounced back. It is not going to be easy to return to the airwaves. We have tremendous support, but powerful enemies. When we put the station on the silent mode, a year ago, it was to protect the lives of our staff. Reopening Radio Haiti Inter would now be suicidal, as those who forced us to close are circulating freely. Some are even vying for a share of the political pie and would do everything they can to stop the truth. But we will return when the conditions allow us to start over. As we

sung on our airwaves, "nou balance, nou pa tonbe" ["we're on a tightrope, but we won't fall"].

NOTES

1. Amy Wilentz, "The Return of Dark Days," *Los Angeles Times*, April 9, 2000, http://www.nchr.org/hrp/jando/return_of_dark_days .htm.

2. "Station of Slain Haitian Journalist Again on Air," Reuters, May 3, 2000.

3. Charles Arthur, "Getting away with murder?" Latinamerica Press, October 23, 2001.

4. "Nòt pou lapres," Fondasyon Eko Vwa Jean Dominique, September 4, 2000.

5. *The International Alliance for Justice for Jean Dominique*, http://www.justiceforjean.com/.

6. Charles Arthur, "The Man Who Gave Speech to the Speechless Is Silenced," *Index on Censorship*, April 7, 2000.

7. Laurie Richardson, "The People's Pen Has No Eraser," *World Association for Christian Communication* (1998).

8. Kapes Kreyol, "The Agronomist: Jean Dominique and Michèle Montas' Story Universal Appeal," http://www.palli.ch/~kapeskreyol/ bibliographie/vedrine/dominique.html.

9. Charles Arthur, author's interview, April 1996.

10. Charles Arthur, "Radio Soleil: Father Hugo Triest Interview," *Unda News* 20, no. 4 (1993).

11. Jonathan Demme, "Jean Dominique Eulogy," April 7, 2000, http://www.nchr.org/hrp/jando/demme_eulogy.htm.

12. Arthur, interview, April 1996.

13. Meg Laughlin, "Haitians Fear for Homeland after Slaying," *Miami Herald*, April 4, 2000.

14. Arthur, interview, April 1996.

15. Charles Arthur, "Haiti's Fallen Warrior," *Global Journalist* (third quarter 2000).

16. Laughlin, "Haitians Fear for Homeland."

17. Arthur, "Haiti's Fallen Warrior."

18. Ibid.

19. Charles Arthur, "Haiti Media Report," *Media Development* (1997).

20. David Gonzalez, "A Haitian Journalist Was Killed, But a Film Keeps His Spirit Alive," *New York Times*, April 20, 2004.

SUGGESTED READING

Amnesty International. "Haiti: Update of the Jean Dominique Investigation and the Situation of Journalists." November 15, 2002. http://web.amnesty.org/library/index/engAMR360132002!Open.

Arana, Ana. "The Case of Jean Leopold Dominique." April 3, 2000. http://www.impunidad.com/cases/jeanleopoldE.html.

Bear, Liza. "Michèle Montas Talks about *The Agronomist*, Haitian History, and Seeking Justice." *Indie Wire*. http://www.indiewire.com/ people/people_040429montas.html.

Haiti Support Group. "Justice for Jean Dominique." http:// haitisupport .gn.apc.org/fea_campaign_index.html.

The International Alliance for Justice for Jean Dominique. http://www.justice forjean.com/.

Kim, Kevin Y. "On an Island of Men." *In These Times*, April 27, 2004. http://www.inthesetimes.com/site/main/article/417/.

Lynch, Marika, and Jane Regan. "Indictment Doesn't Reveal Plot to Kill Haitian Journalist." *Miami Herald*, March 25, 2003. http://www .miami.com/mld/miamiherald/news/front/5474313.htm.

ACKNOWLEDGMENTS

I should like to express my sincerest thanks to the following people who kindly assisted me with the publication of *Silenced: International Journalists Expose Media Censorship.*

First and foremost, I should like to thank the authors of the individual chapters—Charles Arthur, Isabel Arvide, Jasper Becker, Michael Field, Tom Gutting, Gary Hughes, Stephen Kimber, Tim Lambon, Andrew Meldrum, Michael McKinnon, Alexander Pumpyansky, Gerald Ryle, Hans-Martin Tillack, and Stacey Woelfel.

The staff at Prometheus Books also deserves a special mention. I am particularly indebted to Steven L. Mitchell, editor-in-chief at Prometheus Books, who originally suggested this project; Heather Ammermuller, associate editor; Christine Kramer, production manager; Debbie Anderson, proofreader; and Bruce Carle and Roz Gold, typesetters. All of them have worked extremely hard and diligently to ensure that *Silenced* was finished on time.

David Dadge
Vienna
April 25, 2005